RANGERS

An Illustrated History of Glasgow Rangers

RANGERS

An Illustrated History of Glasgow Rangers

Rab MacWilliam

AURUM PRESS

First published 2002 by Aurum Press Limited,
25 Bedford Avenue, London WC1B 3AT

ISBN 1 85410 789 5

Book design by Frank Ainscough @ Compendium
Originated by Global Graphics, Prague
Printed in Singapore by Imago

10 9 8 7 6 5 4 3 2 1
2006 2005 2004 2003 2002

CONTENTS

INTRODUCTION

Rangers are one of the most famous and successful clubs in world football. With forty-nine Scottish league titles, thirty Scottish Cup victories and a European Cup Winners Cup trophy, the club's history is an illustrious one.

Founded in 1872 by a group of young rowers, by the beginning of the 20th century Rangers were the top club in Scotland. Between the two world wars, under the stern leadership of Bill Struth, they won the Scottish league no less than fifteen times and, in the years after World War Two, their famous 'Iron Curtain' defence helped the club to maintain their dominance in the Scottish game. The Jim Baxter-inspired, Scot Symon-managed side of the early 1960s swept everything before them, although it was not until the mid-1970s that they managed to overturn Celtic's nine-year hegemony in Scottish football and capture two 'trebles'. Some lean years followed but, reinvigorated by Graeme Souness and his English imports and then by Walter Smith, in 1997 Rangers famously matched Celtic's 'nine in a row'. Under Dick Advocaat they captured five out of six Scottish trophies between 1998 and 2000 and, at the time of writing, it appears that the managership of Alex McLeish is renewing Rangers' challenge to Martin O'Neill's Celtic.

While exceptional footballers, such as Moses McNeil, Alan Morton, David Meiklejohn, Bob McPhail, Willie Thornton, Willie Waddell, George Young, Jim Baxter, John Greig, Ally McCoist and Brian Laudrup, have all played leading roles in the club's history, Rangers have always prided themselves on their teamwork – their determination, discipline and will to win. Although all the most successful Rangers sides have had their star players, the emphasis at Ibrox has always been on playing for the honour of the club and the famous blue jersey. As the sign on Struth's desk reminded visitors, 'The club is bigger than the man'.

I decided to write this book in order to supply Rangers fans and football supporters generally with what I hope is an accessible, entertaining and informative account of the Gers' history. Much has happened between the club's beginnings on the public pitches of Glasgow Green and the situation today, where a largely foreign contingent of players ply their trade under the imposing stands of Ibrox and in some of the major stadiums of Europe. In the book I have recorded the major triumphs and disappointments, the great matches and unforgettable personalities, and the club's continual jockeying with Celtic for leadership in Scottish football.

I do not concern myself, other than of necessity, with sectarianism and religious affiliation, nor do I seek to analyse Rangers in terms of any socio/cultural/economic framework. I am not a social historian, simply a football fan whose youth coincided with the great Rangers side of the early 1960s and who, as a result, became star-struck by Baxter, Henderson *et al* until the distractions of mid-adolescence began to overtake my devotion to Symon's team. The book is essentially about what happened on the pitch and does not presume to consider the wider issues which are often raised about the connections between football, class and religion in Glasgow. Other writers have comprehensively and lucidly covered the latter aspects of the Old Firm.

Nonetheless, I hope that the reader will find much of interest in the following pages, as the story of Rangers is a fascinating one which deserves retelling. I also hope the evocative photographs will awaken fond memories of Rangers' past glories.

ACKNOWLEDGEMENTS
Thanks to Dave Ash, Anne Beech, Andy Cowie, Sandy Calder, Angus MacWilliam and Jack Murray for their help in the preparation of this book.

CHAPTER ONE:

THE EARLY YEARS: 1872-1899

One afternoon in 1872 four young Scots lads pulled their rowing boat out of the River Clyde and carried it into a boat shed on Glasgow Green. To recover from the effects of a busy morning's exercise, they settled down on the grass to watch two local sides play the increasingly popular sport of Association Football. The rules of the sport had been codified just a few years earlier in a London tavern and its spread across the United Kingdom had been speedy and pervasive, due to the game's elegant simplicity and its appeal to the popular, competitive imagination. Intrigued by what they saw, and fired by a desire to participate in this new and compelling game, these four boys determined to form their own football team in Glasgow. These four students – brothers Moses and Peter McNeil, Peter Campbell and William McBeath – had begun the story of what is now one of the most famous names in world football – Glasgow Rangers.

Playing on the Fleshers' Haugh, a makeshift public pitch on the Green, the newly-formed team – known then as the Argyle – contested their first match, a 0-0 draw with Callander, and took to the game with energy and enthusiasm. These young, athletic players were serious about their football from the beginning, insisting on regular and frequent training sessions, and they played a number of friendly matches against smaller local Glasgow sides as well teams of greater stature, such as Vale of Leven and Clydesdale, who were then among the 'giants' of the Scottish game. Indeed, so confident were they of their abilities that they continually petitioned Queen's Park – formed in 1867 and indisputably Scotland's leading club – to play them on the Green. The haughty Queen's Park refused, on the grounds that playing on a public pitch would be demeaning for their players, but suggested instead that they send the Strollers, their second eleven. This offer was not taken up by Rangers.

By the following year, the structure of the new club had been formalised – including the institution of an annual meeting, the election of officers and the arrangement of fixtures – and 17-year-old Moses, a rugby fan, renamed the club Rangers, after an English rugby club. The year 1873 is regarded by the club as the official date of its foundation.

They were ineligible, however, to play in the inaugural Scottish Cup competition that season as they had left it too late to join the fledgling Scottish Football Association, whose original members were Queen's Park, Clydesdale, Dumbreck, Third Lanark Volunteer Reserves, Glasgow Eastern, Granville, Kilmarnock and Vale of Leven. Rangers, therefore, had to content themselves with friendlies throughout 1873 and much of 1874.

The ambitious Rangers joined the SFA and played their first serious competitive match on 10 October in the 1874/75 Scottish Cup against Oxford, winning 2-0, the goals coming from Moses McNeil and David Gibb. They were beaten in the second round of the tournament 1-0 by a disputed goal in a replay at Dumbarton's impregnable Boghead ground, but they had acquitted themselves well and had demonstrated their potential against one of Scotland's top teams. The line-up against Oxford – the first-ever Rangers side, and therefore of historical importance – was: John Yuill, Peter McNeil, Tom Vallance, William McBeath, William McNeil, Moses McNeil, David Gibb, Peter Campbell, John Campbell, George Phillips, James Watson.

The formation was the then common one of two backs, two half-backs and six forwards, and Rangers were a fast, adventurous side held together at the back by the tackling power and defensive strengths of Peter McNeil and the tall, athletic captain Tom Vallance, while Moses McNeil and Peter Campbell provided the goals. Campbell had persuaded his brother John to join him in the attack and William, playing in the left half-back position, was the third member of the McNeil family to join the side. From the beginning they had sported royal blue shirts with white shorts and, aside from a four-year dalliance with a striped shirt in the early 1880s, the famous Rangers strip has, modern tinkering notwithstanding, remained virtually unchanged since the club's origins.

By now the club had outgrown the Fleshers' Haugh, with the shrubbery acting as the changing room, and they moved in 1875 to Burnbank, on the Great Western Road, where they remained for only one season before upping posts again and relocating to Kinning Park. During this season they played another top team of the era, Third Lanark, in the second round of the Scottish Cup and won 1-0, until it was

The Rangers team of 1876/77. Back: Gillespie, W McNeil, Watt, Ricketts. Middle: Dunlop, Hill, Vallance, Campbell, M McNeil. Seated: Watson, Marshall

pointed out that Rangers had kicked off in both halves! Technically, Rangers had to agree to a replay, and they were beaten 2-0 at Cathkin Park. They also played the Scottish Cup holders Queen's Park, losing 2-0 at Hampden Park but turning in a highly creditable performance against the aristocrats of the Scottish game.

In 1876/77, Rangers reached the Scottish Cup Final for the first time and met favourites Vale of Leven at Hamilton Park, Partick. Both sides played in blue with Rangers adopting a lighter hue. The club's nickname – 'the Light Blues' – stems from this period. The unfancied Rangers, now with George Gillespie to complement left-back Tom Vallance in defence, competed aggressively and, to the surprise of many observers, the game ended goalless. The tie went to a replay. With the score 1-1 in extra time, Rangers scored a 'goal' which was disallowed when the ball seemingly went over the Vale goal line but was cleared by the keeper (nets were not in use at this point in the game's history). A local, noted surgeon, Sir George B MacLeod, was behind the goal and affirmed that the ball had gone over the line. However, a pitch invasion led to the abandonment of the fixture. In the second replay, this time at Hampden Park on 13 April in front of 15,000 spectators, Vale went ahead through an own goal from Rangers forward and school teacher James Watson, but Peter Campbell and Moses McNeil both struck in the second half to put Rangers 2-1 ahead. Vale's superior strength and experience, however, saw them scrape through to a 3-2 victory with their winning goal coming in the last two minutes of a tense and exciting match.

The following season, Rangers met up again with Vale in the Scottish Cup, in the fourth round. Although Vale were held to a goalless draw at Kinning Park, Vale preserved the old order in the replay, winning 5-0. In 1879, the two sides lined up against each other once more in the Cup Final at Hampden Park, Rangers having disposed of Queen's Park 1-0 in the quarter-final, their first ever cup victory over the Glasgow giants. A large crowd attended the match and the crush caused a section of the pavilion to collapse. George Gillespie had now assumed the goalkeeping position (where he was to achieve Scottish international recognition in the years to come) and Tom Vallance was now partnered by his brother Alec. Hugh McIntyre had taken over the right half-back position, while forwards William Struthers and Archie Steel had arrived to support the attacking flair of Moses McNeil and Peter Campbell. The team was: Gillespie, T Vallance, A Vallance, McIntyre, Drinnan, Dunlop, Hill, Struthers, Steel, M McNeil, Campbell.

In the 10th minute of the game, the powerful Struthers set off on a run and opened the scoring for Rangers. Then Struthers, again, converted a cross from Dunlop, only to have it ruled invalid because of Dunlop's adjudged offside. The Rangers section of the crowd loudly expressed their unhappiness with this decision but the referee was unmoved by their vociferous objections. The *Glasgow Herald* dryly commented that the decision was 'somewhat galling for the Rangers'. Rangers, however, held on to their one-goal lead until an error of judgment from Gillespie allowed Vale to equalise.

After the match Rangers protested vigorously about the disallowed 'goal' but the SFA accepted the result and ordered a replay. On the appointed day, Vale of Leven turned up at Hampden but discovered that their piqued opposition had decided in protest not to turn up, having apparently opted instead for the attractions of Ayr races. Vale ran the ball into their opponents' empty goal, and they had won the Scottish Cup for the third consecutive year. Rangers were to salvage some pride the following month, however, when they beat Vale 2-1 in the Glasgow Charity Cup final, the first trophy they had won in their short history. The *Glasgow Herald* summed up the rather fractious nature of the last contest by concluding that it went 'a little beyond what could be described as friendly rivalry'.

After this, their second near miss in the Scottish Cup, the team began to break up. At the time,

Moses McNeil, the lad from the Gareloch who gave Rangers their name

payment to players was illegal in England and would remain so until 1885, while professionalism would not be accepted in Scotland until 1893. However, it was common knowledge among Scottish players that the wealthier English clubs made payments anyway, while offering lip service to amateurism. Indeed, Scottish players – with their intricate passing game and dribbling skills – were in great demand by English

George Gillespie, in Rangers' goal for the 1879 Scottish Cup final

clubs who regularly sent agents over the border to scout for emerging Scottish talent. So Peter Campbell and Hugh McIntyre left Kinning Park to join Blackburn Rovers, and they were followed by William Struthers who took the Bolton Wanderers shilling. Rangers were about to undergo a period of reconstruction.

The first reinforcements to arrive at Kinning Park were James 'Tuck' McIntyre, a half-back, and forward Willie Pringle. Rangers, however, could not repeat their two Cup Final appearances, losing to Dumbarton in the 1881 and 1882 quarter-finals, the latter by 5-1 in a replay at Boghead. The long-serving and popular captain Tom Vallance – by now a successful businessman as well as a renowned artist – left the club in 1882 to take up an appointment in India but returned in 1883 when he assumed the club presidency. In 1882, Charlie Heggie, and forwards Alick McKenzie and Jimmy Gossland joined the Rangers cause, but they could progress no further than the second round of the Cup that season, losing 3-2 at home to Queen's Park.

The next two seasons were little better, although Rangers reached the semi-final in 1883/84, going down 3-0 to old foes Vale of Leven. Their finances were also in a perilous state due mainly to a decline in members' subscriptions. Club President George Goudie stepped in with a £30 loan which was sufficient to keep the club afloat and, although Rangers were £100 in debt at the end of the season, an increase in the membership the following year helped to regain financial stability.

In the summer of 1883 Rangers played their first benefit match. The 500-ton passenger ship 'Daphne' had capsized shortly after its launch on the Clyde four weeks earlier, drowning 146 of the 200 ship workers on board. Rangers played Dumbarton to raise money for the victims' families and won the game 4-2. After the match Rangers were criticised in the press for deducting their expenses from the gate money while Dumbarton waived theirs.

In 1884/85, Rangers faced Arbroath away in the fourth round of the tournament and, in spite of leading 3-0 at half time, collapsed in the second half to finish the tie 4-3 behind the 'Red Lichties'. Ever mindful of escape clauses, Rangers officials measured the width of the pitch after the game and found that it was one foot under the minimum requirements. They demanded a replay – to which the SFA grudgingly agreed – and handed Arbroath an 8-1 trouncing. Renton, however, ended their interest in the Cup in the quarter-final by five goals to three.

Now playing in the 'modern' style with three half-backs and five forwards, Rangers decided to try their luck in England and joined the English Football Association in 1885. That season they were drawn against Rawtenstall but Rangers refused to play the English club on the grounds that they were professional. Rangers were fined 10 shillings by the FA for failing to honour their commitments. In season 1886/87, having been eliminated in the Scottish Cup second round by Cambuslang, Rangers travelled to Liverpool to play Everton in the first round of the FA Cup. A Charlie Heggie goal brought them a shock 1-0 win, after the players' boisterous behaviour had seen them evicted from their hotel the previous evening, and two goals from left-winger Matt Lawrie took them past Church at Kinning Park in the next round.

Scottish club Cowlairs were then beaten, 3-2 in an exciting game, and the Rangers were given a bye in the fourth round. They beat Lincoln City 3-0 in the fifth round to move into the quarter-final. After the game Lincoln had been so impressed by Donald Gow that they made the Rangers forward an offer of two pounds ten shillings per week to join them. Gow refused. Old Westminsters travelled up to Glasgow and returned chastened by a 5-1 drubbing in what was the last official game played at Kinning Park. Rangers faced Aston Villa in the final at Nantwich, almost a home game for the Birmingham side, and were defeated 3-1. Much of the blame was apportioned to keeper Willie Chalmers, something of a trencherman, whose mobility was apparently curtailed by a large meal on the morning of the match. The team which played Villa was: Chalmers, Forbes, Gow, Cameron, McIntyre, Muir, Lawrie, Lafferty, Lindsay, Peacock, Fraser. At the end of the season the SFA, annoyed by various clubs' apparent preference for the FA Cup, banned Scottish clubs from entering the competition.

Having earlier in the year received an eviction notice to leave Kinning Park, Rangers played out the rest of the 1886/87 season on Third Lanark's ground at Cathkin Park. Reasoning correctly that the inevitable development of the

Tom Vallance, captain and club president of Rangers and a noted artist and businessman

city was to the west, Rangers themselves moved westwards, to Ibrox Park in Govan. The new ground had a 300-foot long grandstand, an imposing pavilion in the north-east corner of the ground and an overall capacity for 15,000 spectators. The stadium was located where Edmiston House stands today. On 20 August 1887 they marked the opening of the new ground with an exhibition match against the top English side Preston North End, known as the 'Invincibles'. The exhibition came from Preston who, playing with seven Scots in the team, were 5-0 ahead at half time, and the game was prematurely ended by a pitch invasion with the score 8-1.

Rangers took time to settle into their new surroundings and, in 1888/89, had a bad season, losing 19 of their 39 games. They were also knocked out of the Scottish Cup by Clyde and defeated 6-1 in the Glasgow Cup by Celtic, a newly-formed and equally ambitious club from the east side of the city. That season, Rangers strengthened the team by acquiring two half-backs – Robert Marshall and David Mitchell – and a forward, Andrew McCreadie, while behind the scenes they appointed William Wilton as Match Secretary. In effect Wilton had become Rangers' first manager and he was about to begin a 30-year distinguished career in charge of the club.

The team building continued during the 1890 close season, with forwards Neil Kerr arriving from Cowlairs and

David Hislop from Partick Thistle. Goal-scoring inside-left John 'Kitey' McPherson, who would prove to be a loyal club servant, also arrived from Cowlairs.

Season 1890/91 saw the birth of the Scottish League, with Wilton, the League's first treasurer, working hard behind the scenes to help ensure that this new competition ran smoothly and efficiently. Not everyone welcomed the new league, however. The *Sunday Sport* thundered 'The entire rules stink of finance – money making and money grubbing'. Some clubs, such as Queen's Park, argued that the new arrangement would threaten the future of the amateur ethos and would lead to the demise of the smaller, village clubs who depended on friendlies with the larger clubs for their existence. Queen's Park declined to take part in the league but they were forced by economic necessity to join ten years later.

The original clubs were Rangers, Celtic, Vale of Leven, Renton, Third Lanark, Hearts, St Mirren, Dumbarton, Cowlairs, Cambuslang, and Abercorn, although early in the season Renton were banned for playing a professional team, St Bernards (disguised as Edinburgh Saints). By now the rules of association football had been tightened and the game was beginning to bear a closer resemblance to the sport we know today. Nets had been installed behind the goal and a crossbar had replaced the old goal tape. One referee, armed with a whistle, replaced the old system of two umpires (one provided by each club) and, to add excitement – and controversy – to the game, the penalty kick was introduced that season.

Rangers' first league game was at Ibrox against Hearts on 16 August and they won 5-2. McPherson scored four in their next league match against Cambuslang and they then beat Renton 4-1. Throughout the season, Rangers were neck to neck with Dumbarton and had to beat Celtic on the last day to win the title. A goalkeeping error allowed Celtic to win 2-1 and Rangers and Dumbarton tied on 29 points. Although Dumbarton had a better goal difference – 40 to Rangers' 33 – this was at the time not a factor influencing league position. A decider was held at Cathkin on 21 May 1891 in front of 10,000 spectators. Rangers had full-back William Hodge and outside-left David Hislop out through injury, but the team began promisingly. The crowd, as the *Scottish Sport* observed, were 'rivetted by the magnificent actions of the Rangers who all at once fell into a nice confident stride and seemed like carrying all before them'.

By the interval Rangers were two up, but they began to waver in the second half and Dumbarton fought back to level the score by the end. The *Scottish Sport* concluded: 'It was truly a great struggle'. The SFA decided to declare the clubs joint champions, mainly because there was very little time in the clubs' fixture lists for another replay. The first Scottish League season had altogether been a great success, with 814 goals scored in 180 games, none of which ended goalless.

In the Scottish Cup, Rangers had played their first ever match against Celtic on 8 September, the game finishing 1-0 in Celtic's favour at Parkhead. Thus began one of the most famous, and indeed notorious, rivalries in world football. In the Glasgow Cup, Rangers played Third Lanark in the third round, a tie which took a remarkable four games to resolve. Third Lanark eventually progressed in the competition with a 2-1 victory at Ibrox.

By the 1891/92 season there had been more personnel changes, with winger Tom Wylie having joined Everton, defender Donald Gow gone to Sunderland and forward David Hislop to Aston Villa. The lure of an attractive and legal salary was proving difficult to resist. Incomers included keeper David Haddow from Albion Rovers and, later in the season, Jock Drummond, a full-back from Falkirk who was to prove a stalwart defender in the years to come. A strong tackler and firm exponent of the shoulder charge (an effective and perfectly legitimate tactic right up until the 1960s), Drummond was never seen on the pitch without his cap, ostensibly to keep his head warm but in reality to conceal his greying hair. In spite of this infusion of new players, however, Rangers started the season badly, losing to Celtic, Third Lanark and Dumbarton, and never really found their momentum. They finished the season in fifth place in the league. In the Scottish Cup they were beaten by Celtic 5-3 in the semi-final at Parkhead, and they were beaten again by Celtic, fast becoming a bogey team, 2-0 in the final of the Charity Cup. Of the latter match, *Scottish Sport* noted of Rangers: 'the team's forward play was indifferent and erratic and perhaps had more pluck in it than judgment'.

Rangers' fortunes in 1892/93 were mixed. Although they beat Dumbarton away in the Scottish Cup for the first time, with McPherson scoring the only goal, they were knocked out in the third round of the competition by Edinburgh's St Bernards. However, Rangers triumphed in the Glasgow Cup and recorded their first win over Celtic, and their first Glasgow Cup trophy, at Cathkin Park in the final by three goals to one. The team in this momentous clash was: Haddow, Hay, Drummond, Marshall, H McCreadie, Mitchell, Davie, A McCreadie, Kerr, McPherson, Barker. In the league, Rangers made a bright start, winning their first fifteen games, but defeat at Dumbarton and Celtic left them one point behind champions Celtic at the conclusion of the league campaign.

Two important signings were made by Rangers towards the end of the 1892/93 season. Nicol ('Nick') Smith, who was to form the bedrock of the defence with Jock

Drummond until Smith's untimely death from enteric fever in 1905 at the age of 31, joined to fill the right-back position, and forward James Steel arrived from Linthouse.

At the end of the season, the SFA annual general meeting bowed to the inevitable and sanctioned professionalism, a move which removed the threat of the English clubs' inducements to attract the top Scottish players and which instituted formal and binding contracts between club and player. This belated capitulation by the SFA removed the sham of 'amateurism' from Scottish football, many of whose clubs had been paying players one way or another for several years, and reinforced the commercial ethos fast developing in the Scottish game. The decision was a controversial one and was denounced by many contemporary observers, but the logic of professionalism was inescapable. Apart, that is, for Queen's Park who opted to retain their amateur status.

In the following season – 1893/94 – Rangers at last won the Scottish Cup. Having already retained the Glasgow Cup with wins over Pollockshaws (by eleven goals!) and Celtic (1-0), they made sure of the trophy with a 1-0 victory over Cowlairs at Cathkin Park They also took on Cowlairs at Ibrox in the Scottish Cup and put eight goals past the old club. They then disposed of Leith Athletic and Clyde in subsequent rounds – Steel scoring four in their 5-0 demolition of Clyde – and met Cup-holders Queen's Park in the semi-final at Ibrox. After a 1-1 draw, Rangers opened the scoring through Nicol Smith in the first half of the replay at Hampden, and ensured their place in the Final against Celtic with two second half goals from McPherson and Steel to win 3-1.

Earlier in the season Rangers had played Celtic in the league at Ibrox and won 5-0. Left-winger John Barker scored three of them, while McPherson and Gray added the other two. Barker became the first Rangers player to claim a hat-trick in a Rangers v Celtic match. On 1 January Rangers visited Celtic Park to play the first Ne'er Day fixture, a friendly, beating Celtic 3-2. The Ne'er Day fixture was to become a tradition, and the popular annual match between the two clubs over the New Year period was to continue until season 2000/2001.

John McPherson, scorer of the third goal in the 1893/94 Scottish Cup final and Rangers' Director from 1907-1926

On 17 February 1894 Rangers met Celtic in the Scottish Cup Final at a rain-drenched Hampden Park. By half-time, in a pulsating game, the score remained goalless, with Rangers captain Davy Mitchell in imperious form. In the space of ten second-half minutes Rangers won the game. In the 60th minute Hugh McCreadie opened Rangers' account, converting a Mitchell free-kick, and then five minutes later Barker doubled the lead with a splendid solo goal. In the 68th minute McPherson added a third from twenty yards and, although Willie Maley scored for Celtic, the Celts were well beaten. The Rangers players received a bonus of 3 guineas for their efforts. An amicable presentation of the trophy followed that evening at the Alexandra Hotel with players and officials from both sides warmly joining in the celebrations. At the time the two clubs enjoyed a friendly and mutually profitable relationship, although over the next few years this was to cool off, and the rise of sectarianism in the early years of the 20th century was to engender a bitter and enduring polarisation between supporters of Rangers and Celtic.

Some notable players joined Rangers in 1894. First to arrive was left-winger Alec Smith who was to represent Scotland on 20 occasions and to enjoy an illustrious 21-year career with Rangers. Smith was a supremely consistent player, speedy down the wing and renowned for being an excellent crosser of the ball. Towards the end of the year, the exceptionally talented wing-half Neil ('Neilly') Gibson, whose speciality was his back-heel clearances, joined from Larkhall. Defender David Crawford, from St Mirren, also made his first appearance. Rangers were building a side which was to dominate Scottish football over the coming seasons, although 1894/95 was something of a disappointment. Hearts were in the ascendant and the Edinburgh club won the league, with Rangers finishing third. Hearts also knocked Rangers out of the Scottish Cup at Ibrox 2-1 in the first round. Rangers reached the final of the Glasgow Cup but were defeated 2-0 by Celtic. Season 1895/96 was also uneventful by Rangers' standards although they did finish second to Celtic in the league.

Jock Drummond, long-serving full back distinguished by the cap he wore in every game. He collected fourteen caps for Scotland

Rangers in 1894 with the Scottish Cup and Glasgow Cup. Back: H McCreadie, Steel, Smith, Taylor (trainer), Haddow, Mitchell. Middle: A McCreadie, Boyd, Wilton (secretary), Drummond, McPherson, Barker. Seated: Marshall, Gray

However, everything fell into place in 1896/97. With new keeper Matthew Dickie between the posts, and winger Tommy ('the Boy') Low and forwards James Miller and ex-Guardsman Tom Hyslop teaming up with McPherson and Smith, Rangers now possessed a team of the highest calibre. Firstly they beat Celtic 2-1 in the Glasgow Cup final replay to claim the trophy. In the Scottish Cup, they brushed aside Partick Thistle, Hibernian and Dundee before defeating Morton 7-2 at Cappielow. They faced Dumbarton in the final on 20 March 1897 at Hampden. Two goals ahead early in the second half, Rangers conceded a goal but a three-goal burst in five minutes towards the end of the game ensured that Rangers won their second trophy of the season, 5-1. The team was: Dickie, Smith, Drummond, Gibson, McCreadie, Mitchell, Low, McPherson, Miller, Hyslop, Smith.

Central defender Bobby Neil joined the club before the Charity Cup campaign began and replaced Hugh McCreadie. Rangers eliminated Celtic 4-1 in the first round and then put six past Third Lanark to collect their third cup of the season. This laudable achievement was a result of their diligent defending and their remarkable, high-scoring attack who scored fifty-four goals in the three tournaments, conceding only ten. Rangers were rapidly becoming a coherent, cohesive unit, displaying strength and skill as well as dogged determination and a refusal to capitulate.

In 1897/98 the attack was given a further boost by the arrival of centre-forward R C (Bob) Hamilton. Hamilton began his career with Elgin City in the Highland League, and signed for Rangers while at Glasgow University. At the end of his career, he moved back to Elgin where he eventually became Lord Provost. Although Rangers were beaten early in the league programme, 4-0 by Celtic at Ibrox, they ended the season in second place, four points behind their Glasgow rivals. They retained the Glasgow Cup, having taken three games to defeat Celtic in the semi-final, and beat Queen's Park in the final at Cathkin Park by four goals. In the Scottish Cup they again had to play three games in the semi-final, this time against Third Lanark, to progress to the final where they met Kilmarnock. Smith and Hamilton scored for Rangers and Rangers had their second trophy of the season. A strangely nervous Rangers took to the field for the Charity Cup final against Third Lanark and they lost the match 1-0. Still, two out of three trophies was certainly acceptable, and Rangers moved on to contest their most successful season to date.

Now regularly vying with Celtic for the accolade of best

TOM VALLANCE

Requests the Presence of

Mr J.S. M'Kenzie

TO SUPPER

IN THE

METROPOLITAN

40 HUTCHISON St

on the occasion of the

21st ANNIVERSARY

OF THE

FINAL CUP TIE

PLAYED

13th APRIL 1877.

Vale of Leven Team.
1876-77.
Wm. C. Wood.
Archibald Michie.
Andrew M'Intyre.
William Jamieson.
Alexander M'Lintock.
John Ferguson.
David Lindsay.
John M'Dougall.
Robert Paton.
John C. M'Gregor.
John C. Baird.

Rangers Team.
Thomas Vallance.
George Gillespie.
Wm. B. M'Neil.
Sam. Ricketts.
David Hill.
James Watson.
Moses M'Neil.
J.S. MacKenzie.

IN MEMORIAM
Alex. Marshall.
P. M. Campbell.
W. Dunlop.
J. Watt.

WEDNESDAY, 13TH APRIL, 1898.

An invitation to supper from Tom Vallance to celebrate the 21st anniversary of the 1877 Scottish Cup final. Note that three of the Rangers team had died in the intervening period

team in Scotland, Rangers emphatically asserted their dominance in 1898/99, when they took the league title at a canter, winning every one of the 18 games they played and not dropping a single point. Right-winger John Campbell arrived from Blackburn Rovers to take over from Tommy Low, and Rangers started as they meant to continue, with a 6-2 win over Partick Thistle at Ibrox, Hamilton claiming a hat-trick. They compensated for their 4-0 defeat by Celtic the previous season with a 4-0 win at Parkhead and beat Hearts 3-1 at Ibrox. They did have a scare, however, in the eleventh match at Easter Road when they were 3-2 down but recovered to 3-3. With less than a minute to go, Campbell was fouled in the box, and Bobby Neil coolly stepped up to convert and give a relieved Rangers a 4-3 win.

Rangers captured the title with four league games remaining when Hamilton scored another hat-trick against Dundee in a 7-0 drubbing of the Tayside team. Hibernian visited Ibrox for the fifteenth game and were five goals down after twenty minutes. In a masterful display Rangers ran up ten goals without reply, Alec Smith contributing four. New arrival Campbell scored twice against St Mirren in the 3-2 win at Ibrox, and Hamilton picked up yet another hat-trick in Rangers' 4-1 defeat of Celtic at Ibrox. A 3-0 result away at Clyde brought Rangers their unprecedented winning record, which has never been matched in British football, and is never likely to be. The regular team, with occasional changes, through the season was: Dickie, Smith, Crawford, Gibson, Neil, Mitchell, Campbell, McPherson, Hamilton, Miller, Smith.

Curiously, although Rangers reached the final of all three cup competitions, this prodigiously talented team could not add another trophy to their league triumph. In the Glasgow Cup they went down 1-0 to Queen's Park after a Nicol Smith own goal. In the Scottish Cup first round Rangers beat Hearts 4-1 in a controversial tie. Two Hearts players were sent off in a bad-tempered game and, although the Edinburgh side lodged a protest about the quality of the refereeing, it was rejected by the SFA. Celtic achieved revenge for their league humiliations, beating Rangers 2-0 in the final, and it was Celtic again by the same scoreline in the Charity Cup.

Rangers were growing in stature off the pitch as well as on it. On 27 March 1899 a special general meeting was held where the members voted to transform Rangers into a limited liability company. The club would henceforth be known as Rangers Football Club Limited. Later in the Spring a board of directors was appointed and, on 30 May, William Wilton, until now match secretary, was formally appointed manager, a popular choice and the first manager in Rangers' history. James Henderson, who had filled the role of club president, was elected club chairman. Rangers now embarked on expansion.

Having recognised that the current Ibrox had become too small for Rangers' growing support and the club's ambition, the board had decided to expand and enlarge their stadium. The 'second' Ibrox was opened on 30 December 1899, 100 yards across the road from the old stadium, at a cost of £20,000. The ground's grandstand and pavilion were on the south side, facing a covered terrace to the north which was known as the 'Bovril Stand' from the Bovril advertisement on the roof. The rest of the ground was open, banked terracing, with an overall capacity of around 75,000. Wilton also insisted on a cinder running track around the pitch which would form the basis for the annual summer athletics competition – the Rangers Sports. The Sports in time attracted some of the world's finest athletes – including Eric Liddell, inspiration for the movie *Chariots of Fire* – and were a prestigious and popular event right up till their termination in 1962.

The stadium was inaugurated with a match against Hearts in

Do drop in

the Inter-City league, a short-lived tournament contested by clubs from Glasgow, Edinburgh and Aberdeen. Rangers won 3-1, all three goals coming from forward John Wilkie who had joined the club the previous season from Blackburn Rovers. The club also acquired earlier in the season the left-half Jackie Robertson from Southampton, who was to captain Scotland in April 1900 to the country's memorable 4-1 defeat of England at Parkhead. A stylish, hard-tackling goalscorer, who is reputed to have initiated the pass back to the keeper as a tactic, Robertson replaced David Mitchell in the Rangers line-up.

The question uppermost in the players' and supporters' minds now was how long could this winning league sequence last? Rangers began the 1899/1900 season winning their first four league games – twenty-two in succession – but the run came to an end when they drew 1-1 with Hearts at Tynecastle. But how many games could they continue without a defeat? The team who took both points of Rangers was, inevitably, Celtic, on New Year's Day when they won 3-2. This meant that Rangers had played thirty-five games without losing in the league, an astonishing record. They finished the season with the league title again, seven points ahead of Celtic. In the cups, they won the Charity Cup with a crushing 5-1 win over Celtic, and the Glasgow Cup by 1-0, Celtic again being the victim.

The 20th century had just begun and Rangers, resplendent in their new and imposing stadium, one of the world's biggest, and fielding the finest team so far in their history, had every reason to look forward to the new millennium.

William Wilton, Match Secretary from 1889 to 1899 and Manager from 1899 until his death in 1920

CHAPTER TWO:

WILTON TAKES OVER: 1900-1920

Left: *Finlay Speedie, inside left for Rangers*

Right: *Contemporary drawing of the Ibrox Disaster of 1902.*

Rangers began the 20th century in confident mood, winning their first four league games before stumbling 4-1 to a young Hibernian team and then losing 2-1 to Celtic. The Celtic defeat was the last of their league season and they beat their old enemy at Ibrox, winning 2-1 with the goals coming from McPherson and new signing Finlay Speedie. Speedie, an inside-left from Clydebank Juniors, was to create a powerful left-wing partnership with Alec Smith in the years to come.

Another newcomer was centre-back James Stark, from Glasgow Perthshire. He was a stabilising and dependable presence, and he was fondly regarded by the Ibrox faithful for his subduing effect on the prolific Celtic striker Jimmy Quinn. An apocryphal but revealing anecdote in John Allan's *The Story of the Rangers, 1873 – 1923* has Quinn buying a football in a sports shop and being asked by the salesman 'Will you take it with you?'. 'Oh, no', replied Quinn, 'If I met Jamie Stark, he would be sure to take it from me.'

Rangers won the league by six points, beating St Mirren 4-1 in the final game, and they also claimed the Glasgow Cup. In an exciting first round game in the tournament against Celtic, the Celts were 2-1 ahead with only ten minutes remaining at Parkhead. Rangers then grabbed two goals through Robertson and Campbell, and Celtic equalised with less than twenty seconds left. In the Ibrox replay, although 2-1 down at half time Rangers came back with two goals from Hamilton and one from Campbell. They conceded a late Celtic goal but went through to the semi-final, beating Third Lanark, and in the final faced Partick Thistle, who now had ex-Ger Tom

Postcard celebrating the Glasgow Exhibition of 1901

Hyslop playing inside-left. A comfortable 3-1 win gave Rangers the trophy.

In 1901/02, they beat Celtic 3-1, with two goals from Hamilton and one from Neil, to collect the Glasgow Exhibition Cup, a handsome new trophy. The competition was held to celebrate the Glasgow Exhibition and was contested by the top eight Scottish clubs. Although they were eliminated from the Scottish Cup by Hibernian in the semi-final, they retained the Glasgow Cup, under less than ideal circumstances. After a 2-2 draw in the final at Ibrox, the tournament organisers, the Glasgow FA, decreed that the replay be held again at Ibrox. When Celtic insisted on Parkhead being the venue, Rangers suggested a neutral ground but Celtic refused this attempt at a compromise and the Glasgow Cup was awarded to Rangers by default.

Rangers then won the league for the fourth season in succession, the crucial game being against Celtic at Parkhead on New Year's Day. If Celtic won, they were champions. Celtic went ahead but Nicol Smith equalised from a free kick, amid Celtic protests about its validity. Rangers then scored another through Campbell. Celtic again complained, this time about handling, and Celtic's inside-left McMahon was sent off. With the score 3-2 to Rangers, Hamilton added a fourth which led to Celtic claiming offside but the score finished 4-2. Rangers then had to win their final three games, which they did in style.

On 5 April, events on the pitch suddenly became sadly irrelevant. The Scotland v England international match was held at Ibrox Park and the rain lashed down. The terracing had been built using steel columns on a concrete base, with steel beams carrying wooden joists to support the wooden standing area. As kick-off approached, thousands of fans were streaming into the west terracing, and the terraces and walkways were becoming increasingly congested. Ten minutes into the game, the steel supports began to buckle under the weight, the terracing started to sway and suddenly an 80-foot-long by 13-foot-wide gap appeared, causing dozens of people to fall fifty feet to the ground. In the ensuing panic many more were crushed and badly injured. While rescue workers attended to the casualties, the game was stopped but was then allowed to continue, with many

Above: *Another drawing of the Ibrox Disaster of 1902*

Left: *The collapsed wooden terracing at Ibrox in 1902*

spectators unaware of what was happening. The game ended in a 1-1 draw, with the cries of the wounded mingling with the roars from the crowd.

The authorities had not contemplated the possibility of such a catastrophe in their state-of-the-art stadium, so splints had to be improvised from broken wooden terracing, clothing was ripped up to provide temporary bandages and doors were torn down to serve as stretchers. The major Glasgow hospitals shared in the rescue and care efforts, but 26 people had died in the first Ibrox Disaster and 587 had been injured. The consensus after the game was that terracings now had to be built on earth and gravel to prevent another awful tragedy occurring. The match was replayed a month later with all receipts going to the Ibrox Disaster Relief Fund.

Rangers then generously suggested that they put up the Exhibition Cup for competition in a one-off, knock-out British League Cup with proceeds going to the Relief Fund. The top two English league teams – Everton and Sunderland – were invited to compete against Celtic and Rangers. The two English teams were dismissed and Celtic beat Rangers 3-2 after injury time in the final.

As a result of the disaster, Ibrox had to be rebuilt the following season and the capacity was cut to 25,000. To help finance the project, no less than 22 players were put on the transfer list! The old guard – such as Mitchell and McPherson – were now leaving the club and the team which won four league championships in succession was being dismantled. New players were, however, brought in, including right-back Alex Fraser from Clydebank Juniors, half-back George Henderson from Dundee and winger Angus McDonald. The team's league form was poor and they finished the season in third place behind winners Hibernian. Rangers were also knocked out of the Glasgow and Charity Cups.

Their fortunes improved in the Scottish Cup. They reached the Final against Hearts and drew the first two games. In the second replay, with ticket prices reduced from one shilling to sixpence to attract the crowds, Alec Mackie opened the scoring for Rangers in the 15th minute, but then the redoubtable Jock Drummond was injured and had to go off. Speedie took his place at left-back and the Rangers defence absorbed the constant pressure from the Hearts forwards. A break by Hamilton from a through ball by Stark made the score 2-0 to Rangers and that was the score at the final whistle. Rangers had won their fourth Scottish Cup, but it was to be be another twenty-five years before the Cup returned to Ibrox.

The next few years saw the dominance of Scottish football by a great Celtic side led by manager Willie Maley and featuring the attacking talents of, among others, Jimmy McMenemy and Jimmy Quinn. Rangers were again rebuilding but they had to wait seven years before they won their next

Cartoon in the Scottish Referee, *1904*

league title. In 1903/04 Third Lanark were the form side, winning the league and the Glasgow Cup. Rangers reached the Scottish Cup final and played Celtic. Two strikes from Speedie had Rangers 2-0 in the lead after 15 minutes but Quinn levelled the score by half time. Quinn's winner in the second half meant that he was the first ever player to score a hat trick in a Scottish Cup final.

Shortly before the Cup final, a cartoon had appeared in the *Scottish Referee* which showed an old man with a sandwich board carrying the legend 'Patronise the Old Firm' and signed underneath by 'Rangers, Celtic Ltd'. In his book *The Old Firm*, Bill Murray writes that this seems to be the first time the famous phrase was used and was obviously intended to be a sarcastic reference to the financial interdependence of the two Glasgow clubs. The existence of the four major tournaments meant that Rangers and Celtic could play each other several times a season, and the commercial benefits of these fixtures had clearly not escaped the notice of the respective boards. With attendances at a Rangers v Celtic league game attracting 70,000 or more the gate receipts were extremely lucrative.

However, as Murray notes: 'It was apparent that the two clubs were attracting people to their games who didn't otherwise show much interest in football. This was in part because they played the best football; but it was also because they drew on deeper passions than the spectacle of a thrilling encounter tightly contested. For a game of football between Celtic and Rangers reflected the religious and almost racial divisions that scarred community life in many parts of Scotland'. The sectarian divide between the two clubs was becoming increasingly apparent and growing. In 1912 the arrival on the Clyde of shipbuilders Harland and Wolff from Belfast, with their exclusively Protestant workforce, served to exacerbate the religious tensions between the two sets of supporters.

By season 1904/05, Dickie, Drummond, Crawford, Gibson and Neil had all left the club and Nicol Smith died in January. Jackie Robertson was also to leave at the end of the season to become manager at Chelsea. However, ex-Queen's Park striker R S McColl arrived from Newcastle. McColl, known as 'Toffee Bob' because of his confectionery

business in Glasgow, was also more appropriately lauded as 'the prince of centre-forwards', and he scored three hat-tricks in his thirteen games for Scotland. In spite of McColl's talismanic presence in the forward line Rangers won no silverware for a second year, although they lost narrowly to Celtic in a league decider play-off. Both teams had finished the season on 41 points and Celtic won the play-off at Hampden 2-1. They had, however, beaten the Parkhead side in the Scottish Cup semi-final. With eight minutes to go and Rangers leading 2-0, Jimmy Quinn was sent off for allegedly kicking Rangers full-back Alec Craig in the face. A section of the crowd, incensed by this decision, invaded the pitch and the game was abandoned. Celtic conceded the tie, and Rangers were defeated 3-1 in the final by Third Lanark. Season 1905/6 was also a disappointment. Although Rangers won the Charity Cup, they could only manage fourth spot in the league, 12 points behind Celtic.

In 1906/07, Rangers augmented the squad with two young players who were to make their mark in the next few years. James Gordon, a right-half, arrived from Renfrew Victoria and George Law from Arbroath was to fill Nicol Smith's right-back position. Right-back R G Campbell had been acquired from Celtic in early 1906 and the burly defender was also to prove his worth as centre-forward, scoring 14 goals this season and 35 the next. Rangers won the Charity Cup but the other three trophies were picked up by Celtic, who were to underline their dominance the next season by collecting all four. An interesting piece of good fortune occurred this season for Rangers' reserve goalkeeper Tom Sinclair. In the first game of the season – a testimonial for Finlay Speedie against Celtic – Celtic's keeper David Adams was

Above: RS McColl, Rangers forward known as 'the prince of centre-forwards' in the Scotland strip

Right: Ibrox in the early years of the 20th century

RANGERS F.C.

injured. Obligingly, Rangers loaned them Sinclair, who went on to keep eight consecutive clean sheets for Celtic, win a Scottish Cup medal and also, after his transfer to Newcastle, collect an English league medal, all in the same season!

Beaten by Celtic in the Scottish Cup and Glasgow Cup, and by Queen's Park in the Charity Cup, and third in the

The Rangers squad in 1909. Back: Yuille, McLean, Stark, Campbell, Galt, Gordon, May, Hunter. Middle: Rennie, Waddell, Reid, Gilchrist, Law, Thomson, McPherson, Lock. Seated: Wilson (trainer), Bennett, Miller, Hogg, McKenzie, Craig, Jackson, Smith

league, Rangers had another unfulfilled season in 1907/08. They did, however, late in the season secure the services of ex-Scottish international keeper Harry Rennie from Hibernian as well as persuading inside-left Alec Bennett to move across the city from Parkhead. Bob Hamilton left the club on a free transfer at the end of the season. Left-winger Alec Smith was now the only player in the team who had been part of the famous 1898/99 line-up.

Season 1908/09 is remembered for the infamous Hampden Riot. In April Rangers played Celtic in the Scottish Cup Final at Hampden. With Rangers ahead 2-1. Rennie caught a cross from Celtic right-winger Munro, and swerved to avoid the onrushing Quinn. The referee, apparently believing that Rennie had carried the ball over the line, gave a goal. Rennie vehemently denied that the ball had gone over but a 2-2 result stood.

Before the game Celtic's Willie Maley had suggested that, in the event of a replay, the game should go into extra time even though the laws firmly stated that extra time should only be played after a second replay. The replay finished 1-1, and after the whistle went some of the players remained on the

pitch, thereby suggesting the possibility of extra time. When a section of the crowd realised that extra time would not be played, and suspecting a plot between the clubs to arrange another lucrative play-off, they went on the rampage. Fuelled by outrage and whisky, they attacked and stoned the police, tore down barricades, burnt down the turnstiles, set alight bonfires, cut the fire brigade hoses and generally caused mayhem. Whisky was also apparently used to stoke the fires. The fighting and violence continued until seven in the evening and more than one hundred people were injured. The next day Rangers and Celtic released a joint statement which said: 'On account of the regrettable occurrences of Saturday, both clubs agree to petition the Association that the Final tie be abandoned.' Although the SFA suggested replaying the game outside Glasgow, both clubs refused. They were fined £150 each and the SFA withheld the trophy, the only time this has occurred in the history of Scottish football.

Just before the replay, one of Rangers' greatest ever goalscorers – Willie Reid – joined the club from Portsmouth. Other new arrivals included powerful outside-right Billy Hogg from Sunderland and keeper Herbert Lock from Southampton. Lock became the first Englishman signed by Rangers from an English club. Season 1909-10 was, however, lacklustre, with the club finishing third in the league and being knocked out of the cups. The team finally blended the following season and – bolstered by new recruits

Above: *The players remain on the pitch after the 1909 Cup final replay and the crowd assumes that extra time will be played*

Left: *The 1909 Hampden Riot*

winger Dr James Paterson (as eventual replacement for Alec Smith), centre-half George Chapman and inside-forward Jimmy Bowie – Rangers won the league (Reid scoring 38 times in the competition) and beat Celtic in the finals of the Glasgow Cup and the Charity Cup, Reid claiming both goals in the final of the latter tournament. They exited from the Scottish Cup, however, after a 2-1 defeat by Dundee in the third round.

They won the league again in 1911-12, not losing a game until a 2-1 defeat by Morton in early December and wrapped up the title with a 2-1 victory over Raith Rovers in March. In the Scottish Cup they played Clyde in the second round at Shawfield in front of a record crowd of 52,000. With Clyde 3-1 ahead after 75 minutes there was a pitch invasion by 2,000 or so Rangers supporters and the match was abandoned. Rangers conceded the tie. At the end of the season, Rangers' president and chairman for the previous fourteen years, Bailie James Henderson, died and was succeeded by Sir John Ure Primrose.

In spite of keeper Lock missing virtually the entire 1912/13 season through injury, Rangers retained the league title, finishing four points ahead of Celtic. However, they were surprisingly eliminated from the Scottish Cup by Falkirk, with John Hempsey,

Lock's replacement in goal, having a nightmare performance. Falkirk went on to win the trophy while Rangers picked up their tenth Glasgow Cup. New faces appeared early in the next season. Billy Hogg had moved to Dundee and he was replaced on the right wing by Scott Duncan from Newcastle. Skilful inside-right James Stewart also arrived from Newcastle. Paterson moved to the left-wing position, with Reid still occupying the centre-forward role, and the club won the Glasgow Cup for the fourth consecutive year. Another newcomer, inside-forward Tommy Cairns, soon to be a hugely influential playmaker, goalscorer and captain, played his first game in December 1913. The only tournament Rangers won that season was the Glasgow Cup, beating Third Lanark 3-0 at Hampden. In 1914 James Wilson, club trainer for the past seventeen years, died and he was replaced by William Struth, coach at Clyde, physiotherapist and an ex-professional runner. One of the most momentous appointments ever made by Rangers, Bill Struth was to become one of the true legends in the club's history.

Before season 1914-15 could get under way, the Great War broke out. The SFA immediately cancelled the Scottish Cup for the duration of the conflict but unaccountably continued with the league and the Glasgow Cup competitions. Players were discouraged from playing full-time football and entered active service or worked in war-related industries in Glasgow, while Struth and Wilton devoted much of their energies to helping out at Bellahouston Hospital. With so many joining up, attendances suffered and many of the best Scottish players were fighting for their country in the trenches of France. Although the league was somewhat debased, Celtic were dominant throughout the period and Rangers won the league only once between 1914 and 1918, in 1918 when they beat Celtic by one point.

The Light Blues, however, were building the side which would sweep all before it in the 1920s. While Alec Smith retired in 1915, bringing to an end Rangers' last great era, full-back Ulsterman Bert Manderson arrived as did the goalscoring inside-forward Andy Cunningham, who was to remain with the club until 1929. Two years later they were joined by outside-right Sandy Archibald, wing-half Tommy Muirhead, centre-half Arthur Dixon and full-back George McQueen. That year, 1917, King George V visited Ibrox for an investiture of war heroes in front of thousands of spectators, and the Lord Provost presented Wilton to the king.

By the end of the War several Rangers players had been decorated and fought with distinction but the only death was Walter Tull, the first coloured player to sign for the club, but who never had the oportunity to play for Rangers. Tull was killed at the Second Battle of the Somme in March 1918.

The War ended on 11 November 1918, and Rangers finished the first season of peace in second place to Celtic in the league. In 1919/20, with the league expanded from 18 to 22 clubs and the crowds flocking back to football, Rangers won the league, losing only two games, and they scored 106 goals, conceding only 25. They tied up the title in April, drawing with Dumbarton. The previous month a young half-back David Meiklejohn had joined the club, and he was about to begin a distinguished career with Rangers. In their fourth round Scottish Cup tie against Celtic, in front of a record attendance of 83,000 at Ibrox, a Muirhead goal early in the second half put Rangers through to play Albion Rovers, to whom they lost after a replay in a shock result. The team against Celtic was: Lock, Manderson, Gordon, Bowie, Dixon, Walls, Archibald, Muirhead, Cunningham, Cairns, Paterson.

In early May, just after the final game of the season, Wilton decided to spend the weekend at Gourock, just down the Clyde, on a 19-ton yawl, the Caltha, owned by John Mair, one of the club directors. In the early hours of Sunday 2 May a fierce storm blew up in the harbour and the boat was broken free from its moorings by the increasingly treacherous seas. Wilton's companions climbed up the mast and managed to scramble on to the quayside but, in trying to get ashore, Wilton lost his grip and fell under the waves. Although Mair dived into the water in an attempt to save him, Wilton drowned and his body was never found. The next day's *Glasgow Herald* expressed shock at the accident, concluding: 'To the members of the club his death will bring a sense of personal bereavement. It is a loss not only to Scottish football but to the game.'

In June Bill Struth was appointed the new manager of Rangers, a position he was to hold for the next thirty-four years and from which he oversaw Rangers' domination of Scottish football over the coming decades. He was also to become the most successful manager in the club's history.

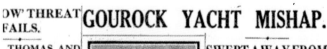

The Daily Record *reports the death of William Wilton in its Monday 3 May edition*

CHAPTER THREE:

BETWEEN THE WARS: 1920-1945

Alan Morton, the 'wee blue devil'

After Wilton's drowning, Bill Struth took over responsibility for matters on the pitch while the board appointed J Rogers Simpson as company secretary. This division between the administration of the club and the responsibility for results on the pitch suited Struth's personality and inclination. A stonemason by trade, Struth had been a highly successful professional runner – a 'pedestrian' – in his youth and had developed a strong interest in training methods and techniques. After a spell on the coaching staff at Hearts, he became trainer at Clyde in 1907 and his insistence on fitness and training had taken the club to two Scottish Cup Finals, including 1909/10 when they had eliminated Rangers 2-0 on their way to Hampden. Rangers, impressed by his achievements, unofficially approached him in 1910 about taking over from their then trainer James Wilson but, although pleased to be asked, Struth declined, probably out of professional respect for Wilson. However, on the death of Wilson in 1914 he accepted the job with alacrity.

He had worked closely with Wilton and had introduced high disciplinary standards, in terms of players' appearance and conduct, as well as working with the players on their fitness, introducing dedicated training regimes. He had also bought wisely, securing the services of full-back Billy ('Bucksy') McCandless, keeper Willie Robb, and his finest ever acquisition, the 5ft 4in outside-left Alan Morton from Queen's Park. An austere, dapper mining engineer, Morton was arguably the greatest left-winger Scotland has produced and he was to go on to become a national footballing legend. Naturally right-footed, he had worked on strengthening his left foot until he was equally adept with both. He was an excellent crosser of the ball and his speciality was lobbing the keeper from distance, managing to impart a wicked spin on the ball which deceived many opposing custodians. Nicknamed 'the wee blue devil' later in his career by an English journalist awestruck by his speed, skill and ability to ghost through defences, Morton was to play 495 games for the Light Blues and score 115 goals for the club before becoming a Rangers' director on his retirement thirteen years later. He is specially remembered in Scotland for his inspirational role in the 'Wembley Wizards' Scottish side who beat England 5-1 at Wembley in 1928.

In June 1920 Struth, realising Morton's potential, signed him on terms which made him the highest paid player in Scottish football, and Morton began to repay the investment. Rangers swept all before them in the league that season and claimed the league title with 76 out of a maximum 84 points. They lost only once, at the Ne'er Day fixture against Celtic when an injury-weakened side let in two goals without reply. Rangers would not lose another Ne'er Day match at Ibrox under Struth's 34-year management career, and it would be 62 years before Celtic triumphed at Ibrox in the traditional fixture.

The Light Blues also reached the final of the Scottish Cup against Partick Thistle, regarded as rank outsiders. Without the services of dependable left-half James Walls, who had broken his leg at Clyde in a Charity Cup game, Rangers replaced him with Jimmy Bowie. Bowie had to leave the field to change his strip during the Final, and Thistle took advantage of his absence to score the only goal of the game through John Blair. The Rangers team that day was: Robb, Manderson, McCandless, Meiklejohn, Dixon, Bowie, Archibald, Cunningham, Henderson, Cairns, Morton.

Rangers were back in the Final the following season where they faced Morton at Hampden in what was their jubilee year. The Scottish Cup jinx continued. Rangers

Presented with FOOTBALL FAVOURITE, October 28th, 1922.

OUR FOOTBALL
BOYS—No. 11.

J. BOWIE (Glasgow Rangers). One of Scotland's star forwards, played in the Victory Internationals against England—in 1919 and again in 1920. North of the Tweed his name ranks with such stalwarts as Charlie Shaw and Alec McNair.

J BOWIE
(Glasgow Rangers)

attacked from the outset with Alan Morton in sparkling form but the Greenock side's James Gourlay scored from a free kick in the 12th minute after keeper Willie Robb carried the ball outside the box. The Rangers defence mistakenly believed the kick to be indirect but Gourlay knew otherwise. Ten minutes later Rangers captain Andy Cunningham broke his jaw and had to go to hospital, accompanied by Bill Struth, and the Gers were down to ten men. Rangers threw themselves forward at the Morton goal but Morton's defence held out to lift the Cup. The *Sunday Mail* headline was 'Rangers beaten by dour Cappielow team', and the newspaper and Scottish football observers again wondered why it was that Rangers – with virtually a full team of internationals – still could not achieve the main prize in the game. Rangers, however, had the consolation of winning the Glasgow Cup and Charity Cup – both against Celtic in the Final. They missed out on the league, finishing one point behind Celtic. That season, a Second Division had been created in Scottish football, with three teams going down. As a reflection of how the old order had changed over thirty years, the three teams relegated were the once-mighty Queen's Park, Dumbarton and Clydebank.

Earlier in the season Rangers had acquired the services of Carl Hansen, a Danish international who had impressed Struth in a close season tour of Scandinavia. The 'Great Dane', a centre-forward, was the first Scandinavian to play for Rangers and quickly became a favourite with the Ibrox faithful. However, he broke his leg the following season and had to return home to Denmark. Hansen opened the

scoring in the 1923 Ne'er Day fixture, Rangers winning 2-0, and they went on to win the league, five points clear of an exciting Airdrie side who could boast Hughie Gallacher in attack. Gallacher scored 33 goals in 34 appearances that season. They also picked up the Glasgow Cup and Charity Cup but the Scottish Cup continued to elude them, going down 2-0 to Ayr United in the second round.

Early in the 1923/24 season, Tom Hamilton arrived from Kirkintilloch Rob Roy to replace Willie Robb in goal. Hamilton was to become a dependable fixture between the posts and would go on to make 399 appearances for the club. Joining him was Tom ('Tully') Craig, a wing-half. Rangers retained the league title, nine points ahead of Airdrie, but stuttered again in the Scottish Cup. On 16 February they met Hibs at Ibrox and, although 1-0 ahead at half time through Meiklejohn, they allowed Hibs to score twice in the second half and were again out of the tournament. Rangers' performances in the Scottish Cup were becoming the butt of music hall gibes but Ibrox fans didn't appreciate the joke.

Rangers' fourth Glasgow Cup victory in succession was achieved the following season in a 4-1 win over Celtic at Parkhead, the goals coming from Henderson (2), Morton and Cairns. After Rangers' fourth goal, captain Cairns suggested to his players that they take it easy till the final whistle. The Light Blues ran up the same scoreline in the Ne'er Day match at Ibrox, Henderson again claiming a brace. Henderson ended the season with 27 league goals, helping Rangers to another league title, with Airdrie again the runner-up. The Scottish Cup, however, continued to prove a problem. A crowd of over 101,000 packed Hampden to watch the semi-final against Celtic towards the end of March. Rangers, perhaps a shade over-confident in the light of their previous two victories that season, allowed Jimmy McGrory to open the scoring in the first half. In the second half they were overrun by Celtic, the game ending in a 5-0 defeat. There is no record of Cairns' instructions to his players in this match.

In the close season more new faces entered Ibrox. Right-back Dougie Gray came from Aberdeen Mugiemoss, and he was to go on to play 940 games for Rangers in a career spanning twenty-two years. Doctor James Marshall, an inside-right, arrived from Shettleston, and the high-scoring centre-forward Jimmy Fleming from St Johnstone completed the intake. In 1925/26 – one of the most disappointing seasons in the club's history – Rangers slumped to a final 6th position in the league and lost an unprecedented 13 games. The club also failed to win any of the three cups. Injuries were partly the cause – the long-term injury list at various points of the season included

Meiklejohn, McCandless, Cairns, Morton, Muirhead, Archibald and Cunningham. But just as importantly, the team was ageing and this was recognised at the end of season 1926/27 by the departure of Cairns and Manderson to Bradford City and the retirement of Dixon. That season, however, Rangers regained the league title, five points ahead of Motherwell, and were to embark on a run of five championships in succession.

The Scottish Cup continued to be an elusive prize. Rangers reached the fourth round and played Falkirk at Brockville where a last-minute McCandless penalty, to even the tie 2-2, spared their blushes. In the replay at Ibrox, the game was goalless when, close to the final whistle, McCandless was injured and Cunningham moved to left-back. In the dying minutes of extra time, Falkirk scored and Rangers' Cup hoodoo remained.

One of the greatest goalscorers in the club's history, arrived at Ibrox in the spring of 1927 from Airdrie for the then massive transfer fee of £4,500. Bob McPhail, a big, powerful inside-left was to become a Rangers and Scotland footballing legend, and he held the Rangers scoring record until Ally McCoist's goal exploits in the 1990s. He was about to build a lethal left-wing partnership with Alan Morton. Jimmy Simpson (father of Ronnie, Celtic goalkeeper in the 1967 European Cup-winning team) was

Above: An aerial view of a match taking place at Ibrox in 1922

Left: Bob McPhail, legendary goalscoring inside forward from 1927 to 1939. His 230 league goals for Rangers was a club record until overtaken by Ally McCoist in 1996

Goalmouth action from the 1928 Scottish Cup final

also brought in to the team to replace the departed Arthur Dixon in the centre-half position.

With their re-modelled team, Rangers roared into the 1927/28 season, winning their first six games and scoring twenty-four goals in the process. In late September Fleming established a club record when he scored six goals in Rangers's 7-0 defeat of Clyde at Ibrox in a Glasgow Cup tie. He was to end the season with the remarkable total of 45 goals.

Rangers fought their way to the Scottish Cup Final on April 24, beating Hibs 3-0 in the semi. Their opponents at Hampden in April were Celtic, in the first Old Firm final for 19 years, and 118,115 supporters crammed into the stadium with thousands turned away outside. The crowd was easily a record for a UK football match up till then. Celtic piled into the attack in the first half, with a strong wind behind them, and outside-right Paddy Connolly unleashed a shot which was quite brilliantly saved by Tommy Hamilton, diving full length to his right. Celtic forward Adam McLean skyed the rebound over the bar and Rangers could breathe again. Although Morton was causing Celtic all sorts of trouble down the wing, the half ended with Rangers massed in defence and Hamilton being called on to make some daring saves to keep Celtic at bay.

Then, in the 55th minute, Celtic defender Willie McStay punched out a Fleming shot, which had beaten keeper John Thomson, and a penalty was awarded. Rangers insisted that the ball had crossed the line but the referee pointed to the spot. Up stepped Govan-born David Meiklejohn, captain for the day in the absence through injury of regular captain Tommy Muirhead. The pressure on this man was enormous and the vast stadium fell silent. As quoted in John Allan's *Eleven Great Years*, Meiklejohn described his feelings: ' I saw, in a flash, the whole picture of our striving to win the Cup. I saw all the dire flicks of fortune which had beaten us when we should have won. That ball should have been in the net. It was on the penalty spot instead. If I scored, we would win; if I failed, we could be beaten. It was a moment of agony'. 'Meek' smashed an unsaveable shot into the corner of the net and Rangers were one ahead. It took him at least ten minutes to stop shaking.

The goal proved cathartic. Bob McPhail made the score 2-0 in the 66th minute from an Archibald cross. A rampant Archibald added a third two minutes later, and within a further couple of minutes Archibald, again, hit a screaming 25-yard shot high into the net to make the final score 4-0. 'Belhaven', writing in the *Sunday Mail*, described the shot as 'like an arrow from a bow the ball went from his toe to the net. Thomson touched it but it would have taken a stone wall to stop it'. Celtic were magnanimous in defeat, the Celtic captain Willie McStay commenting 'I don't grudge Rangers the victory. They played a great game and deserve their cup'. The music hall jokes could now stop. The team on this historic day was: T Hamilton, Gray, R Hamilton, Buchanan, Meiklejohn, Craig, Archibald, Cunningham, Fleming, McPhail, Morton.

In this memorable season Rangers also completed the club's first ever 'double' when, in the month after the Cup final, a 5-1 win over Kilmarnock, helped by a Fleming hat-trick, gave them the league title. To round off matters, Rangers also retained the Charity Cup, beating Queen's Park 2-1.

In May and June of 1928 Rangers travelled to America and Canada for a close season tour. They played ten games and received a warm welcome from the many exiled Scots in the continent. Back in Glasgow for the start of the 1928/29 season, they were defeated by Celtic in the Glasgow Cup final but defeated the old enemy twice in the league, the second time by 3-0 in the Ne'er Day fixture with Fleming scoring twice and Archibald netting the other.

Before the latter game, the new Main Stand was officially opened by Lord Provost David Mason. The Archibald Leitch-designed red brick stand, now a Grade 2 listed building on Edmiston Drive, held 10,000 seated spectators, with room for thousands more in the enclosures, and contained a spacious blue-tiled dressing room for the players with a five-foot deep communal bath entered by a ladder. The dressing room today has changed little since 1929, although the bath has gone. Struth's team, the best that Scotland had produced for many years, deserved appropriately first-rate facilities.

The stand boasted an entrance area fitted out in marble and oak panels, the wood originally being intended for fitting out the Queen Mary, with thick, expensive carpeting. In the years to come three art deco lamps were to be added to the reception and a Hall of Fame was introduced halfway up the staircase. Today, there are twenty-eight players' names inscribed on the memorial, from Moses McNeill to Brian Laudrup. A portrait of Alan Morton dominates the stairwell.

The exterior was equally sumptuous, with arched windows on the upper floors and pedimented windows at each end, and at each end of the stand were mosaics of the club crest with the Lion Rampant and the club's motto 'Aye Ready' picked out in blue and gold. Two huge ironwork gates were built at what are now the Copland and Broomloan stands.

On the pitch side of the stand a distinctive castellated Press Box was erected on the roof.

Struth himself had a well-appointed office in the stand, looking out over Edmiston Drive. A dapper man and proud of his appearance, he kept several tailored suits in the office and was often known to change his suit at least once a day. Also in the office he kept a canary in a cage. The little songbird had flown in through the window and it had been caught by Struth who kept it mellow and in good voice by feeding it an occasional nip of whisky.

Struth, however, was far more than just a dandy and a mild eccentric. His influence over his players was now absolute. A remote and somewhat dictatorial figure, he rarely interfered with tactics, leaving the playing of the game to his senior players on the pitch. Although he treated 'his boys' well and insisted that they ate well and travelled in style, he also demanded respect and insisted on obedience, with any miscreant, idler or refusenik being summoned up the marble staircase to his office at Ibrox to be summarily admonished. A light was placed on the wall outside Struth's office, and when it was switched on a player was allowed admittance.

He also liked to see his players well turned-out in suits

A smiling David Meiklejohn with the Scottish Cup in 1928

Bill Struth

and bowler hats. In his book *Legend – Sixty Years at Ibrox*, Bob McPhail relates how Struth would insist that the players, when at away games, walk from the railway station to the ground, partly to loosen up their muscles but also for the psychological impact of their distinguished appearance on the opposing fans and players. Struth was, for good or ill, mainly responsible for the almost palpable atmosphere of authority, discipline and hierarchy which was to permeate Rangers right up until the 1960s when younger, more tolerant managers began to break the Struth mould.

Struth used to tell a story against himself which revealed the opportunistic side of his character as well as suggesting a hint of duplicity in his make-up. In his running career he attended a meeting to find out that he was, in his opinion, over-handicapped for the race, He surreptitiously stole twenty yards on his position, sprinted over the winning line, grabbed the credit note from the organiser and had taken the money from the bank before the race committee discovered his deception. He was out of town on the next train.

He could also be an remote man, with little awareness of the realities of his players' lives. Ian Peebles' book *Growing with Glory* relates that, before a visit from Arsenal in the early 1930s, Struth promised his team a canteen of cutlery each if they won. Although the players were relatively well

paid by the standards of the time, they still had to live with the continuing effects of the Depression. When Bob McPhail heard about the cutlery incentive, he visited Struth in his office and said indignantly 'There's no much use having a knife and fork, Boss, if ye canny afford a steak'. Struth took the point.

Rangers won the league in 1928/29 losing only 1 game, and the 3-1 win over Dundee in April marked the introduction of Jimmy Smith to the first team. Smith was to become another Rangers legend and run up 299 goals in his time at Ibrox and finish his career as chief scout. Rangers also reached the Scottish Cup final where, after Tully Craig had missed a 17th minute penalty, they were defeated 2-0 by Kilmarnock. Gers right-half Jock Buchanan was sent off for dissent near the end of the game and became the first player to be sent off in a Scottish Cup final.

In 1929/30 Rangers embarked on the most successful season in their history to date, winning the league and all three Cups. They disposed of Celtic in October in the Glasgow Cup final replay, winning 4-0 with Fleming contributing a hat-trick. They won the league again – their fourth consecutive championship – by March, and ended five points clear of Motherwell. They also contested the Scottish Cup final against Partick Thistle in April, having eliminated Hearts 4-1 in the semi thanks to another Fleming hat-trick and a goal from McPhail.

Although the *Sunday Mail* stated that 'the general opinion before the start was that Rangers had only to appear on the field to demoralise and whack their opponents', a jittery performance by the Light Blues, and their containment by an assured and confident Thistle defence, saw the game end 0-0. In the replay, Morton was injured after fifteen minutes and was a virtual passenger throughout the match. Doc Marshall opened the scoring in the 41st minute while Thistle's Torbet equalised mid-way through the second period. In the 86th minute Tully Craig's speculative lob deceived the Thistle keeper and Rangers were 2-1 up. The keeper later claimed that he had been blinded by sunshine, but Rangers had another trophy. They ended the season by adding the Charity Cup to their collection.

In the summer Rangers travelled again to America and Canada where they played fourteen games, winning them all. That was the last season for Tommy Muirhead and Billy McCandless, who left the club. However, Rangers had acquired a new keeper – James Dawson (nicknamed 'Jerry' after the famous Burnley and England keeper) from Camelon Juniors – as an eventual replacement for Tom Hamilton, and left-half George Brown, who had played his first game for Rangers in November. Dawson was to became one of the

George Brown, half back for Rangers who ended his career as a Director of the club

finest keepers in Rangers' history, and earn the title 'the prince of goalkeepers'. His only weakness was an inability to kick a dead ball, often falling over after the kick and alarming his teammates, but this role was soon taken over by the full-backs. Brown was a multi-talented half-back who could play with equal fluency and flair in the inside-forward position. A teacher by profession, Brown finished his Rangers career as a director of the club.

Rangers won the league title for the fifth time in succession in 1930/31 but had to wait until the last game of the season to make sure of the trophy. Having to beat East Fife away, they scored four goals in the first half, Jimmy Smith scoring twice, and ran out 4-0 winners. A 2-1 win over Queen's Park secured them the Glasgow Cup, but they lost to Celtic 2-1 in the Charity Cup final. Rangers played Dundee in the second round of the Scottish Cup on a water-logged pitch. The conditions should have ensured the immediate abandonment of the tie but the referee went ahead with the game. Dundee won 2-1 by the clever expedient of restraining themselves to the wings while Rangers struggled to play their normal game in the centre of the boggy park.

Centre-forward Sam English from Coleraine had arrived in July 1931 and he made his mark on his first season by scoring no less than 44 league goals, including a five-goal burst against Morton. On September 5 1931 80,000 expectant fans filled Ibrox for a league game against Celtic, most of whom were hoping to see English, Fleming and McPhail inflict on Celtic the Parkhead club's first defeat of the season. In the event, they were to witness one of the great tragedies in the history of Scottish football. Jerry Dawson was making his Old Firm debut in goal for Rangers, and the first half was fairly uneventful and ended 0-0. Five minutes into the second half, a through ball from Fleming found English. English, ten yards from goal, prepared to shoot and the Celtic keeper, John Thomson, dived at his feet. Thomson's head connected with English's knee and the keeper lay prone on the ground while English limped away. Some heckling and jeering arose from the Rangers fans behind the goal but Meiklejohn, realising the seriousness of the situation, ran over and motioned them to stop. Thomson was stretchered from the ground, his head swathed in bandages.

The 23-year-old keeper – possessor of eight international caps and predicted to be one of Scotland's great goalkeepers – was diagnosed with a depressed skull fracture and died in the Victoria Infirmary later that evening. In spite of Celtic

manager Willie Maley's irresponsible comment at the hearing – 'I *hope* it was an accident' – newsreel footage confirmed that it certainly was. English was completely exonerated of any blame but, although he continued his goalscoring form that season, he was deeply affected by Thomson's death and opposing fans never let him forget about the accident. He left the club the following season to play for Liverpool and eventually returned to Ireland. He

Left: *Sam English, scorer of 44 league goals for Rangers in 1931/32*

Above: *John Thomson dives at the feet of Sam English on 5 September 1931. The goalkeeper was fatally injured in the collision*

retired from football at the age of 28. The tragedy shocked Scotland and thirty thousand people attended Thomson's funeral in Cardenden in Fife. All the Rangers playing staff were at the service and Meiklejohn read one of the lessons.

Later in the season Rangers beat Hearts 1-0 in a thrilling Scottish Cup third round game at Tynecastle and disposed of Hamilton 5-2 in the semi-final to meet Kilmarnock in the final. At Hampden 112,000 spectators saw Killie take the lead in the first half but a Bob McPhail long-range effort enforced a replay. Fleming was on for the injured Morton and opened the scoring in the 10th minute. McPhail and English added another two and the Cup came back to Govan. The team in the replay was: Hamilton, Gray, McCauley, Meiklejohn, Simpson, Brown, Archibald,

Marshall, English, McPhail, Fleming. After a five-year ownership of the league trophy, however, Rangers relinquished the title to an excellent Motherwell side, five points ahead of the Light Blues, although the Ibrox club retained the Charity Cup. Motherwell were to become the only team other than Rangers and Celtic to win the league between 1905 and 1948.

Season 1932/33 was notable not only for Rangers' regaining the league title – which they did by winning eighteen and drawing seven of their last twenty-five games – but also for the retirement of Alan Morton in January. In May they added to their squad by acquiring 17-year-old inside-right Torrance ('Torry') Gillick from Petershill. He was to become a great Ibrox favourite in the years ahead. In

118 goals, Smith scoring six in their 9-1 win over Ayr United (newcomer Irishman Alec Stevenson claimed a hat-trick in the same game). In the Scottish Cup, the first round saw poor Blairgowrie receive a 14-2 drubbing with Fleming setting a club record by scoring nine of them. In the final Rangers easily beat St Mirren 5-0 at Hampden, outclassing the Paisley side. The team for the final was: Hamilton, Gray, McDonald, Meiklejohn, Simpson, Brown, Main, Marshall, Smith, McPhail, Nicholson.

In September Herbert Chapman's famed Arsenal team had come to Ibrox for the first leg of the 'British championship', and Jimmy Smith and Bob McPhail ensured a 2-0 win. At Highbury a week later, Fleming scored twice and Marshall added another in Rangers' 3-1 victory. New signing Alex Venters, a Scottish international inside-forward, had joined from Cowdenbeath in November and Doc Marshall left at the end of the season to join Arsenal and set up a medical practice in London.

Strengthened by the arrival of outside-left Davie Kinnear from Raith Rovers, Rangers continued their winning ways in 1934/35. Although they failed to retain the Glasgow and Charity Cups, they won the league and Scottish Cup 'double' again. Their 3-2 defeat by Dundee in April was their first league defeat in nine months and they took the title by three points over Celtic. Smith again scored six in one game, this time in the 7-1 defeat of Dunfermline Athletic. In front of a crowd of 102,000 at Hampden, Rangers drew 1-1 with Hearts in the Scottish Cup semi-final, but goals from McPhail and Main in the replay saw them through. In the Cup final, McPhail missed a first-half penalty and Smith struck twice in an exciting and entertaining 2-1 win over Hamilton Academicals, whose teenage keeper Peter Morgan performed heroics in goal. This was the first time that Rangers had successfully defended the Scottish Cup in the 20th century.

The old guard were now leaving the club, with Jimmy Fleming transferring to Hearts and Sandy Archibald, after seventeen years of loyal service, departing to Raith Rovers. Tully Craig, too, left at the end of the season to become manager of Falkirk. In the autumn Rangers played friendlies against Rapid Vienna, winning 3-1, and Arsenal at Highbury. With Doc Marshall outstanding in the Arsenal team, McPhail and Arsenal left-winger Cliff Bastin scored in a 1-1 draw. FA Cup holders Manchester City travelled to

Celtic goalkeeper John Thomson punches the ball clear in the Rangers v Celtic game in September 1931

January Rangers played their first ever game against a foreign side at Ibrox, when they were hosts to Rapid Vienna. The game finished 3-3, Smith (2) and McPhail the scorers. During their summer tour of Germany and Austria they played Rapid again in Vienna, losing 4-3.

Struth's team, with its irresistible strike force of McPhail, Smith, Fleming and Marshall, its dominant defence centred around centre-half Jimmy Simpson and the dependable Jerry Dawson in goal, was now one of the most formidable in British football. Its strength, organisation and discipline, allied to its prodigious goalscoring, set it apart from any other club then playing in Scotland. It came as no surprise, then, in season 1933/34 that Rangers again won all three cups and retained the league title. They lost only two of their 38 league games and were beaten only twice in the 50 games they played overall. They ended with 66 points and

Ibrox in the 'British championship' and lost 1-0, but they beat the Ibrox side 4-2 back at Maine Road.

The exodus of older players continued in 1935/36, with Torry Gillick joining Everton for £8,000. Gillick, however, was to come back to Ibrox immediately after the Second World War. Also leaving was David Meiklejohn. 'Meek' retired after Celtic's 4-2 defeat of Rangers in the Charity Cup final having played 635 first-team matches for the club. Celtic won the league that season, five points ahead of Rangers, their first league title for ten years. Rangers, however, lifted the Scottish Cup for the third year in succession, eliminating Clyde 3-0 in the semi and beating newly-promoted Third Lanark 1-0 in the final through a Bob McPhail goal, McPhail's seventh and last Cup winner's medal.

Rangers opened the 1936/37 season with an emphatic 4-1 defeat of Austria Vienna in early August, Bob McPhail scoring a hat-trick, and reclaimed the league title from Celtic, finishing seven points ahead of an impressive Aberdeen side. There was, however, something of an embarrassment for the Light Blues in the Scottish Cup when they succumbed 1-0 to Queen of the South.

Two young forwards joined the club this season. Willie Waddell, a powerful, well-built outside-right, whose career

Hamilton Academicals teenage keeper Morgan saves from Davy Main in the 1935 Scottish Cup final

with the club was to include player, manager and managing director over the next fifty years, signed professional forms for Rangers. A 16-year-old Willie Thornton also made his first appearance in a game against Partick Thistle in January. Thornton, a skilful, left-footed centre-forward with exceptional ability in the air, was to form a devastating goalscoring partnership with Waddell in the years to come.

In October Rangers played a fundraiser against Stoke City for the Holditch Colliery Disaster Fund. After the game the Stoke chairman presented the club with a 'loving cup', cast to commemorate the Coronation of George V in 1937, with the request that the current monarch be toasted from the cup before every New Year game. This tradition continues to the present day.

It was a poor season by Rangers' recent standards. Although they won the Glasgow Cup, they lost the league title, ending in third place behind Celtic and Hearts. Their bad start to 1938 – losing within a month to Celtic, Partick Thistle and Dundee (the last by 6-1) – effectively ended their interest in the campaign. They were also knocked out of the Scottish Cup

Main, Nicholson, Meiklejohn, Smith and McPhail pose with the Scottish Cup after Rangers' 5-0 win over St Mirren in the 1934 final

4-3 by Kilmarnock in the semi-final. Killie, managed by ex-Celtic legend Jimmy McGrory, scored the winner in the closing minutes but were fortunate that a dominant Rangers were so abysmal in their finishing on the day. Killie went on to defeat in the final by East Fife who became the only Second Division team ever to win the Scottish Cup.

However, a transitional Rangers side was continuing to build for the future and the side which, alongside Waddell and Thornton, was to dominate Scottish football in the late 1940s and early 1950s was beginning to take shape. Ginger-haired inside-left Jimmy Duncanson arrived, as did the small, combative full-back Jock ('Tiger') Shaw from Airdrie. Elegant centre-half Willie Woodburn, whose career was to end abruptly in deeply controversial circumstances, had already joined the club from school. The abrasive Woodburn was to prove a skilful creator as well as a tough-tackling defender, and his style of play in many ways prefigured the modern sweeper. Both Shaw and Woodburn made their club debuts at the start of the 1938/39 season. Waddell also made his first team debut in August 1938, scoring the only

goal in a friendly fixture against Arsenal. He made 27 league appearances that season and was rapidly becoming an indispensable provider and goalscorer. In August Scot Symon added another piece to the jigsaw when he transferred from Portsmouth. Symon, a tough-tackling wing-half, was the only man to represent Scotland at both football and cricket until matched by Andy Goram. Symon was to become Rangers' manager and the architect of the Jim Baxter-inspired Rangers side of the early 1960s.

At the end of the season Ibrox hosted the Exhibition Cup, a tournament set up to celebrate the Empire Exhibition taking place at the city's Bellahouston Park, opened by King George VI and Princess Elizabeth. The knock-out tournament featured four top Scottish sides – Rangers, Celtic, Hearts and Clyde – and four English – Everton, Sunderland, Brentford and Chelsea. Everton, with ex-Ger Torry Gillick and English international centre-forward Tommy Lawton in the attack, eliminated Rangers 2-0 in the first round, with centre-half and captain Jimmy Simpson having to take over in goal from an injured Jerry Dawson. The tournament was won by Celtic who defeated Everton 1-0 in the final. The Exhibition came to an end in October having attracted over 12.5 million visitors.

On Ne'er's Day 1939, 118,561 spectators filled Ibrox for the traditional game against Celtic, the ground's highest-ever attendance. Both sides fielded young attacks and the game was an exciting and skilful contest under the winter sunshine. An impressed *Glasgow Herald* noted that 'the display of subtle, cultured and effective football was equal to the best of the great Rangers and Celtic teams of the past'. In the 17th minute Kinnear swept down the left and shot past Celtic keeper Joe Kennaway for Rangers' first goal. Thornton was in dazzling form in the centre of attack and he made the second goal, volleying a pass to Venters with the outside of his right foot. The inside-left made no mistake with his shot. Joe Carruth scored for Celtic but Rangers

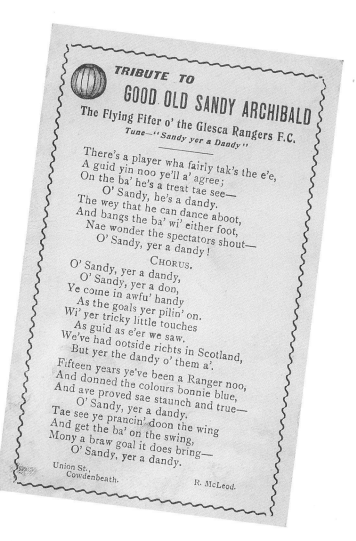

won 2-1. Rangers finished the season by winning the league, eleven points ahead of Celtic.

In February, however, they were overcome 4-1 by Clyde in the third round of the Scottish Cup. A disappointing display by the Light Blues was exploited by Clyde centre-forward Willie Martin who became the first visiting player to score four goals at Ibrox.

War was declared against Germany on 3 September 1939 and the SFA suspended league and Scottish Cup football three days later. However, realising that people would welcome the entertainment provided by football as a diversion from the austerity and grimness of the War, they soon changed their minds and decided to set up a two-division league for 1939/40 based on the east/north and south/west clubs. This lasted one season, and the clubs were then divided into northern and southern regional groupings, partly due to lobbying from Hibs and Hearts who were dependent on the income from Rangers and Celtic fixtures. Rangers were to dominate wartime Scottish football, winning 25 out of the 34 competitions they entered in the six years, including seven league titles and five Glasgow Cups.

At the start of the conflict, players' contracts had been cancelled because of conscription and wages had been cut to two pounds per week. Struth managed to find many of his players work in the 'reserved occupations', such as shipyards, engineering works and local factories, while several others – such as David Kinnear and Willie Thornton – went on active service. Indeed, Thornton returned from service the proud possessor of the Military Medal for his activities in Sicily. Obviously, the six-year war interrupted the careers of several players and some of the old heroes – Bob McPhail, Jimmy Smith, Doug Gray and Jerry Dawson – were to leave the club before the post-war season began. Struth, however, had been replenishing his team and had bought a player in September 1941 who was to become a true Ibrox great – George Young.

Young, from Kirkintilloch Rob Roy, was a six foot two inch, fifteen stone, long-legged defender who made his debut against Hamilton Academicals in 1941/42. A skilful player, adept at quickly turning defence into attack, Young was also a formidable and tough tackler. In his long career with Rangers, which was to continue until 1957, Young was never sent off and was booked only once. Although a natural centre-half he spent much of his club career in the right-back position, because of the presence of Willie Woodburn at centre-half, and he was to become an integral part of the famous Rangers defence of the coming ten years. He also went on to achieve an illustrious career with Scotland, captaining his country 48 times in his 52 appearances.

As well as the southern league, Rangers played numerous charity matches in aid of the war effort and continued to compete in the Glasgow and Charity Cups. Guest appearances by well-known players were common at the time, and the great winger Stanley Matthews appeared for the Light Blues in their 3-0 Charity Cup final defeat of Partick Thistle in 1941. The War period also saw Rangers' biggest ever defeat of Celtic. On Ne'er Day 1943 at Ibrox, Rangers were 2-1 ahead at half time.

Early in the second half they were 4-1 up, when Celtic's Malcolm MacDonald and Matt Lynch were sent off for dissent. The game ended 8-1 in Rangers' favour.

Perhaps the most famous match Rangers played in the period before the official league and cup tournaments began again in 1946/47 was their friendly against Moscow Dynamo on 28 November 1945. The Russians, coached by Mikhail Yakushin, had already beaten Arsenal and Cardiff

Rangers v Moscow Dynamos
IBROX STADIUM, GLASGOW
INCLUDING TAX
WEDNESDAY, 28th NOVEMBER, 1945
KICK-OFF 2.15 p.m.

Section M
Row E
Seat No. 201

15/6

THIS PORTION TO BE
RETAINED BY HOLDER

Left and below: Action from the 1945 match against
Moscow Dynamo. Left:. Tiger Khomich, the Dynamo keeper,
lies injured. Below: Khomich clears a Rangers attack

City, and drawn with Chelsea on their tour, and they lined up against the Light Blues at Ibrox on a Wednesday afternoon. This was Dynamo's first visit to Britain and they had impressed observers with their clever interpassing, speedy movement and accuracy in front of goal. Such was the attraction of these mysterious foreigners that over 90,000 spectators watched the game in the first-ever all-ticket match at Ibrox. Productivity levels in Glasgow must have slumped on what was a working day.

Within two minutes Dynamo were ahead through inside-right Kartsev's free-kick. Five minutes later keeper Tiger Khomich saved a Waddell penalty, which Waddell shot too close to the keeper, deflecting the ball onto the bar. In the 24th minute Dynamo went 2-0 up after their forwards had weaved the ball between themselves around the penalty area, bewildering the Rangers defence. The ball eventually reached Kartsev who claimed his second. In the 40th minute Jimmy Smith scrambled the ball over the line to get a goal back for Rangers. The score was 2-1 at half time.

With the Russians tiring in the second half, Billy Williamson was penalised in the box and big George Young converted the penalty. During the second half, the sharp-eyed Torry Gillick noticed that Dynamo were playing with twelve men, as a substitute had omitted to leave the field! The game ended two each and Rangers had demonstrated they had the ability to compete on level terms with top European sides. The Dynamo trainer agreed, saying 'Rangers are easily the best footballers we have met in Britain. We have no complaints'. The team was: Dawson, Gray, Shaw, Watkins, Young, Symon, Waddell, Gillick, Smith (Duncanson), Williamson, Johnstone.

Struth, with his gifted forward line and his strong, dependable defence, could look forward to the new campaign with considerable optimism.

Chapter Four:

The Iron Curtain and Europe: 1945-1960

The immediate post-War years saw interest in football booming, with remarkable attendances at the major football grounds in Scotland. Rangers retained their position as the country's top club but a new challenger – Edinburgh's Hibernian – was emerging. Hibs had been assembling a forward line which would become renowned as the 'famous five' – Smith, Johnstone, Reilly, Turnbull and Ormond – and which would help the club to three league titles in the next seven years. The other four would go to Rangers.

As a foretaste of the coming duel, in the 1946/47 season Rangers and Hibs met in the semi-final of the Scottish League Cup – a new competition which had taken over from the wartime southern league cup, with a trophy donated by Scottish league president John McMahon – in front of 125,000 at Hampden. Torry Gillick scored the first in the 19th minute and by half time Rangers were 3-0 ahead, through Thornton and Waddell. An injured Waddell played

Jock Shaw, full back and captain of Rangers' 'Iron Curtain' team

Willie Woodburn

no part in the second half but ten-men Rangers held on to win 3-1. The Light Blues beat Aberdeen 4-0 in the final to become the first holders of the new trophy. However, Hibs had earlier handed Rangers their first league defeat and had also bundled them out of the Scottish Cup 2-0 at Easter Road. Nevertheless, Rangers won the league, edging Hibs by two points.

Struth had been laying the foundations of his defence – which famously became known as the 'iron curtain', after the Cold War rhetoric of the time – by acquiring right-half Ian McColl, left-half Sammy Cox and keeper Bobby Brown. First to arrive in June 1945 was McColl, a tall, tough-tackling but gifted player from Queen's Park who was to become captain of the club and go on to manage Scotland in the 1960s. Sammy Cox and Bobby Brown both signed for Rangers on the same day in May 1946. Cox was a graceful and technically accomplished half-back, who could also play in the full-back and inside-forward positions and, in spite of being on the small side, he possessed sophisticated and effective defensive and tackling skills. He was to remain with the club for the next ten years. Something of a showman, but a reliable keeper, the blond, curly-haired

Brown was replacement for Jerry Dawson and, because of this, took some time to win over the Ibrox fans for whom Dawson was a hero . However, although he was an amateur and made his living as a PE teacher, Brown was also to stay with the club for ten years and, at his peak, he played 179 league games in succession. He, like McColl, became manager of Scotland and was in charge of his country when Scotland beat the English World Champions 3-2 at Wembley in 1967, a game which has passed into Scottish footballing mythology. The 'iron curtain' – Brown, Young, Shaw, McColl, Woodburn and Cox – was now complete and ready to contest the growing threat of the 'famous five'.

While the team was changing, so too was the composition of the Ibrox board. Chairman James Bowie had suggested to Struth that he resign his managership to bring on a younger manager, and that Struth join the board. Keen as he was to become a director, Struth had no intention of resigning as manager. The obstacle he faced was Article 74 of the club's constitution which stated that a director could not have any other role in the club. A boardroom battle ensued, with Struth and his allies calling an extraordinary general meeting to vote on the abolition of Article 74. After behind-the scenes lobbying and adroit canvassing of shareholders' votes, Struth and club secretary J Rogers Simpson were elected to the board on 12 June 1947, and the following evening at the AGM Bowie was voted off. A hurt and bitter Bowie severed his connections with Ibrox and Struth was now at the peak of his power with Rangers.

In 1947/48, Rangers began their league campaign promisingly but a 1-0 defeat by Hibs at Easter Road affected their rhythm and they ended the season in second place, two points behind the Edinburgh club. They were knocked out of the League Cup by Falkirk, now managed by ex-Ger Tully Craig, going down 1-0 in a disappointing semi-final at Hampden. A miscued backpass from Woodburn with two minutes to go allowed Archie Aikman to nip in and score for the 'Bairns'. The Light Blues played Hibs in the semi-final of the Scottish Cup at Hampden, in front of what is still a British record attendance of 143,570. Brown was unbeatable in goal and the game was won by a powerful Thornton header from a Waddell cross.

Morton were the opposition in the final and another huge crowd saw the teams contest a 1-1 draw. The largest ever British crowd for a midweek game – 129,176 – gathered at Hampden for the replay and Billy Williamson, playing his first Scottish cup tie of the season as replacement for Willie Findlay, headed in the only goal of the game from an Eddie Rutherford cross in the dying minutes of extra time. The team for the replay was: Brown, Young, Shaw, McColl, Woodburn, Cox, Rutherford, Thornton, Williamson,

Duncanson, Gillick. In February 1948 Rangers flew to Lisbon to play a friendly against Benfica. They won 3-0, but Waddell's fondest memory of the trip was surely meeting his future wife Hilda, an air hostess on the flight.

The following season –1948/49 – was an historic one for the Ibrox club, as they won their first 'treble'. They defeated Celtic 2-1 in a League Cup qualifying group decider at Ibrox and beat Raith Rovers 2-0 in the final. Brown had to be alert to keep out the Raith forwards in the first half and the Kircaldy side had a goal disallowed. Early in the second half Thornton centred and Gillick headed home. In the 60th minute another Thornton cross found Willie Paton who scored the second. They met East Fife in the Scottish Cup semi-final and the contest was won 3-0 by Rangers, the flashing head of Willie Thornton providing a hat-trick.

On 23 April they played Clyde in the final. With Waddell in brilliant form on the right wing for Rangers, Young scored a penalty in the 40th minute and Williamson headed in from a Waddell cross just before half time. Clyde then scored in the 48th minute through Galletly but Young again converted from the spot six minutes later, With six minutes to go, Duncanson made the score 4-1. Young became the only player ever to score two penalties in a Scottish Cup final. At the post-match celebration dinner, a waiter handed Young a champagne cork and told him it would bring Scotland luck in the home internationals. Scotland won all

Above: *Willie Waddell*

Left: *Woodburn rises to head clear a Celtic attack*

three and from then on Young, never without the little lucky mascot, was affectionately nicknamed 'Corky'.

Their league triumph was a much tenser affair. On the last day of the season Dundee were leading the table by one point. Rangers played Albion Rovers and won 4-1, with Thornton contributing a hat-trick and Duncanson scoring the other. They then had to wait for news from Brockville Park where Falkirk were entertaining Dundee. Dundee must have suffered a collective loss of nerve as they went down 4-1, with ex-Ger Jerry Dawson making a crucial penalty save for Falkirk, and Rangers were champions. Thornton ran up a total of 36 goals during the season, many from the crossing of Waddell. Dundee scored more league goals than Rangers that season but the Light Blues conceded significantly fewer than the Tayside club, a testimony to the security of their defence.

The league title race went to the wire again the following season. Rangers' second last game was against fellow contenders Hibs at Ibrox, where 101,000 spectators – a post-War British record attendance for a league game – watched the fast, high-scoring Hibs forward line fail to

Waddell scores from the spot against Celtic in 1949

penetrate the Rangers defence in a 0-0 draw. Rangers final match – a 2-2 draw with Third Lanark – gave them the title by one point ahead of Hibs.

In the Scottish Cup, Rangers had met and eliminated East Fife in the quarter-final and semi-final in the previous two years. This year they were to meet the men from Methil – now managed by Scott Symon – in the final. Within thirty seconds from the kick-off Rutherford crossed and Willie Findlay scored with a diving header from eighteen yards. East Fife came back strongly in the second half but another cross from Rutherford connected with the head of Willie Thornton and Rangers were two up, then a Willie Findlay chip was met by Thornton and the score was 3-0, where it remained until the final whistle. Rangers had produced an

Jock Shaw with the Scottish Cup in April 1949 after having beaten East Fife 3-0 in the final

excellent display of fluid, attacking football and deserved their result. Although known primarily as the 'iron curtain' team, the Rangers forwards Waddell, Thornton, Rutherford and Duncanson could certainly turn it on when required. When irked by constant references to the excellence of the defence, Thornton was wont to remark wryly 'We scored a few too, you know'.

In July 1949 tiny, 5 foot 4 inch Johnny Hubbard arrived at Ibrox from South Africa. An unprepossessing, fragile-looking figure, Hubbard did not impress Struth on the first meeting, but when Struth saw his skill on the ball he signed him immediately. A tricky, dribbling left-winger, and a master of the penalty kick, Hubbard rapidly became a favourite of the Rangers fans and he was to remain at the club until 1959. Another addition to Struth's forward line joined in October 1950. Northern Ireland international Billy Simpson was acquired from Lingfield for a club record fee of £11,500. An inside-forward, and primarily a goalscorer, Simpson had little fear of opposing defences and his heading ability was almost on a par with Thornton. He opened his account for Rangers by scoring a hat-trick against East Fife in December 1950 and later in the season he scored four in a match against Third Lanark.

Generally, however, 1950/51 was a poor season for the Light Blues. Their only trophy was the Charity Cup and they were second in the league, ten points behind a distant Hibs. In November 1950 Jimmy Duncanson left to join St Mirren, having scored 162 goals in 342 games for Rangers. In the close season Struth bought left-back John Little from Queen's Park as a replacement for the ageing Jock Shaw. Canadian-born but Scots-bred Little was an energetic, speedy and effective defender and he made the left-back position virtually his own during the early 1950s.

The skilful, stylish forward Willie Thornton, who scored 188 league goals in his Rangers career between 1937 and 1954

Johnny Hubbard, small South African left winger and master of the penalty kick

In spite of Struth's new players, 1951/52 was not much of an improvement. Rangers were runners-up in the league to Hibs this year by four points and they were knocked out of the Scottish Cup in a fourth round replay by Motherwell, the eventual winners of the competition. In the League Cup they met Celtic in the semi-final. In an inspired display of attacking football, Rangers ran out 3-0 winners. Thornton opened the scoring with a header from a Young cross and inside-left Joe Johnson scored another just before half time. Findlay scored the third goal in the second half. However, they could not maintain this momentum in the final and went down 3-2 to Dundee. This season was the first since 1895 in which neither Rangers nor Celtic won a trophy.

It was beginning to appear that Struth was losing his touch and that his period of dominance in the Scottish game was coming to an end. Nevertheless, he continued to strengthen and refresh his squad, and in the summer of 1952 he signed inside-right Derek Grierson from Queen's Park. Two stars of the future – defender Eric Caldow and keeper George Niven – also arrived at the club. Caldow would not make his first-team debut until the beginning of the 1953/54 season but Niven was pitched into action almost immediately.

Rangers began that season disastrously, losing their first game of the season – a League Cup tie – 5-0 to Hearts. The 'terrible trio' of Conn, Bauld and Wardhaugh did the damage for the Edinburgh side. Bobby Brown had a torrid time in goal and was blamed for the humiliation. The unforgiving Struth told Brown after the game that, unless he

agreed to turn full-time, he was out. 'I didn't, and I was dropped', said Brown. Niven took over and became first choice keeper for the remainder of the season. A smallish but dependable goalie, Niven became the regular keeper through the 1950s, giving way to Billy Ritchie in the early 1960s.

The league campaign was a close struggle with Hibs throughout the season. In the final game Rangers had to secure at least one point from Queen of the South to win the title. With fifteen minutes to go, Queen of the South were 1-0 ahead and Rangers looked in trouble. Suddenly Waddell broke on the wing, powered his way towards goal and unleashed a shot past the opposing keeper. The game finished 1-1 and Rangers were champions.

In the Scottish Cup semi-final, Rangers secured revenge for their humiliation by Hearts in the League Cup, with over 116,000 watching the game at Hampden. Although Jimmy Wardhaugh opened the scoring in the 11th minute from a cross by ex-Ger Eddie Rutherford, Derek Grierson equalised in the 37th minute after a fine solo run. With fifteen minutes to go, a John Prentice shot was deflected past the Hearts keeper and Rangers were in the final.

The opposition was Aberdeen at Hampden. In the 27th minute Niven dived at the feet of Dons' forward Paddy Buckley and had to be helped off with a bad head wound. George Young took over in goal, and by half time Rangers were 1-0 ahead through big inside-left John Prentice. The courageous Niven came back on for the second half, having received four stitches and with his head heavily bandaged. He played magnificently and, although Aberdeen equalised

Right: George Young and Jock Shaw lead the players on a training run

Far right: George Young is held aloft by Willie Waddell and Willie Woodburn after the 1953 Scottish Cup final win against Aberdeen

with seven minutes remaining, the game ended in a 1-1 draw. In the replay Niven wore a leather helmet to protect his head wound. Billy Simpson scored the only goal of the match and Rangers had the 'double'.

At the end of the season, a one-off tournament – the Coronation Cup – was held in Glasgow to celebrate the coronation of Queen Elizabeth II. In the first round Rangers, without the injured McColl and Cox, were drawn against the English champions Manchester United. In the 11th minute Hunter McMillan (cousin of Ian, inside-right in the 1960s team) gave Rangers the lead with a header. Just after half time, Stan Pearson equalised for United and Jack Rowley scored the winner for United three minutes later. The English side were beaten by eventual winners Celtic 2-1 in the semi-final.

An ignominious fourth place in the league, nine points behind winners Celtic, was the best Rangers could manage in 1953/54. They were also beaten in both cups in the semi-finals, going down by a particularly humiliating 6-0 to Aberdeen in the Scottish Cup and 2-0 to Partick Thistle in the League Cup. At the end of the season, two of Rangers old campaigners left the club. Jock Shaw retired, having made 578 appearances, and Willie Thornton, with 248 goals in 406 appearances, became manager of Dundee. However,

young full-back Eric Caldow had made his first team debut in September 1953. A speedy, well-balanced, intelligent defender, Caldow was to become club captain and was to play a major role in the all-conquering side of the early 1960s. He was to finish his career without a single booking or sending-off.

By now Struth was an ill man and in his seventies. His influence over his players, several of whom were also advancing in years, was waning and discontent was becoming increasingly apparent in the dressing room and on the terraces. The once unassailable Rangers were now being eclipsed by Hibs, Aberdeen and Celtic. Something had to be done.

In April 1954 Struth bowed to the inevitable and resigned as manager, although he was to remain as director until his death two years later. Struth's remarkable 34-year career had encompassed 18 league titles, 10 Scottish Cups, 2 League Cups, 18 Glasgow Cups and 20 Charity Cups, but it was now time for control of Rangers to pass into the hands of a younger man. A month earlier, a Glasgow builder, John Lawrence, had been elected to the board and he was to be instrumental in introducing far-reaching changes to the club. He announced his intentions in his appointment speech: 'Rangers cannot, and never shall be, second best. No matter the cost, no matter the effort, and no matter the

sacrifice, we shall go on to make Rangers respected and feared throughout the soccer world.' To achieve this aim, the board announced, on 15 June 1954, that ex-Rangers player Scot Symon would be the club's next manager, only the third in their long history.

Symon arrived back at his old club to a fulsome welcome from Struth, hailing his ex-player as a 'a man of indomitable courage, of unbreakable devotion to purpose; a man, indeed who became a true Ranger, and no more imposing accolade could be given to anyone'. The wing-back had enjoyed an impressive managerial career since he left the club. He had taken unfashionable East Fife to League Cup victory and to a Scottish Cup final and had the previous season guided Preston North End to the FA Cup final, narrowly losing to West Bromwich Albion. But the board had selected a man in Struth's image. Symon was a dignified, aloof man with a respect for tradition, discipline and the Rangers way of doing things. He was also somewhat guarded, particularly in his relations with the world outside Ibrox. Kevin McCarra, in his book *Scottish Football – A Pictorial History* recounts the story of a journalist attempting to find out about the possible postponement due to bad weather of a Rangers home game. He got through to Symon on the telephone and asked him 'Is it foggy at Ibrox?'. Symon considered this

question for a moment and replied 'No comment'. However, he had a good eye for players and he was to become an extremely successful manager in his thirteen years in charge.

Early in the season, 'Big Ben' Woodburn was sent off, in a game against Stirling Albion at Ibrox, for the fifth time in his career. Believing such a record to be unacceptable, the SFA suspended the player *sine die*, ie indefinitely. The decision was a harsh one. Woodburn was undoubtedly hot-headed and argumentative, and would not shrink from a challenge or a confrontation. But he was not a particularly dirty or cynical player. In today's climate, a similar suspension would be unthinkable. However, the SFA were not to be swayed and Woodburn would not return to the game until April 1957. But he was never again to play in the first team. Symon was fortunate to have another outstanding centre-half already at the club, and George Young took over Woodburn's position.

Although Rangers did not lose a home game in the league, they lost away on eight occasions and finished the season in third place behind Aberdeen, who celebrated their first ever league title. They were also knocked out of both cups, 2-1 by Aberdeen in the Scottish Cup and 3-2 on aggregate in the League Cup by Motherwell. They did, however, beat Celtic 4-1 in the Ne'er Day fixture, Simpson

The Lord Provost of Glasgow presents Bill Struth with his portrait which now hangs in the Trophy Room at Ibrox

scoring first and little Johnny Hubbard netting three in the last 18 minutes.

Floodlights had been installed at Ibrox and they had been inaugurated on 8 December 1953 in a game against Arsenal, the London side winning 2-1 in front of a crowd of 70,000. Although Symon was determined to recapture domestic honours, he was also aware of the increasing importance of European football and of the inevitability of competitive fixtures on the continent. To prepare his players for the forthcoming new era, he arranged midweek matches under floodlight against continental opposition. Rapid Vienna and Racing Club de Paris both visited Ibrox and the European sides were beaten, respectively, 1-0 and 5-1. Rangers also visited Highbury in March, drawing 3-3 with two of the goals scored in the first 25 minutes by recently-signed, 18-year-old outside-right Alex Scott whose brilliant performance drew comparisons with the legendary Alex James. Symon now had his replacement for Willie Waddell, who was to retire in 1956.

Scott had made his first-team debut six days previously in a game against Falkirk and had scored a hat-trick in Rangers' 4-1 win. He was devastatingly fast and physically powerful, with the ability to deliver pinpoint crosses as well as finish off in style. Scott was to occupy the right wing slot until he was dislodged by Willie Henderson in 1962. Symon added to his new line-up by buying centre-forward Max Murray from Queen's Park, inside-left Sammy Baird from the manager's old club Preston and Jimmy Millar, a half-back from Dunfermline. Murray was a tall, reliable player with an

outstanding goalscoring record and the blond Baird was a strong, physically imposing forward. Millar was brave, skilful and, for such a relatively small man, an astonishingly effective header of the ball with impeccable timing. He was to blossom into one of Rangers' finest ever centre-forwards.

At the beginning of the new season 1955/56 Don Kitchenbrand came to Ibrox from South Africa. Soon nicknamed 'The Rhino', Kitchenbrand was a big, bustling centre-forward who made up in enthusiasm for what he lacked in skill, and his accuracy in front of goal was not exactly reliable. David Mason, in his book *Rangers: The Managers*, quotes Symon as saying 'I know he misses a lot, but what impresses me is that he is usually in the right place to miss them'.

Rangers won the league that season, six points ahead of Aberdeen, helped by Kitchenbrand's 24 goals, which included five in Rangers' 8-0 win over Queen of the South. This game, incidentally, was the first Scottish league fixture to be played under floodlights. Kitchenbrand won over many of his Ibrox critics by scoring the only goal against Celtic on 2 January at Parkhead. Tough-tackling, fiery, red-haired right-back Bobby Shearer – soon to earn the soubriquet of 'Captain Cutlass' – also joined from Hamilton Academicals, and Caldow, although naturally right-footed, switched to left-back. The story is told of Shearer that, during a friendly match in Menorca, he launched a typically crunching tackle on the touchline, only to discover that he had upended a substitute. Although not exactly a flair player, Shearer was an effective stopper. Shearer and Caldow were to create the formidable last line of the Rangers defence in the great team of the 1960s.

The away game against Airdrie on 28 January 1956 is notable for the fact that Hubbard missed his first penalty in 23 attempts. In his Ibrox career, Hubbard converted 54 out of the 57 penalties he took. Equally worth noting is that Rangers' defeat at home by Clyde in the last game of the season was the club's first home defeat in the league for two years.

Rangers lost out on all the cups that season, falling 2-1 to Aberdeen in the semi-final of the League Cup. Celtic had beaten them 4-1 at Ibrox in a qualifying game. Four days later Rangers won 4-0 at Parkhead to qualify from the section. They went down 4-0 to Hearts at Tynecastle in the Scottish Cup. Own goals by Caldow in the Charity and Glasgow Cups aided the Ibrox club's elimination from both tournaments. The Light Blues also played Dinamo of Yugoslavia in a floodlit friendly, drawing 3-3, but competitive European football was waiting next season.

The European Cup had been initiated by French journalist Gabriel Hanot and ratified by UEFA in time for the start of the 1955/56 season. Sixteen teams from different European countries were to play each other in midweek fixtures on a home and away basis in a knock-out tournament to determine the best team in Europe. In the opening season the competition was won by Spanish masters Real Madrid who were to dominate the competition until 1960. The Scottish entrant had been Hibs who had overcome Germany's Rot Weiss Essen and Sweden's Djurgarden to reach the semi-final against French side Reims. They were beaten 3-0 on aggregate but had bolstered Scotland's footballing reputation. Now it was Rangers' turn to carry the saltire into Europe.

Rangers drew a bye in the preliminary round of the competition. Their first appearance in the European Cup came on the evening of 24 October 1956 in the wind and pouring rain in front of 65,000 at Ibrox, where they faced French champions Nice. Shearer set the tone for what was to become a fractious and unpleasant evening by clattering into Nice left-half Nurenberg in the first minute, and the game degenerated from there. The *Glasgow Herald*, commenting on the body-checking, reckless tackling and kicking, described the game as 'a bear-garden…a disgraceful exhibition of fouling and other misbehaviour'.

Rangers missed several chances in the opening twenty minutes and the French team went ahead through outside-left Faivre in the 23rd minute. A Max Murray header just before half time and a 60th minute strike from Billy Simpson saw Rangers take a 2-1 lead to France. Referee Arthur Ellis, rapidly losing control of the game, had to lecture the teams about their behaviour in the 55th minute. The same official, who claimed that his watch had been broken by the ball,

A young Alex Scott, Rangers' goalscoring regular right winger until the arrival of Willie Henderson

blew for time five minutes early but soon realised his mistake and called the players back onto the pitch. Caldow, heading to the bath and looking forward to his brother's wedding reception, had to change back into his strip.

The first attempt at the second leg in France was cancelled owing to torrential rain. Two weeks later – 14 November – in Nice, in another bruising and bad-tempered encounter on a mudbath of a pitch, Hubbard scored first with a 40th minute penalty, after Gonzalez had flattened Murray in the box, but the French replied with two goals in two minutes from Foix and Bravo early in the second half to level the tie on aggregate. Rangers should have scored and the forwards, particularly Scott and Simpson, missed several chances. Towards the end, Bravo and Logie were sent off for fighting, Niven's goal was pelted with fireworks and only the wire fencing prevented a crowd invasion. The referee was shepherded off by a police escort.

The deciding match was held in Paris on 28 November.

Rangers in 1956/57. Back: Shearer, Caldow, Niven, McColl, Davis. Front: Scott, Simpson. Murray, Young, Baird, Hubbard

Young was injured and was replaced by Korean War veteran and ball-winning hardman Harold Davis, a tough right-half signed a month previously from East Fife. Rangers again went on the attack and were continually foiled by Nice keeper Colonna, in excellent form. On half-time Foix scored from twelve yards. After the interval, Nice right-back Bonvin turned a Sammy Baird shot into his own net and Rangers were level. However, Muro and then Faivre scored to put Rangers out of the European Cup. In the 75th minute Shearer bundled Muro over the touchline, knocking him unconscious, and, in the ensuing chaos, Shearer and Bravo were sent off for fighting although they both stayed on the pitch till the end of the game! There was pandemonium in the stadium and the Rangers players were relieved to reach the safety of the dressing room. The Rangers team for the deciding match was: Niven, Shearer, Caldow, McColl, Davis, Logie, Scott, Simpson, Murray, Baird, Hubbard.

Back in the Scottish league, Rangers started in a faltering manner but won 14 of their last 16 league games to pip Hearts to the title by two points. During the season, in a particularly

striking demonstration of the team's steeliness and ability to fight back from apparently hopeless situations, they were 4-1 down to Queen's Park and came back to win 6-4. For good measure they also won the Glasgow and Charity Cups although Celtic were victorious in the League Cup and Falkirk took the Scottish Cup. At the end of the season, George Young retired. 'Corky' had played 678 games for the club, and this modest and likeable man who was such an influential and charismatic player for Rangers can be considered as one of the greatest ever Light Blues. He went on to manage Third Lanark for three years and he died in 1997.

Rangers, as Scottish champions, were back in the European Cup in 1957/58. On 4 September 1957, 90,000 spectators – at the time a British record for a floodlit match – crammed into Ibrox for the first leg of the first round against French champions St Etienne. As early as the 14th minute 'Les Verts' were ahead after a Davis mistake allowed Rachid Mekloufi to

score a stunning goal. Five minutes later the massive Kitchenbrand backheaded in from a Hubbard cross. Early in the second half Davis atoned for his error by sending through Scott who scored from the edge of the penalty box. Billy Simpson then added a third from a Kitchenbrand header with eight minutes to go. Rangers, however, should have found the net more often than they did as they were on the attack throughout the match, but the forward line, with the exception of Scott, spurned several chances.

For the second leg in the Stade Geoffroy-Guichard, with temperatures touching 90F, Rangers had introduced Billy Ritchie, newly-acquired centre-half John Valentine and Jimmy Millar in place of Niven, Davis and Kitchenbrand. A reliable and dependable keeper, Ritchie was bought from Bathgate Thistle in 1954 as reserve to Niven but he was to replace him in 1961. With Johnny Hubbard unwell, the South African winger's place was taken by 18-year-old Davie Wilson. Wilson was a rare talent. A small, fair-haired outside-left, he was a speedy supplier and a deadly finisher whose pace and opportunism were to delight the Ibrox fans over the coming years.

Above: Ian McColl and George Young in action

Below: The St Etienne defence keeps out Rangers' attack in September 1957 at Ibrox

AC Milan keeper Buffon saves an Alex Scott corner under the challenge of Sammy Baird in November 1957 at Ibrox.

St Etienne mounted an onslaught from the start and the clever French forwards deserved their 11th minute goal on the half-volley from Oleksiak. Rangers packed their defence and weathered the storm, with Ritchie particularly outstanding in goal. In a 71st minute breakaway, Rangers forced a corner, and Davie Wilson stooped to head into the net from Alex Scott's kick. Four minutes later, St Etienne keeper Abbes made a fine save from a McColl penalty, with McColl distracted by the stones and fireworks hurled at him by the crowd. Urged on by their frantic support, St Etienne piled forward again and Fevrier added a second for the French with three minutes to go. Rangers, however, withstood the pressure and held on till the final whistle, a mightily relieved team.

The champions of Italy – AC Milan – were the second round opponents at Ibrox, with their hugely talented forwards Ernesto Grillo and Juan Schiaffino and the defensive flair of captain Cesare Maldini, father of today's Milan left-back and captain, Paolo. Rangers opened the scoring through an early Max Murray strike and were 1-0 ahead at half time. Milan's clever counter-attacking game proved effective,

however, in the second half. The floodgates opened and Milan scored four times in the last 15 minutes, two of them coming from Grillo. The Ibrox crowd, impressed by the Italian side's devastating finishing, cheered Milan off the pitch, while the *Glasgow Herald* said of Rangers: 'The poverty of ideas in attack was painful to behold'.

In Milan, with only 3,000 turning up to watch, mainly because of the pouring rain and deplorable conditions, Baruffi and Grillo scored in a 2-0 win for the Italians. Rangers had been outplayed again by a superior side. Dominance in Scottish football was one thing, survival in Europe another.

Meanwhile, back in Scotland Hearts finished the league season 13 points ahead of second-placed Rangers having scored 132 goals and conceded only 29. Hearts were also about to discover the technical inadequacy of Scottish football on the continental stage in the next season's European Cup, going out 6-3 to Standard Liege in the opening round.

Ralph Brand had established himself as a regular in the Rangers team this season. He had made his debut in the Rangers first team in November 1954 at the age of 18 against Kilmarnock and had scored twice in their 6-0 win.

National Service had then intervened. Brand was a high scoring inside-forward with a sharp tactical brain and a predator's eye for goal. He was to establish a legendary partnership – known as the 'M&B' – with Jimmy Millar in the 1960s. In the Scottish Cup Rangers met Hibs in a semi-final replay on 9 April 1958. With Hibs 2-1 up and with two minutes to go, McColl sent in a high cross to the box and Brand rose his full 5 foot 7 inch height to challenge the keeper in the air. The ball fell to Murray who smashed it into the net. The referee pointed to the centre circle but then he spotted the linesman with his flag in the air. The linesman claimed to have seen Brand handle the ball and Hibs were awarded a free-kick. Rangers were out of the competition and Hibs were beaten 1-0 by Clyde in the final.

Earlier in the season Rangers had suffered one of the most deeply humiliating defeats in their history. On 19 October 1957 they met Celtic at Hampden in the final of the Scottish League Cup. At half time they were lucky to be only 2-0 down. By the end of the game they were on the wrong end of a 7-1 drubbing, with Billy McPhail scoring a second-half hat-trick. McPhail was in superb form throughout and his marker, centre-half John Valentine, was blamed for the debacle. Valentine never again played for the first team and he was transferred to St Johnstone shortly afterwards. When asked the time after the game, Celtic's Charlie Tully said 'Seven past Niven', although Niven was not responsible for the defensive shortcomings. A new centre-half, 32-year-old Willie Telfer, was brought in from St Mirren as a stop-gap till Rangers could rebuild the defence.

At the end of the season Billy Simpson, after 262 appearances and 262 goals, left the club to join Stirling Albion and wee winger Johnny Hubbard, 116 goals in 258 games, went south to Bury. Arrivals included Andy Matthew, Billy Paterson and Ian McMillan. Matthew was an outside-left from Fife who was to stay only two years. Paterson was a tall, elegant centre-half, who perhaps lacked the bite and aggression to make the position his own although he was first choice until the emergence of Ronnie McKinnon in the early 1960s. Scottish international Ian McMillan was signed from Airdrie and his influence on Rangers was immediate. A slight inside-right, with close dribbling skills, vision and inch-perfect distribution, McMillan was the playmaker supreme. Although he avoided physical contact where possible, he was fortunate to play alongside Harry Davis, and then John Greig, who provided the defensive cover for his talents to flourish.

On his debut match in 1958/59, McMillan scored twice in Rangers' 4-4 draw with Raith Rovers. 'The Wee Prime Minister' (as McMillan was dubbed in a reference to the then Prime Minister Harold McMillan) helped guide Rangers to

Ralph Brand

twenty-four league matches with just one defeat between October and April. Although Rangers lost their last game of the season, Celtic beat Hearts, Rangers' main challenger, and the Light Blues won the title by two points. They failed, however, to qualify for the League Cup and were beaten 2-1 by Celtic in the third round of the Scottish Cup.

Rangers also played a couple of friendlies with European clubs in November. They were 2-0 down to Napoli after 23 minutes but Davie Wilson scored twice and Rangers won 5-2. Against Grasshoppers Max Murray scored in the 56th minute and Caldow converted a penalty towards the end. Brand made the score 3-0 in the 87th minute. They also played Arsenal again at Highbury on 21 April 1959. With McMillan superbly orchestrating his side, Brand opened the scoring in the 12th minute. In the 53rd minute a piece of trickery from McMillan led to him being brought down in the box. Caldow scored from the penalty spot and Brand scored his second ten minutes from the end.

Left-half Billy Stevenson was now partnering Harry Davis in the team. Stevenson was to be supplanted by Jim Baxter in 1960 and he joined Bill Shankly's Liverpool in 1962, where his career flourished. He played in the close season

Ian McMillan, the 'wee Prime Minister'

with pennants and flags presented by opponents and the Scottish league championship pennants cover one wall, under the watchful eyes of an oil painting of Bill Struth.

Season 1959/60 saw Rangers back in Europe attempting to improve on their record in the previous two campaigns. In the first round at Ibrox on 16 September Rangers met Belgian champions Anderlecht. Rangers were 2-0 ahead within three minutes. Jimmy Millar headed in an Alex Scott free kick in the 2nd minute, with keeper Meert rooted to the spot, and Scott scored from twelve yards from a Davis through pass one minute later. The game quickly turned into a hostile and bruising encounter with the Belgian side engaging in vicious tackles and even physical assault. Within the first half hour Anderlecht had twelve free-kicks awarded against them.

A Van den Bosch goal was disallowed for offside in the 30th minute and Danish referee Helge, having a nightmare game, was surrounded by the Anderlecht team. The decision stood. The fouling and kicking escalated and at one point Anderlecht's star player, the bespectacled Joseph Jurion, had the temerity to kick Harry Davis, the tough man of the Rangers side, to the ground. The outraged Davis chased Jurion behind the goal but soon saw the funny side of his actions. In the second half McMillan was fouled and Andy Matthew scored with a header from his rebounded penalty. Anderlecht retaliated within two minutes with a Stockman goal and then de Waele added a second. Anderlecht were back in the game although Rangers were guilty of missing several chances. Sammy Baird sealed victory with two goals in six minutes, the first after a McMillan dummy, the second a 73rd minute penalty.

In the replay at the Parc Astrid on 23 September, an intimidating Anderlecht went on the all-out attack but the game was goalless at half-time. Alex Scott had been stretchered off just before the interval with blood pouring

tour of Denmark, which saw Jimmy Millar make the permanent move from right half to centre-forward when he scored four goals from the striker's position in one game.

On a visit to Real Madrid, Symon had been impressed by the Spanish club's trophy room. In 1959 he converted the players' billiard room in the Main Stand next to the manager's office into the Ibrox Trophy Room. Today there are six glass cabinets full of glittering crystal, china, silverware and medals from Rangers' history, the earliest being a small bronze cup awarded to Moses McNeil in 1876 for his athletic endeavours on behalf of Rangers Football Club. The walls are resplendent

Jimmy Millar shoots for goal, watched by Celtic's Bobby Evans

from his head after a crude tackle had sent him crashing into the boundary wall. He returned in the second half, his head bandaged, and sent over a cross in the 65th minute which Andy Matthew headed between the keeper's legs. Ian McMillan added a second ten minutes later from a Matthew cross and Rangers were through. The Anderlecht president apologised for his team's behaviour after the match, while Rangers chairman Bailie John Wilson said 'I've never been more proud of the boys. They were wonderful.'

Red Star Bratislava, with four Czech internationals in the team, were the visitors to Ibrox in the second round. Ian McMillan opened the scoring after 90 seconds but by the half-hour mark Rangers were 2-1 down, the goals coming from Scherer and Dolindky. Two minutes before half time, Baird and Red Star keeper Hlavaty collided and Scott lobbed into the empty net. The keeper was carried off unconscious but returned in the second half. In the 68th minute Scherer scored again and Rangers were losing 3-2. Caldow missed a penalty but Davie Wilson equalised in the 74th minute and, with seconds of the game remaining, Jimmy Millar scored the winner.

In the away leg in a hostile atmosphere Rangers put up an effective defensive performance. Scott scored with a thumping header in a second-half breakaway but Red Star drew level in the last minute. Millar was sent off for punching Tichy. Rangers' 5-4 aggregate victory had taken them to the quarter-final of the European Cup where they were drawn against Sparta Rotterdam.

In Rotterdam Wilson and Baird had Rangers 2-0 ahead after 35 minutes. De Vries pulled one back but Murray increased Rangers' lead to 3-1. In the dying seconds De Vries scored again for Sparta. At Ibrox an 81st minute strike from Van Ede was the only goal and the sides were level on aggregate. As there was then no away goal rule in operation, the game had to go to a playoff, at Highbury, a ground with which Rangers were familiar.

In pouring rain and muddy conditions, Sparta went ahead after only 6 minutes through Verhoeven. In the 27th minute Wilson crossed to the far post, Baird dummied and the ball was deflected into his own net by Verhoeven. Hero to villain. In the 57th minute another Wilson cross found Baird unmarked and the big inside-left scored with a 20-yard left-foot rocket. Millar made the score 3-1 and, although Sparta scored from a penalty near the end, Rangers were through to the semi-final.

Eric Caldow watches as George Niven makes a one-handed save from Erwin Stein in the European Cup semi-final against Eintracht Frankfurt at Ibrox in 1960

The other three clubs left in the tournament were Real Madrid, with Di Stefano, Puskas and Gento, the undisputed champions of Europe; Barcelona, managed by Helenio Herrera with the feared Hungarian attack force of Kubala, Kocsis and Czibor; and German champions Eintracht Frankfurt who were making what proved to be their only appearance ever in the competition. Rangers drew Eintracht in the semi-final and were no doubt pleased to escape the other two giants.

The relief, however, did not last long. Rangers were handed a footballing lesson in the first leg in Germany. They were unable to cope with the speed, movement and tactical understanding of the Germans, with young centre-forward Erwin Stein, inside-forward Albert Pfaff and right-winger Richard Kress outstanding, and they were crushed 6-1. Eric Caldow's penalty conversion did little to cheer Rangers. It wasn't much better at Ibrox in the return. Although Rangers scored three – McMillan with two and the other coming from Wilson – Eintracht again put six past the shell-shocked Rangers side, who were rapidly discovering the yawning tactical gulf between Scottish and European football. Billy Stevenson, quoted in Motson and Rowlinson's book *The European Cup*, admitted 'When you look back at that year our lack of knowledge was laughable. We lost 6-1 but it could easily have been ten'.

Eintracht played Real Madrid in the final at Hampden, often described as the best game of football ever played. Real enthralled the huge 130,000 crowd with a magnificent display, the goals coming from Puskas (4) and Di Stefano (3), and collected their fifth European Cup in succession.

Drained by their European adventures, Rangers had a poor league season. They finished in 3rd place, twelve

Ian McMillan's shot beats Frankfurt keeper Loy in the 1960 European Cup semi-final at Ibrox.

points behind Hearts, the team of the moment. They also failed to qualify for the League Cup. The Scottish Cup, however, was more fruitful. Having beaten Hibs in the quarter-final 3-2, Jimmy Millar scoring the winner, they faced Celtic in the semi-final. Chalmers opened the scoring for Celtic with a 25th minute header. In the second half Wilson crossed to Millar on the edge of the penalty box and Millar sent the ball soaring past keeper Haffey with an outrageous header. In the replay Celtic were swamped 4-1 although honours were even – 1-1 – at half time, Wilson scoring in the 10th minute. In the second half Wilson and Millar (2) inflicted the damage.

Kilmarnock, second in the league and managed by Willie Waddell, were the opposition in the final on a sunny 23 April. McColl was in for Rangers, a replacement for Davis,

sidelined with a back injury. Rangers went on the attack from the kick-off. Millar put Rangers ahead with a 22nd minute double header, deceiving keeper Brown with his second attempt, but Caldow missed a penalty early in the second half, after Scott had been fouled in the area, blasting the ball over the bar. Rangers continued their onslaught and it was Millar again with another header from a Stevenson cross in the 67th minute. Rangers had convincingly won the Cup 2-0 and they should have scored more against a disappointing Killie. In what had been an exhausting season for Rangers, they had managed to pick up only one major trophy, although they did collect the Glasgow and Charity Cups, beating Partick Thistle on both occasions. The team for the Cup final was: Niven, Caldow, Little, McColl, Paterson, Stevenson, Scott, McMillan, Millar, Baird, Wilson.

A new name was to be added to the team sheet in 1960/61. James Curran Baxter was on his way from Raith Rovers to Ibrox and five years of glory lay ahead.

CHAPTER FIVE:

FROM BAXTER TO BERWICK: 1960-1967

'Slim Jim' Baxter joined Rangers on 21 June 1960 for £17,500, a then Scottish record transfer fee, having impressed Symon in Raith Rovers' defeat of the Gers the previous season. Over the next five years he was to be the inspiration behind what was arguably the greatest Rangers side of the modern era. A young ex-miner from Hill o'Beath in Fife, who had given up the game for a while as a teenager, Baxter's audacious and cocky talents marked him out as a player of genius. Not overly keen on defensive duties (which he tended to leave to his full-back, Eric Caldow), and unwilling to spend too much time in the air, he was nonetheless an outrageously gifted player with a sublime left foot, and he teamed up with Ian McMillan to

'Slim Jim' Baxter

Jim Baxter and Eric Caldow run out of the tunnel at Ibrox carrying the Scottish League Cup

form the creative heart of Scot Symon's team. His work rate and application could vary depending on his mood and motivation but it is very unlikely that, without his presence on the park, Rangers could have achieved what they did between 1961 and 1965. Described by Willie Waddell as 'the most skilful left-half ever produced by Rangers', Baxter could lay claim to being the best left-sided player to have played for Rangers since the little winger Alan Morton in the 1920s.

Baxter's first season at Ibrox was hardly interrupted by his National Service with the Black Watch, as the left-half was based in Stirling and Perth, but the team suffered from the prolonged absence of Jimmy Millar in the latter half of the season with slipped disc problems. Rangers began their league programme briskly, opening with a 6-3 win over Partick Thistle and following that up with a 5-1 hammering of Celtic at Parkhead. In this latter game, Alex Scott scored first and then Rangers claimed four goals in 21 second-half minutes through Millar, Brand, Wilson and Davis. In November at Ibrox, McMillan made history by scoring the club's 5,000 league goal against Raith Rovers.

In the final game of the season, an Alex Scott hat-trick helped the club to a 7-3 win over Ayr and they grabbed the league title by one point over Kilmarnock. Killie had been their opponents in the League Cup Final, and a 37th minute goal from Brand and a strike from Scott with six minutes to go had brought the trophy back to Ibrox. They disappointed in the Scottish Cup, however, going down 5-2 to a spirited Motherwell in a third-round replay, a game which Baxter missed due to Army duties.

This season, Rangers produced their best performance to date in Europe. The European Cup Winners Cup – a knockout, two-legged competition between the domestic cup winners in Europe – had been initiated by UEFA at the beginning of the season. Unlike in Britain, where the cup competition preceded the league and was considered of at least equal importance, many European countries afforded their cup competitions little status or did not even have a domestic cup tournament, and so only ten countries entered the new tournament.

Rangers' first game in the competition was against Ferencvaros, with the Hungarian international Florian Albert their charismatic captain and centre-forward. At Ibrox, although the Hungarian side were 1-0 ahead at half

John Greig and Jimmy Millar lead a training run with Jim Baxter, Bobby Shearer and Alex Scott taking up the rear

time through Orosz, Davis equalised after the interval. An increasingly confident Rangers took control and scored through Millar (2) and Brand, to leave a 4-2 scoreline. In Hungary Rangers were 2-0 down until Wilson narrowed the difference in the 61st minute, taking advantage of defensive sloppiness.

The Light Blues proceeded to the second round 5-4 on aggregate to play Borussia Moenchengladbach. The Germans were expected to provide tough opposition but they crumbled at home and collapsed in Glasgow. In Germany, Millar, Scott and McMillan had their names on the scoresheet without reply, and back at a rain-soaked Ibrox a rampant Rangers ran up an 8-0 victory against the embarrassed and outplayed Germans. Baxter opened the scoring in the 2nd minute and Ralph Brand claimed three, becoming in the process the first Rangers player to score a hat-trick in Europe.

Their next opponents were Wolverhampton Wanderers in the semi-final. Wolves were coming to the end of their impressive domination of English football, under the dour, long-ball management of Stan Cullis, but they had won the English league twice in the previous three seasons, and were still a strong, determined side. The two-leg tie was billed as the 'Battle of Britain'.

Eric Caldow puts his penalty wide in the European Cup Winners Cup final at Ibrox in May 1961. Observe the position of Fiorentina keeper Albertosi just inside his six-yard box when the kick is taken

At Ibrox, with new signing from Airdrie, centre-half Doug Baillie, playing in the centre-forward position due to the injured Jimmy Millar's absence, Rangers suffered an early blow when Davis pulled a thigh muscle in the 9th minute and had to move out to the wing. Davie Wilson had to pull back to the right-half position to act as cover. Rangers, however, seized the advantage when Alex Scott capitalised on an error by England international half-back Ron Flowers to lash into the net from 20 yards. Wolves were on top throughout but, with only six minutes remaining, Brand made the most of another Wolves' defensive mistake to pinch a second goal.

In the snow at Molineux, with more than 10,000 Rangers fans noisily making their presence felt, Wolves again moved onto the offensive. Scott, however, made the aggregate score 3-0 from a Brand pass just before half time and, although Peter Broadbent equalised on the night for Wolves in the second half, Rangers held on to their winning margin. Wilson was the most threatening player on the park and Billy Ritchie had a memorable evening in goal, the high point being his

Willie Henderson floats in a corner kick

exceptional, acrobatic save from a thunderous Flowers drive from thirty yards. Rangers were now through to the final, the first British club to have reached a European final.

Italian cup winners Fiorentina, with the outstanding Swedish winger Kurt Hamrin their main danger man, lined up against Rangers in front of 80,000 spectators in the first leg of the final at Ibrox. Fiorentina got off to a good start when a bad pass-back by Davis in the 11th minute was intercepted by Petris who found Milani in space. The Fiorentina forward swept the ball into the net. The Italians were making their intentions clear, indulging in fouling, body-checking and cynical obstruction, and a particularly clumsy tackle by Fiorentina captain Orzan on McMillan in the 17th minute resulted in a penalty award. As Rangers captain Caldow stepped forward to take the kick, the Italian keeper, Albertosi, ran from his goal line towards the 6-yard line gesticulating and shouting, and an astonished Caldow shot wide. The referee refused to allow the kick to be retaken, in spite of the protests of the Rangers players. Milani, capitalising on another Davis error, scored his second in the last few minutes and Rangers faced a trip to Italy carrying a 2-0 deficit, a difficult task ahead of them.

Jimmy Millar was back for the second leg and, although Rangers turned in a stirring performance, their defence was

again breached twice. Milani opened the scoring in the 12th minute and, although Scott equalised in the 60th minute from a Wilson cross, Hamrin scored another when he surged from midfield to blast a wicked, curling shot past Ritchie from a tight angle. Baxter and McMillan spurred on a determined Rangers team, but they could not find the net again. The game ended 2-1 and Fiorentina had won the first European Cup Winners Cup.

At the end of the season, Ian McColl left the club after fifteen years at Ibrox. He was to become Scotland manager, where he would renew his acquaintance with several of the present team, and he ended his career as manager of Sunderland. Other departures included Willie Telfer and Sammy Baird. Symon, however, had some remarkable, young emerging talents – in particular Willie Henderson, John Greig and Ronnie McKinnon – in his squad, and these players would soon establish themselves as Ibrox legends.

'Wee Willie' Henderson was a schoolboy footballing prodigy who was one of the youngest players to play for Scotland. A tiny (5 foot 4 inch), fast, outside-right, he possessed tight dribbling skills which bewildered defenders

Left to right: Ralph Brand, Jimmy Millar and Davie Wilson

as he sped down the wing to deliver crosses to Millar, Brand and Wilson. He could also score goals. He made his debut in the 1960/61 season and duelled for the right-wing position with Alex Scott until the latter's departure for Everton in February 1963, when Henderson made the position his own. In his autobiography, *Forward with Rangers*, Henderson disclosed the lack of warmth between the two wingers and his relief at Scott's decision to move to England.

Willie was also extremely myopic. His short-sightedness can best be illustrated by the possibly apocryphal episode, later in his career, when he lost his contact lenses during a game against Celtic. With the game drawing to a close, he ran over to the dug-out to find out how much time remained.

'Ask at your own bench', roared Celtic manager Jock Stein, pointing the hapless winger in the correct direction.

John Greig, a strong, determined Edinburgh lad with an eye for goal and a powerful shot, was about to begin a remarkable career with the Ibrox club as a long-serving player, captain and, eventually, manager. And Ronnie McKinnon, a relatively small but stylish centre-half, was soon to take over from Bill Paterson in the central defensive position. He was also about to embark on a long and productive Ibrox career.

For all their new talent, however, Rangers could not hold on to the league title in 1961/62. That honour went to Dundee, who won their last seven games to clinch the title by three points, and had underlined their superiority by beating Rangers 5-1 at Ibrox, centre-forward Alan Gilzean scoring four of them. After the game, centre-half Bill Paterson was blamed for the scale of the defeat and was replaced by the giant Doug Baillie, although McKinnon was soon to assume the position. Dundee were to do themselves and Scottish football proud in the following season's European Cup, when they reached the semi-final only to lose to AC Milan, the eventual winners.

Davie Wilson outdid Gilzean's total in an away match at Falkirk in March. Relocated into the centre-forward position as Jimmy Millar had dropped back to the half-back line, Wilson scored six in Rangers' 7-1 crushing of the Bairns, including three in eight minutes. Three of the goals came from his left foot, three from his right. A disingenuous Wilson reflected after the game that 'the ball kept hitting the net'. Four days later, he scored a hat-trick in the Scottish

Jimmy Millar finds the net against Hibs

League's 4-3 defeat of the English League at Villa Park. Nine goals in two games was some achievement, even for the prolific little winger. Rangers had a poor run-in, however, taking only seven points out of their last seven games and had to be content with the runner-up spot.

The Light Blues did, however, pick up both cups that season. They drew 1-1 with Hearts in the League Cup final, the Edinburgh side equalising Jimmy Millar's 15th minute goal with a penalty in the 78th minute in a dull match. In the replay at a fog-shrouded Hampden, Rangers were at their attacking best and were 3-1 ahead by the 21st minute. Jimmy Millar scored first with a header in the 7th minute but Hearts replied immediately. Then Brand made it 2-1 in the 15th minute and McMillan added a third, smashing in a rebound from the crossbar with his left foot. No more goals were scored although Rangers hit the woodwork four times.

In the Scottish Cup final on 21 April, with Baxter in masterful form and Henderson, the replacement for Scott, cutting his way at will down the right wing, Rangers flooded into attack against St Mirren. Although St Mirren defended bravely, Brand scored in the 40th minute, forcing in a Wilson cross. In the second half Wilson took advantage of a McMillan pass to score another and, although Saints came back briefly, Rangers won 2-0. It was an exciting and dramatic match, and Rangers returned to the pitch after the game for a deserved lap of honour. 'Rex', writing in the *Sunday Mail*, said 'The game belonged to Baxter more than anyone. He moved all over that field with the polite affability of a young curate looking up his parishioners and patting a head generally here and there.' An on-song Baxter could certainly attract the metaphors.

They were also back in the European Cup. Drawn away to Monaco in the first round first leg, they were 2-0 ahead by half time. The match ended 3-2 in Rangers' favour, the goals coming from Scott (2), and Baxter. Baxter's accomplished and assured performance in this game, acting as the link-man between defence and counter-attack, marked him out as one of the finest footballers in Europe. At Ibrox, reserve centre-forward John Christie, in for the injured Jimmy Millar, scored twice and Scott added a third in another 3-2 win.

The second round found them paired with East Germany's Vorwaerts. At the time, Iron Curtain clubs were refused permission to visit NATO countries. The Warsaw Pact were concerned about the possibility of their Eastern European players being seduced by the temptations of decadent Western culture and by the consequent risk of defections. Vorwaerts' opponents in the first round – Linfield – had been unable, largely for financial reasons, to arrange their second round tie in a neutral country. The Irish team

Jim Baxter and Billy Ritchie share a joke

had to withdraw and Vorwaerts progresssed to round two. Rangers travelled to the Walter Ulbricht Stadium in East Berlin on 15 November and came away with a 2-1 win, through a Ralph Brand goal and an Eric Caldow penalty. Malmo in politically neutral Sweden was selected as the venue for the second leg one week later. With a crowd of just over 3,000 in the stadium, Rangers went ahead in the 40th minute when Willie Henderson, making his European debut, took advantage of a rebound to score. Rangers were ahead 3-1 by the interval and cruising. However, fog descended at

Scott Symon and assistant trainer Joe Craven in the Ibrox dressing room

half time and the referee, having waited a fruitless half an hour for it to clear, abandoned the game.

With Rangers' flight home booked for the next day, and Vorwaerts' visas running out, the clubs agreed to replay the game the following morning. The match kicked off at 10am, in front of a 1,800 crowd, and early in the second half Rangers went ahead through an own goal. McMillan, after a splendid piece of individual skill, made it 2-0 three minutes later. With ten minutes to go McMillan claimed another and, although Caldow put the ball into his own net, Henderson wrapped it up with three minutes to go. Rangers went through 6-2 on aggregate.

On 7 February 1962 Rangers faced Standard Liege in Belgium in the quarter-final first leg. Caldow had to pull out just before kick-off with a bruised toe and 19-year-old Bobby King took his place. Captain Caldow's authority was missed by Rangers who went down 4-1 to the Belgian champions, with Irishman Johnny Crossan scoring twice for Liege. At Ibrox, they lined up with Ian McMillan replacing John Greig who had made his European debut in the first leg. Henderson's name was on the teamsheet, but he was held up in Glasgow traffic from his Airdrie home on his way to the game and missed the kick-off. His place was taken by Alex Scott. Rangers won the game 2-0 – the goals coming from Caldow and Brand – but Liege held on to go through on aggregate 4-3.

In the summer of 1962 Rangers arranged a series of friendlies in the Soviet Union, the first Scottish club to visit the country. They played three games in ten days, beating Lokomotiv Moscow 3-1 and Dinamo Tbilisi 1-0, and drawing 1-1 with Dinamo Kiev. The Russian fans initially were hostile to Rangers but, towards the end of the tour, they warmed to the Glasgow side. Henderson's fast, tricky wing play, in particular,

was much appreciated by the enthusiastic crowds who were captivated by the little winger's impudent skills. Jim Baxter was on National Service in the Far East, and John Greig replaced him at left-half for the trip. Rangers had been concerned about their playmaker's absence. Their worries proved unnecessary. Until then regarded as an inside-right, Greig's robust and effective performances in the half-back role established him as a regular in the following season's first team and he took over in the right-half position from Harry Davis. An effusive and emotional crowd of over 10,000 welcomed Rangers back to Renfrew Airport and, in the confusion, all flights were delayed for nearly an hour. The players remember the homecoming with astonishment and no little pride, although the airport staff perhaps did not share their high spirits.

It was during the Russian tour that Caldow lost his captaincy. A man who had admired and respected Struth,

The crowd at Renfrew Airport as Rangers return from Russia

Early in the 1962/63 season the clearout of the older players continued at Ibrox. Billy Paterson was given a free transfer and Billy Stevenson joined Liverpool for £20,000. In November Max Murray was transferred to West Bromwich Albion while Alex Scott, scorer of 117 goals in 347 games for the club, moved to Everton for a fee of £39,000 in February.

The regular, first-choice team was now a settled one: Ritchie, Shearer, Caldow, Greig, McKinnon, Baxter, Henderson, McMillan, Millar, Brand, Wilson. Many Rangers fans of a certain vintage regard this line-up as one of the finest the club has ever produced: the dependable 'quiet man' Ritchie in goal; the aggression and fearsome tackling of 'bluenose' Shearer matched on the other wing by the speed and finesse of Caldow; Greig and McKinnon cooly and effectively controlling the centre of defence; the superlative skills of the peerless Baxter and the calm, mature authority of McMillan; and the industry and goalscoring flair of Millar and Brand, supplied by the marauding, speedy wingers Henderson and Wilson. This blend of all the talents was a powerful and intoxicating one, and this exceptional side was to dominate Scottish football over the next two years.

The astute Scot Symon continued to control matters behind the scenes, aided by his lieutenants Davie Kinnear

Ralph Brand avoids Celtic centre half Billy McNeill's tackle

Caldow did not extend the same courtesy to the dour and reclusive Symon. The antipathetic nature of their relationship came to the surface after Caldow, with some other players, opted for some decent food and beer and spent an evening at the British Embassy rather than attend an official, post-match dinner with the Russians. At a photographic shoot to mark the opening of the 1962/63 season, Symon pointedly handed the ball to Bobby Shearer, and the right-back became skipper. Not a vindictive man, Symon nevertheless would not forgive disobedience from his players. During the season two familiar and long-serving faces left Ibrox. George Niven, who had lost his place to Billy Ritchie and had played 368 games in goal for the club, moved to Partick Thistle in February and full-back John Little moved to Morton.

(trainer) and Bob McPhail and Jock Shaw (youth coaches). Continuity and tradition were all-important at Ibrox, and who better to take the club into the future than famous ex-players, imbued with Struthian values and principles? Like his predecessor, Symon was not a man to concern himself with tactics and strategies of play, preferring to pick the best players he had and let them make their own decisions on the field. His aloofness did not universally endear him to the players but most of the squad respected his footballing knowledge and his perceptive team selection skills. This talented team, however, was one which virtually selected itself.

Rangers stormed the league in season 1962/63, losing only two matches – to Kilmarnock and Dundee United – and ended the season nine points ahead of nearest challenger Kilmarnock. They were also thirteen points ahead of Celtic whom they beat 4-0 on the Ne'er day fixture at Ibrox, the goals scored by Davis, Millar, Greig and Wilson. Millar had a particularly outstanding season, scoring 44 goals in 52 matches, and Millar, Brand and Wilson scored between them a total of 106 goals. In the Scottish Cup they reached the final but were nearly undone by Dundee in the quarter-final. After a 1-1 draw at Dens Park, the replay at Ibrox was 2-2 with two minutes to go, but Brand connected with a low cross from Henderson to score the winner.

After overcoming Dundee United 5-2 in the semi-final, on 4 May they faced Celtic at Hampden in the first Old Firm final since 1928. Brand scored for Rangers in the 41st minute and Murdoch equalised within three minutes. The game ended in a 1-1 draw, although a Willie Henderson

Bobby Shearer and Tottenham's Cliff Jones rise to challenge for the ball in the 1962 European Cup Winners Cup second round first leg at White Hart Lane in October 1962

shot hit the crossbar with Celtic keeper Frank Haffey nowhere. Rangers would surely have won had it not been for an exceptionally commanding, bravura performance from Haffey. George McLean, a tall inside-forward who had been bought from St Mirren in February for a record transfer fee between Scottish clubs of £26,500, was in the side in place of McMillan. Eric Caldow was absent, having suffered a triple fracture in his leg in the 6th minute of the Scotland v England international the previous month at Wembley. In that game, Davie Wilson moved from left-wing to left-back and Baxter scored twice in a memorable victory for the ten men of Scotland.

In the cup final replay, Baxter and McMillan, replacing an injured McLean, were again the instigators of an outstanding Rangers display. Baxter, in particular, often seemed to save the best of his club performances for the Old Firm encounters. In his eighteen appearances for Rangers against Celtic between 1960 and 1965 he was only twice on the losing side. 'I loved to turn it on against Celtic', he said later in his career. At

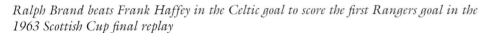

Ralph Brand beats Frank Haffey in the Celtic goal to score the first Rangers goal in the 1963 Scottish Cup final replay

John White scores Spurs' first goal at White Hart Lane while Billy Ritchie remains rooted to the spot

Hampden, Brand opened the scoring in the 7th minute, sidefooting the ball into the net from five yards, and just on half time Wilson made it 2-0 after Haffey had failed to hold a Brand shot. During the interval, many Celtic supporters, sensing their team's inevitable defeat, began streaming out of the stadium. Brand added a third in the 73rd minute, his speculative 20-yard shot deceiving an off-form Haffey, and Rangers had retained the Scottish Cup. Celtic were poor, particularly in attack, and were fortunate to lose by only three. During the game, Baxter had emphasised his and Rangers' superiority by sitting on the ball and inviting the Celtic players to come and get it.

In recognition of McMillan's sparkling performance, Baxter stuffed the ball up his jersey after the final whistle, refused to hand it to referee 'Tiny' Wharton and proudly presented it to McMillan in the Rangers dressing-room. Just under 250,000 people had attended the two games, an indication of the massive appeal of the Old Firm in the early 1960s and the strength and appeal of Scottish club football generally during the period.

Earlier in the season, Rangers had an easy win at Ibrox over the Spanish cup holders Seville in the first round first leg match of the European Cup Winners Cup, Millar scoring a hat-trick and Brand claiming the other in their 4-0 win. In Seville, they were the victims of a disgraceful display of kicking, butting, spitting and gouging from the Spaniards, but Seville could only score twice. Baxter was kicked as he lay injured and Henderson, ill-advisedly but in the heat of the moment, belted the Seville left-back on his jaw. Henderson fled, pursued by his much bigger opponent, and did not stop until he reached the reassuring safety of Bobby Shearer. Punch-ups were breaking out across the pitch, with substitute Doug Baillie getting off the bench to join the melee. The referee stopped the game two minutes early and Rangers had to be escorted off the pitch by the police. In his autobiography *The Party's Over*, Baxter wryly comments that 'in the dressing room we counted heads, just to make sure nobody was still lying out there'. Rangers survived the 'Battle of Seville' to go through to round two 4-2 on aggregate.

English cup holders Tottenham Hotspur, with their feared attack force of Jimmy Greaves, Les Allen, John White and wingers Terry Medwin and Cliff Jones, lined up against Rangers in the second round first leg in an electric atmosphere at White Hart Lane. Spurs went ahead after only four minutes. Massive centre-half Maurice Norman rose for a Greaves corner kick, distracted the Rangers defence and White expertly headed in to the net. Almost immediately, Rangers equalised when Brand intercepted a poor back pass, shot, and the rebound was converted by Henderson. By half time, however, the tie was virtually over and Rangers' defensive frailties in the air, and particularly from the corner flag, had been cruelly exposed. Spurs scored three further goals, two from corner kicks, and Billy Ritchie and Ronnie McKinnon had been tested and found wanting. In the second half, a header from Jimmy Millar brought the score back to 4-2 but Rangers lost another goal, a Norman volley from yet another corner, and a 5-2 scoreline promised a testing time for the Light Blues in Glasgow.

The Saturday before the second leg, Rangers had turned in a devastating performance to crush Kilmarnock 6-1 and confidence was high at Ibrox. In front of 80,000 supporters

at Ibrox, Rangers met Spurs again on 11 December. The London side had replaced centre-forward Allen with big Bobby Smith. A clever dummy from Smith let in Jimmy Greaves to open the scoring in the 9th minute with a superb individual goal, running from the halfway line and leaving McKinnon, Davis and Caldow for dead before slotting the ball past Ritchie. The tie was now effectively over for Rangers.

Rangers, however, continued to play with courage and flair but the tightly-organised Tottenham defenders were the equal of the Rangers attack. Brand headed in the equaliser just after half time from a Henderson cross, and five minutes later Smith fired in a White cross for Spurs. Wilson made it 2-2 with fifteen minutes to go. With only three minutes remaining, Smith scored his second of the night, heading home a Dave Mackay cross. The result gave Tottenham victory on the night and Rangers exited the competition 8-4 on aggregate. Small consolation for the Gers, but Tottenham won the trophy, beating Atletico Madrid in the final.

Although Baxter had been continually complaining about the relatively low wages on offer at Ibrox, he signed a new

Jim Forrest wheels away in triumph after scoring against Celtic

contract before the 1963/64 season began which stipulated that, in the event of a club making an offer for him, the Rangers board would seriously consider it. Baxter's wages had moved from £22 per week in 1960 to £35 per week, and he was well aware that players in England were earning at least double this. Baxter was not particularly greedy, but he believed his considerable drawing power should be appropriately rewarded.

Jim Forrest, an athletic, young centre-forward, made his scoring debut in the first team in the opening game of the 1963/64 season against Celtic at Parkhead in a League Cup game on 10 August. He replaced the injured Jimmy Millar and scored twice in Rangers 3-0 win. His first goal came in the 29th minute when he took advantage of a poor passback from McNeill to Haffey and his second was a second-half conversion of a Henderson cross. In between times 'Dandy' McLean had buried a sweet pass from Baxter past Haffey. Tall full-back Davie Provan had taken over Eric Caldow's

Rangers celebrate their 5-0 1963 Scottish league Cup final win over Morton. From left (standing): Forrest (four-goal hero of the game), Brand, Ritchie, Willoughby, Provan, Shearer, Watson, McKinnon, Greig. Sitting: Henderson, Baxter

position at left-back. In the second leg a fortnight later, Rangers repeated their 3-0 victory. In the 38th minute Wilson headed in a Henderson cross, and just after half time Brand converted a penalty after Forrest had been upended by McNeill. Forrest smashed in an 18-yard left-foot shot seven minutes later. Two weeks later they beat Celtic again in the league. Chalmers opened the scoring in the 11th minute but McLean fired in the equaliser just before half time. Brand made the final score 2-1.

Rangers were unbeaten in their first thirteen league games, winning ten and drawing three, until the run was ended in a 3-0 defeat by Hearts at Ibrox. In spite of an extended injury list – which at various times included Caldow, Wilson, Baxter, Millar, Forrest and Henderson – they made sure of their 34th league title on 4 April, beating Dundee United 2-0. They ended the season six points ahead of second-placed Kilmarnock.

In late September 1963 they had the misfortune to be drawn against Real Madrid in the first round of the European Cup. Real – with their glittering, international forward line of Ferenc Puskas, Alfredo Di Stefano and Paco Gento – were not the force they once were in European football, but they remained one of the best sides on the continent. In the first leg at Ibrox on 25 September, Rangers pressurised the Spanish aristocrats, with Henderson in particularly effective raiding form down the right and McKinnon ably containing the threat of Di Stefano. However, with three minutes to go, Real keeper Jose Araquistain punted the ball up to Puskas, till then having a quiet game. The tubby Hungarian fed Gento on the left and, when Gento centred, Puskas' left foot was waiting. Real were 1-0 ahead.

In Madrid on 9 October, none of the Rangers forward line – Henderson, Willoughby, Forrest, McLean and Watson – was over the age of twenty-one, and Wilson was out with a broken leg, sustained in a League Cup semi-final against

Berwick. Their youthfulness, and the naivety of the defence, were ruthlessly exploited by the veteran Spanish side. Rangers were demolished by Madrid's speed and tactical awareness, and by Di Stefano's genius. Puskas scored Real's first goal in the third minute, smashing the ball into the net from the underside of the bar, and by the 24th minute Real were four up. Puskas claimed a hat-trick and the game ended 6-0, although such was Real's superiority that it could have been ten. After the match, a chastened and defensive Symon said that the score could have been different had Forrest not missed a simple chance in the 3rd minute. 'Yes, it would have been 6-1', observed a realistic Scottish journalist. Hugh Taylor, in *The Scottish Football Book No 10*, witheringly assessed Rangers' European status: 'Once again, Rangers had failed sadly in Europe. Once again they had shown that while cocks of the walk in Scotland they were merely fluttering chicks among the giants of Continental soccer, babes in arms in the war that is the European Cup'.

Domestically, the 'cocks of the walk' were enjoying their most successful season for many years. The team had already made sure of the League Cup, and reached the final by beating Berwick Rangers 3-1 in the semi-final (the 'wee Rangers' would get their revenge in 1967). In the final they met Morton (in the Second Division but to be promoted as champions at the season's end), who had eliminated Motherwell and Hibs. In front of 105,000 spectators, Rangers put five second-half goals past Morton without reply, with four coming from new goalscoring sensation Forrest. The other was collected by Forrest's cousin, blond-haired inside-forward Alex Willoughby, who had joined the

Ralph Brand watches the ball enter the net for Jimmy Millar's and Rangers' first goal in the 1964 Scottish Cup final...

club at the same time as the centre-forward. Although Morton had been overwhelmed by another sparkling display from the Rangers attack, they had played with spirit and determination and scarcely deserved to lose by five goals.

The club's second 'treble' – League, League Cup and Scottish Cup – was now on the cards. Rangers had begun their Cup trail with a 5-1 win over Stenhousemuir and a 9-0 humbling of Duns. Partick were next to be eliminated from the tournament, 3-0. In the quarter-final Rangers once again faced Celtic. The Light Blues were 1-0 ahead at half time after Forrest had dived to direct a header past Celtic keeper John Fallon. A piece of magic from Henderson – when he cut infield in the 46th minute, dribbled past three Celtic defenders and blasted a shot into the right-hand corner of Fallon's net – gave Rangers a 2-0 win on the day. In the semi-final, a Davie Wilson goal just on half time was enough to beat Jock Stein's Dunfermline Athletic, and Rangers met Dundee at Hampden in the final on 25 April 1964.

With a crowd of 120,000 in Hampden, the game kicked off and the first half, although goalless, was a tense and exciting affair. Rangers were on top but the superb goalkeeping of Bert Slater defied the Rangers attack. 'Rex' praised Slater in the *Sunday Mail*: 'A wonderful exhibition. You felt that Rangers would need a traffic cop to direct them past Slater.' In the 71st minute, Millar broke the deadlock with a header from a Henderson corner, Brand's dummy confusing Slater. Dundee, however, equalised almost straight from the kick-off. Without a Rangers player touching the ball, centre-forward Kenny Cameron finished off the move by shooting into the roof of the net from twelve yards. With under two minutes to go of a heart-

...and Millar heads in another for the second

A celebration soaking after the 3-1 win over Dundee in the 1964 Scottish Cup final. From left: Brand, Ritchie, Provan, McKinnon (holding Shearer with the trophy), McLean, Millar, Greig, Baxter. On the ground: Henderson and Wilson (wearing a bowler hat)

stopping final, a clever Baxter free-kick found Henderson in space on the left. The winger crossed and Millar rose to loop in a header for Rangers' second.

It was still not finished. On the stroke of full time, Henderson delivered a perfect lob to Wilson on the six-yard line. Wilson shot but Slater, deservedly the man of the match for his courageous and inspired control of the Dundee goal area, pulled out a splendid save. He could not hold it, though, and the ball fell to Brand on the goalline. Brand's shot hit the foot of the far post and rolled into the net. Rangers had won their eighteenth Scottish Cup 3-1 and Brand had become the first player to score in three consecutive Scottish Cup finals (four, if replays are considered). The *Sunday Mail* headline, 'Wonderful Willie' confirmed Henderson, creator of the three goals, as the best outfield player in the match. Rangers, in their change strip of blue and white stripes, hoisted captain Shearer aloft and paraded the trophy to the thousands of their fans in the old stadium. The 'treble' had come back to Ibrox, and in style. The team at Hampden was: Ritchie, Shearer, Provan, Greig, McKinnon, Baxter, Henderson, McLean, Millar, Brand, Wilson.

In March, Rangers chairman John Lawrence had said of Scot Symon that 'he will be our manager as long as he wants to stay' and the Cup triumph and 'treble' confirmed Symon's unassailable position at Ibrox. The team, however, as with all great sides, was beginning to break up. The exodus began with Ian McMillan who returned to his original club, Airdrie. The hugely influential inside-forward had played 205 games and had scored 55 goals for Rangers, and at the age of 34 felt his future lay elsewhere.

Season 1964/65 was to mark the domestic decline of Symon's side, although they were to acquit themselves fairly well in the European Cup. They were drawn at home to Red Star Belgrade in the first round, first leg, and travelled to Yugoslavia with a 3-1 lead, two of the goals scored by Brand. In Belgrade, Rangers conceded three goals in ten minutes and were 4-1 down with only eight minutes to play. A 5-4 aggregate defeat was looming, until a Davie Wilson corner kick was headed against the crossbar by Forrest. Centre-half Ron McKinnon got his head to the rebound and the ball went into the roof of the net for McKinnon's first-ever goal for Rangers. The deciding game was held at Highbury where two goals from Forrest and one from Brand brought Rangers a 3-1 win.

Austrian champions Rapid Vienna travelled to Ibrox for the first leg of the second round, and a through ball from Baxter to Wilson in the 55th minute was turned into the net by the winger for the only goal of the game. In the Prater (now Ernst Happel) Stadium in Vienna on 7 December, Jim Baxter had probably the game of his life. Clearly reveling in the thrilling and still exotic atmosphere of European football, he taunted and teased the Austrians, directing play in his own seemingly languid yet incisive manner. He made Rangers' first goal, beating two defenders and passing to Forrest in the 19th minute for the centre-forward to open the Light Blues' account. Willie 'Bud' Johnston, an ebullient and exciting 17-year-old inside-left, had joined Rangers three months previously and he made the second goal, dribbling past two defenders and cutting back for Wilson to score. The pacy Johnston was to make his mark as a regular winger with Rangers and Scotland but, for all his talent, his hot-headedness and temper were to do him no favours in the years to come.

With the game virtually over, and Rangers holding a 3-0 aggregate lead, Baxter was eyeing the dressing room when he was badly tackled by Vienna right-half Walter Stocik. He fell to the ground and whispered to trainer Davie Kinnear 'It's broken'. Baxter would be out of action for three months with a broken leg just above the ankle, retaliation for his humbling of Austria's top players. *The Times* quoted the referee as saying of Baxter: 'He played like Pele'.

Baxter-less Rangers were drawn against Inter Milan in the first leg of the quarter-final at the San Siro Stadium in Milan. Inter, under the authoritarian direction of coach Helenio Herrera, had developed the defensive *catenaccio* system, with a defender playing behind the back four, and were difficult to break down. The system, however, depended on counter-attacking, and full back Giacinto Facchetti and stylish forwards Luis Suarez, Sandro Mazzola and Jair were lethal on the break. Rangers discovered this at the beginning of the second half when Inter scored three times in three minutes, Suarez scoring the first and inside-forward Piero adding two more. Rangers replied with a 65th minute Forrest goal from a Wilson Woods pass – becoming the first British team to score in the San Siro in the European Cup – but the score stayed 3-1.

Three young Rangers forwards: from left Jim Forrest, Alex Willoughby and Willie Henderson

Back at Ibrox in front of an 80,000 crowd, Forrest raised Rangers hopes with a 6th minute strike and the team now needed one more goal to take the tie to a playoff in Stuttgart. The Italians massed in defence and effectively killed the game, although McLean nearly made the breakthrough in the 70th minute when he thundered in a shot which beat keeper Sarti but rebounded off the underside of the crossbar. Inter went on to win the trophy, beating Benfica in a disappointing final, but Rangers were once again out of Europe.

By their recent high standards, Rangers had a dismal season in the league. With Henderson out for the first half of the season recovering from an unglamorous bunion operation, and Baxter unavailable after his leg injury in Austria, the team was playing significantly below their form of the previous three seasons. They finished in fifth place in the league, their lowest position for 39 years. They won only one trophy, the League Cup, which they contested against Celtic in the final on 24 October. The game was goalless until early in the second half when Forrest gave Rangers the lead. Just prior to this, Celtic's Bobby Murdoch had seen his shot slip out of Ritchie's hands and Murdoch claimed that the ball had gone over the line. Ritchie protested this and the referee sided with the keeper, much to the anger of the Celtic team. Forrest secured the cup for his club with another goal later in the half from a Baxter through ball.

A poor season for the Light Blues had some bright spots, principally the goalscoring of Jim Forrest who proved himself more than an adequate replacement for Jimmy Millar with 57 goals in all competitions, a new club record.

More bad news was to come, however, with the departure in May of Jim Baxter to Ian McColl's Sunderland for £72,500. The gifted left-half had decided to cash in on his talents in the English game and immediately moved from a basic of £45 to £80 per week plus a share of the signing-on fee. As further evidence of the disintegration of the team, Bobby Shearer was given a free transfer and, before the beginning of the next season, Ralph Brand followed Baxter to England, joining Manchester City for £30,000.

Across the city, Jock Stein had taken over as manager of Celtic and the Parkhead team were about to dislodge Rangers as the top team in Scotland. It would be several more years before Rangers could rebuild a side which would bring them back to the heights of Scottish football. Stein – 'The Big Man' – was busy effecting a revolution at Celtic. In contrast to Symon's detached, formal and bowler-hat management style, Stein was an involved, track-suit manager and a motivator supreme. His forceful personality, attacking football philosophy and rigorous training methods were to create a Celtic team which would eclipse Rangers well into the 1970s.

As well as the increasing threat of Celtic, Rangers were experiencing other, internal, problems at the beginning of the season. Ralph Brand, now with Manchester City, had penned an article in the *News of the World* which was highly critical of the Ibrox set-up. Brand had condemned the

training methods as old-fashioned, revealed the tensions in the club between management and players and had denounced the club for only playing Protestant players. This last charge was perfectly true and had been an unwritten rule at Ibrox for several decades. Celtic, although essentially a Catholic club, had no such constraints and had benefited from the comparison in the eyes of neutral fans. Jock Stein, for instance, was a Protestant. The Rangers board refused to comment on Brand's article but were apparently privately furious about Brand 'breaking the ranks'. Allan Herron, writing in the *Sunday Mail*, agreed with Rangers in an article entitled 'Come off it, Ralph'. Herron's view was that 'Brand is castigating the very heritage of Rangers FC...greater players than Brand have had the opportunity to reveal what goes on at Ibrox but have chosen to remain silent...I have defended his play on many occasions...now I can defend him no longer.'

In June 1965 Symon paid Morton £20,000 for the services of talented Dane Kai Johansen, an attacking full-back, to replace Bobby Shearer. Rangers began the 1965/66 season well and did not lose in their first fifteen league games. The contest throughout the season was with Celtic, whom they beat 2-1 in September at Ibrox. The

Kai Johansen scores the only goal in the 1966 Scottish Cup final replay. Tommy Gemmell, Billy McNeill and George McLean watch the ball beat Celtic keeper Ronnie Simpson

goals came in the first 20 minutes. Forrest scored in the 6th minute and twelve minutes later John Hughes equalised from the spot. Within two minutes McLean scored the winner, again from a penalty. By the end of 1965 the Old Firm were neck-and-neck at the top of the league.

In the Ne'er Day fixture on 3 January at Parkhead, however, although Davie Wilson opened the scoring within the first two minutes a revitalised and fast-improving Celtic drubbed the Light Blues 5-1, with Stevie Chalmers claiming a hat-trick. Rangers effectively conceded the title in March, when they lost 3-2 to Falkirk and 1-0 to Dundee United, and could only draw with Hearts and Kilmarnock. Although they won their last seven games, they finished in second place in the league, two points behind Celtic, and the Parkhead side had won their first league title for twelve years.

Rangers had faced Celtic in October at Hampden in the League Cup final. In the 17th minute McKinnon handled in the box and Hughes scored from the resulting penalty. Then Provan brought down Jimmy Johnstone, a constant torment to the left-back, in the area and Hughes again converted from the spot. Rangers pulled one back with seven minutes to go but the cup went to Parkhead.

Consolation awaited Rangers in the Scottish Cup. They reached the final on 23 April and lying in wait for them was, yet again, Celtic. The game ended in a 0-0 draw and, although Wilson and Henderson switched wings in an attempt to wrong-foot Celtic early in the game, the match remained inconclusive. It was replayed the following Wednesday. Bobby Watson was at inside-right, in front of John Greig, Scotland's Player of the Year, while Jimmy Millar filled the left-half position. Something of an anti-climax, the match was sealed by Rangers when, with ten minutes to go, Willie Johnston beat three Celtic defenders on the left, crossed low into the centre and found Henderson. Willie's shot was cleared by Bobby Murdoch and right-back Johansen unleashed a twenty-yard drive past Ronnie Simpson in the Celtic goal. Rangers held on to their lead and collected the cup, guaranteeing themselves European football the following season. In the dressing room, Symon, aware of the symbolic importance of a victory over Celtic, told his players 'this is Rangers' most important victory'. The team for the replay was: Ritchie, Johansen, Provan, Greig, McKinnon, Millar, Henderson, Watson, McLean, Johnston, Wilson.

To say that 1966/67 produced a season of mixed fortunes for Rangers would be seriously to understate the glaring contrast between their European achievements and their disastrous performance in the Scottish Cup. So far as the latter competition is considered, older Rangers fans will not need reminding of the events of 28 January 1967, one of the blackest days in the history of the club.

The Rangers team after the 1966 Scottish Cup final replay

Rangers had been drawn away to Second Division Berwick Rangers in the first round of the Scottish Cup – a formality, surely. Berwick's keeper and manager was Jock Wallace who was, a few years later, to become coach and manager of the Light Blues. In the opening half hour Rangers forced a flurry of corners and Alex Smith and Willie Henderson came close to scoring. So far, so good, until little Sammy Reid in the 37th minute walloped the ball past Norrie Martin, who had taken over in goal from Partick Thistle-bound Billy Ritchie at the beginning of the season. As the second half wore on, Jock Wallace was unbeatable, making fine saves from Wilson – on as a substitute for Willie Johnston who was stretchered off with a broken leg after a collision with Wallace – McLean and Greig, and Rangers could not find the net. The *Sunday Mail* commented 'this was the game of a lifetime for Wallace'. It could have been worse with five minutes to go when Berwick's Christie was denied a clear chance by Martin. The whistle went and Berwick had won 1-0, one of the great shock results in the history of the Scottish Cup.

The recriminations were swift and predictable. Symon was quick to dust any blame off his shoulders for his role in the debacle: 'I am at a loss to understand how professional players can go into a game like that and apparently fail to understand the consequences of a defeat for the club. Our prestige has received a shattering blow. They (the players) were found wanting completely in ability and intelligence'. Chairman John Lawrence also waxed righteous. 'There is no doubt in my mind', he fulminated, 'that the only people who can be blamed for the defeat are the ones on the field – the players'. Although there were eight Scottish internationals in the Rangers side, the team's application and effort in the game was at best minimal and the fact remains that freak results do happen. The minnows Berwick, in what to them was a huge game, had played to their best and beaten a superior side, as happens from time to time in football. The Glasgow side had been too complacent for their own good and had grievously underestimated a fighting Berwick team.

The Rangers' management and board, however, needed scapegoats. Rangers' pride was at stake and, although many criticised Symon's tactical naivety, the manager was to remain in control, at least for the time being. The *Sunday Mail* was quick to apportion blame: 'If there are any brickbats flying – and there are bound to be after this disaster – then they must be aimed at inside men McLean and Forrest'. Although Jim Forrest had scored 145 goals in 164 games, and was about the only consistent centre-forward at the club, he was blamed for the defeat and transferred to Preston North End for £38,000 only a few weeks later. He was later to return to Scottish football and enjoy five productive years at Aberdeen. George McLean was also deemed guilty and he was quickly transferred to Dundee, as part of an exchange deal for Scottish international midfielder Andy Penman. The club now had only two recognised goalscorers – Alex Willoughby and new £55,000 signing from Dunfermline, inside-right Alex Smith. Rangers were to regret these punitive disposals as the season progressed.

The fact that Symon had abdicated responsibility for the defeat and had sided with the board to the detriment of his players was unfortunate. How much better for all concerned had Rangers and the manager accepted the blow to the club's self-image, swallowed the hurt and continued with the season, where they were, after all, in with a chance of the league as well as the European Cup Winners Cup? This was not, however, the Rangers' way. The aftermath of the shocking defeat by the battling Second Division side led the club to failure in the league championship race and was a crucial factor in Rangers missing out on their first European trophy.

Earlier in the season, Rangers had met Celtic in the League Cup final. A Bobby Lennox goal was the difference between the sides, but Alex Smith managed to miss an empty goal to equalise. In the league, 16 unbeaten games between mid-December and the end of March gave hope to Rangers, and Alex Willoughby compensated to some degree for the loss of McLean and Forrest. Celtic, however, claimed the title by three points and captured the 'treble'.

A week after the Berwick disaster, an 18-year-old right-half, William 'Sandy' Jardine made his debut for the first team against Hearts at Ibrox, where Rangers recovered some self belief by inflicting a 5-1 defeat on the Edinburgh side, Willoughby scoring a hat-trick. Jardine was a cool and collected player who was to develop into one of the finest full-backs in the British game, and he was to form a formidable partnership with Celtic's Danny McGrain in the Scottish international team.

This season, both Celtic and Rangers reached the finals of Europe's two competitions, Celtic famously becoming the first British club to win the European Cup when they beat Herrera's Inter Milan 2-1 in Lisbon. Rangers' campaign began in Belfast, their first trip to Northern Ireland, when they played Glentoran. The Irish players, managed by ex-Celtic player John Colrain, were virtually all Rangers supporters, but hero worship was not in evidence as they held the Light Blues to a 1-1 draw, McLean scoring for Rangers. Back at Ibrox, goals from Johnston, Dave Smith, Denis Setterington and McLean saw Rangers progress 4-0.

In the second round they were drawn against European Cup Winners Cup holders, Borussia Dortmund, with West German internationals Sigi Held, keeper Hans Tilkowski and goalscoring winger Lothar Emmerich the stars of the team. No British team had beaten Borussia in two years of European football.

At Ibrox in the first leg, Kai Johansen opened the scoring with a low shot from an acute angle in the 10th minute. In the 30th minute Dortmund equalised in the most outrageous manner. Held hared down the left on the attack and ran over the bye-line, where he remained fearing an offside decision. He then came back onto the pitch, without the referee's permission, picked up a John Greig deflection and passed to inside-right Trimhold, who scored. Spanish referee Daniel Zariquiegui, who seemed ignorant of the laws of the game on at least two counts, awarded the goal, in spite of Rangers' heated protestations. Justice was served when Alex Smith headed a late winner.

In the second leg at the Rote Erde Stadium, Rangers courageously defended their lead, with Greig and McKinnon superb at the heart of the defence. Bobby Watson broke his ankle – after what seemed to be a deliberate kick from Emmerich – and Alex Smith dropped back to midfield to replace him. Forrest shot wide when he should have scored and Martin made a fine save with only minutes to go. Rangers' magnificent rearguard display was the equal of any of their performances to date in Europe, and the final 0-0 scoreline deservedly moved them through to the quarter-final against Spain's Real Zaragoza.

At a wet Ibrox, a goal apiece from Dave Smith and Alex Willoughby within the first twenty-seven minutes of the match gave Rangers a cushion for their trip to Spain. Ronnie McKinnon was out for the second leg, having broken his nose in a league match against Ayr, and was replaced by Colin Jackson. Lapetra scored for the Spaniards in the 24th minute

and Santos levelled the aggregate score with a penalty towards the end. The game went into extra time and Dave Smith had his penalty saved in the extra period. The overall score remained 2-2 when the final whistle blew. As at the time there were no penalty shoot-outs (these would not be introduced into European competition until season 1970/71), the tie was decided by the toss of a coin. Captain John Greig guessed correctly and Rangers were in the semi-final.

On a bumpy and grassless pitch in the Vasilij Levski Stadium in Bulgaria, Rangers took on Slavia Sofia for the right to contest the final. Favourites Rangers went ahead in the 31st minute when Willoughby set up Wilson to score with a low shot. This was the first home goal which Slavia had conceded in European football and, slighted by the dishonour, they took the attack to Rangers. What appeared a perfectly good Dave Smith goal was disallowed in the 55th minute and Rangers held on to win 1-0. In Glasgow, with 70,000 fans in Ibrox, Johnston was back from injury but, mystifyingly, Symon had selected Roger Hynd as centre-forward in place of Alex Willoughby. Hynd, a capable central defender, had scored four goals from the centre-forward

Roger Hynd watches as Sandy Jardine's shot goes over the bar in the 1967 semi-final second leg match against Slavia Sofia at Ibrox

position in a reserve game the previous week, but his lack of experience and pace up front was a problem, as he himself admitted. Slavia played badly but Rangers could only score once, when Henderson took advantage of a Hynd header to volley in the winner from outside the penalty box in the 31st minute. Nevertheless, the Light Blues had reached their first European final and were to play the Bayern Munich of Franz Beckenbauer and Gerd Muller in Nuremberg on 31 May.

Although Hynd had acquitted himself with a degree of competence in the centre-forward position, Symon made a serious tactical error in preferring him to top scorer Alex Willoughby in the line-up for the final. Indeed, Willoughby was left out of the squad for the game and the aggrieved forward immediately requested a transfer. Symon and his new coach Bobby Seith were hoping that the game would be won by the speed of wingers Henderson and Johnston. They were closely marked, however, and without a recognised striker Rangers could not breach the German defence, marshalled

Bayern Munich's keeper Sepp Maier saves from Roger Hynd in the European Cup Winners Cup final in May 1967 in Nuremberg

impeccably by Beckenbauer sweeping up in defence. In the 30th minute Hynd missed Rangers' only clear-cut chance from six yards and the game went into extra time. Towards the end of the second period Franz Roth scored for Bayern and the Germans had won the Cup. The *Sunday Mail* praised Rangers' defence but criticised the leaden forwards: 'The attack flopped completely. Rangers were slow in the break. When the scoring chances were created, no forward had reflexes sharp enough to cash in.' The Rangers team for the final was: Martin, Johansen, Provan, Jardine, McKinnon, Greig, Henderson, A Smith, Hynd, D Smith, Johnston.

The players' acute disappointment was made much worse by Celtic's triumph in the previous week's European Cup final. They were also dismayed by the comments made by John Lawrence in a press conference before the game, when he criticised the team saying that Rangers needed new forwards and that three half-backs in attack was not good enough. John Greig in his book *A Captain's Game* says: 'It has been suggested that these remarks and the heavy press coverage of the affair affected our play. It didn't. We didn't even know about the conference until after the game when

someone gave us the papers from home.' Nevertheless, the club and its supporters were in disarray and trouble was deepening at Ibrox.

Clyde manager Davie White had travelled to Nuremberg with Rangers as an observer. White had spent all his career with the Shawfield club and he was admired within Rangers for his modern training methods. On his return from Germany White was appointed Rangers' assistant manager with a view eventually to take over from Symon and introduce younger blood into the management.

The squad was also refreshed in the close season. Old stalwarts Jimmy Millar and Davie Wilson both left to join Dundee United. There was a feeling among the fans that Rangers had got rid of Wilson too early, a view confirmed by Wilson's consistent form for the Tayside club over the next five seasons. The talented Swedish winger Orjan Persson arrived at Ibrox from Dundee United. Danish keeper Eric Sorensen – known as 'the man in black' – joined from Morton. And Alex

Scott Symon with Dave White on White's appointment as assistant manager

Ferguson, who would become one of the most successful and controversial figures in football management, came from Dunfermline for a Scottish record £65,000. Ferguson was a classic, direct centre-forward, with a no-holds-barred style, and he had scored 66 goals in 88 matches for the Fife club.

The 1967/68 season kicked off with Rangers in a league cup draw with Aberdeen, Dundee United and Celtic. The first game against Celtic on 16 August attracted a huge crowd of 95,000 with thousands more unable to get in. The three new signings plus Andy Penman, a clever, visionary midfield player, were making their Old Firm debuts. In the 38th minute Dave Smith fouled Bobby Lennox in the area and Tommy Gemmell's penalty sent new keeper Sorensen the wrong way. Rangers had most of the pressure throughout the game but Celtic keeper Ronnie Simpson saved a Penman penalty. Dead ball expert Penman finally achieved a deserved equaliser in the last minute when his 25-yard free-kick deceived Simpson.

The second game at Parkhead two weeks later was watched by a capacity crowd of 75,000. Willie Henderson put Rangers ahead in the 7th minute amid offside appeals from Celtic, and the home team were provoked into attack. A Lennox 'goal' was disallowed just on half time. Rangers defended grimly and, on the break, Johnston's shot hit Celtic's crossbar midway through the second half. With twelve minutes remaining, John Clark fouled Henderson in the Celtic box. Johansen's penalty kick hit the underside of the bar and the Dane illegally hit the ball as it rebounded, oblivious to the presence of the waiting and expectant Andy Penman. Celtic, now re-energised by their good fortune, pressed forward and levelled the score with a Willie Wallace header two minutes later. In the 83rd minute a twenty-yard strike from Bobby Murdoch gave Celtic the lead and Lennox made the score 3-1 in the last minute. Rangers were eliminated from the tournament, and they lost the services of David Provan who broke his leg in a collision with Celtic's Bertie Auld. Celtic went on to win the League Cup, beating Dundee 5-3 in the final.

Jock Stein's men were now confirming their dominance of the Scottish game. Nonetheless, Rangers were progressing well in the league and, by the end of October, were ahead in the title race. They had won six and drawn two of their first eight games and were three points ahead of Celtic, whom they had beaten 1-0 at Ibrox in the second league game of the season thanks to a fine individual goal from Persson who rounded four Celtic players and scored from a tight angle from eighteen yards. Many of the supporters, however, were unhappy with Rangers' continuing defensive play, and, after a 0-0 draw with Dunfermline at Ibrox, on 28 October, when fans' favourite Alex Willoughby was substituted, they vocally made their displeasure felt at Symon and the board.

On 1 November, Symon stunned Scottish football with the news of his resignation. Symon's statement to the press was brief: 'I was informed by a Glasgow businessman that at a meeting of the directors of Rangers football club it was decided to terminate my appointment forthwith. I am awaiting confirmation of this.'

There was little doubt that Rangers needed a new, younger manager but the shoddy actions of the board, and in particular John Lawrence, did them little credit in the affair.

Above: *Alex Ferguson (centre) scores his first goal for Rangers in a friendly against Eintracht Frankfurt in August 1967, watched by Andy Penman*

Left: *Symon after his sacking*

Lawrence had not informed Symon personally about the dismissal, preferring to leave it to a business colleague, accountant Alex McBain, who had no formal connection with Rangers. Symon was clearly losing the confidence of the club,

and he had to go. Lawrence, however, could have offered him a position on the board or some other role within Rangers, if only because of his successful record over the years and his unquestioning commitment and loyalty to the club. Symon was deeply hurt and cut all connections with Rangers. He was not to return to Ibrox for eight years. Coach Bobby Seith also resigned in protest, saying 'I no longer want to be part of an organisation which can treat a loyal servant so badly'.

Symon had brought the club fifteen trophies in his thirteen seasons at the helm and had introduced gifted footballers, in particular Greig, Baxter, McMillan and Henderson, to Ibrox. Although his personality and methods did not always endear him to the players, the team were shocked at his departure. The board acted precipitately, almost certainly as a panicked reaction to Celtic's increasing, and seemingly unstoppable, hegemony over Scottish football. As David Mason wrote in *Rangers: The Managers*, 'Symon paid the price of Jock Stein's success more than he paid for Rangers' failure'.

And the new manager – 34-year-old Davie White – was charged with bringing back the trophies.

CHAPTER SIX:

WHITE, WADDELL AND WALLACE: 1968-1975

Davie White was a very different personality to Scot Symon. Young, untested in international football and informal with his players, White had made a name for himself by taking unfashionable Clyde to third spot in the league the previous season before he had joined Rangers as assistant manager.

He was also not a 'Rangers man', having only ever played for Clyde, but this was a mixed blessing. On the one hand, he was unencumbered with the baggage of the past and could introduce fresh methods and tactics into Ibrox without genuflecting to tradition. On the other, he was to be continually scrutinised by the old guard – notably by Willie Waddell, now a football journalist – to ensure that he was upholding the standards and values which they firmly associated with Rangers. Many observers felt that he lacked

Rangers team group, 1967. Back: Jardine, Johansen, Martin, Provan, McKinnon, Greig. Front: Henderson, A Smith, Hynd, D Smith, Johnston

the qualities and experience to continue in the patrician line of Rangers managers, although Symon gave him his blessing, saying 'Davie is a very fine man. I wish him all the best. He is with a wonderful club.' He quickly developed a rapport with the players, many of whom found his engaging personality and willingness to talk tactics a refreshing change from the remote Symon. White was a track-suit manager and hands-on when it came to training, but off the pitch he maintained the Ibrox tradition of insisting that his players dress formally and smartly and behave in ways appropriate to their standing in the world of football.

John Lawrence had blamed the lack of goals as one of the reasons behind Symon's departure (although others detected the hangover from Berwick as a more important factor). The view within the club was that, as Celtic seemed unbeatable, goal average could decide the destination of the league championship. White agreed, and preached an attacking philosophy to his receptive team. White came through his Old Firm baptism at the Ne'er's Day fixture at Parkhead when a last minute strike from Johansen secured Rangers a lucky 2-2 draw, coming back from 2-0 down. His forwards embarked on a impressive goal spree through the Spring but, despite maintaining their unbeaten record, they dropped points at Dundee United and Morton towards the end. Rangers were still unbeaten by the last league game of the season at Ibrox against Aberdeen. David Smith opened the scoring but Sorensen fumbled a high ball which dropped into the net. Ferguson restored Rangers lead early in the second half with a header but Aberdeen added two, the last in the 89th minute, to end

Ronnie McKinnon (left) and Kai Johansen defend their goal

Rangers' title hopes. The team was jeered off the park and Celtic won the league by two points.

Symon had been in charge for Rangers' first game in the Fairs Cup earlier in the season. The competition – full title European Inter Cities Fairs Cup – had been established in the 1950s and was originally contested by clubs from cities which hosted annual trade exhibitions. By the mid-1960s it was open to the best clubs from European countries who had not won the cup or league, and Rangers qualified because of their second place in the league the previous season. The competition changed its name in 1972 to the UEFA Cup.

Rangers had travelled away to East Germany, where they played Dynamo Dresden in the first round. Ferguson scored early in the second half but it was the excellence of Sorensen in goal which allowed Rangers to take a 1-1 draw back to Ibrox. Penman scored in the first half in Glasgow and, just before the final whistle, Kreische equalised for Dresden. The

game was won in injury time by a John Greig goal.

With White now the manager, Rangers entertained a defensive Cologne, with their German international inside-left Wolfgang Overath, in the second round first leg. Rangers came away 3-0 winners, the scorers being Henderson and Ferguson (2), the centre-forward directing in a stunning header from the edge of the penalty box for the third goal. In the Hungersdorf stadium, Overath opened the scoring for Cologne, and Webber and Ruhl added two more within four minutes in the second half. With two minutes remaining of extra time, Henderson was the matchwinner with an excellently taken goal.

An all-British quarter-final was now set up with Leeds United on 26 March, with the first leg at Ibrox. Rangers had been knocked out of the Scottish Cup by Hearts two weeks previously but were still two points ahead of Celtic in the

---

Dave Smith

league. Leeds, managed by Don Revie, were a formidable side. Steely and ruthless, they could also turn on the skill, with Billy Bremner, Peter Lorimer and Johnny Giles creating the chances, and Norman Hunter and Jackie Charlton taking no prisoners in the centre of defence. The game was watched by 80,000 spectators on a wet evening and Rangers, without the injured Penman and Willoughby, attacked from the outset but could not penetrate the Yorkshire side's defence. Persson was denied a last-minute goal by the acrobatic Gary Sprake in the Leeds goal and the game finished 0-0.

With nearly 20,000 Rangers fans in the 43,000 crowd at Elland Road two weeks later, and over 43,000 watching the game on close circuit at Ibrox, Leeds went ahead in the 25th minute when Giles converted a penalty after Ferguson had handled a Bremner header in the penalty area. Six minutes later they were two up when a seemingly offside Lorimer slotted home a simple opportunity. Leeds, with Bremner and Giles controlling midfield, were on top for the rest of the game and should have scored more through Lorimer and Charlton. The game ended 2-0 and Leeds went on to win the Fairs Cup, beating Ferencvaros 1-0 in a two-leg final.

Rangers had failed to win a trophy for the second successive season and, although White could take some comfort from the goalscoring of Alex Ferguson who bagged 23 in the campaign, it was clear that the existing squad needed to be improved. It was now the start of White's first full season in charge of the club and, early in the season, he was about to make some changes. But before he could follow through with his transfer dealings, there was still the little matter of meeting Celtic, yet again, in the League Cup sectional games in August.

The first game at Ibrox was unfortunate for John Greig whose defensive mistakes allowed Celtic's recent signing

from Hearts, Willie Wallace, to score twice in the first half. Rangers dominated in the second half but Celtic keeper Simpson's performance ensured a 2-0 scoreline. At Parkhead, Wallace scored again and it was only Martin's performance in the Rangers goal, saving at one point a Gemmell penalty, that restricted Celtic to a 1-0 win. Rangers failed to qualify for the quarter-finals and the Parkhead side won the competition for the fourth year in succession, beating Hibs by an emphatic 6-2 in the final.

In the second league game of season 1968/69, Rangers visited Parkhead and came away with a fortifying 4-2 victory, courtesy of two goals from Johnston and one apiece from Penman and Persson. Towards the end of October, however, the club were fifth in the league and it was clear that new blood was required. On 31 October White unveiled his new signing, Colin Stein, bought for a Scottish record £100,000 from Hibs. A blond, bustling centre-forward, Stein made an immediate impression, scoring a hat-trick on his debut at Arbroath and

Colin Stein

Alex MacDonald

then another hat-trick at Ibrox in Rangers' 6-1 win over Hibs. In mid-November White again entered the transfer market, securing the small, combative Alex MacDonald from St Johnstone for £50,000. A ball-winning midfielder or inside-forward, 'Doddie' eventually became a great favourite with the Rangers fans and was to enjoy a long career with the club.

Rangers had reached the second round of the Fairs Cup, beating Vojvodina Novi Sad 2-1 on aggregate, although John Greig had been sent off for retaliation in the away leg. In a politically sensitive tie, they faced Ireland's Dundalk in the second round at Ibrox and romped home 6-1. In the away game, Stein was available and he scored twice in Rangers' 3-0 win. A defensive DWS Amsterdam were easily overcome 4-1 and the quarter-final tie drew the club against Athletic Bilbao. At Ibrox Rangers were 2-1 ahead near the end of the match, through Ferguson and Penman, and two goals from Stein and Persson gave the team a comfortable 4-1 result to take to Spain. They went down 2-0 in Bilbao and the volatile Willie Johnston, whose career was to be littered with dismissals, was sent off.

Colin Stein was also prone to retaliation. Both Stein and Johnston received bans for their dismissals in the league in January, and in March Stein was again sent off, in a game against Clyde where he had scored a hat-trick. He again appeared before the SFA and received a five-week suspension, which meant he missed the last seven games of the season. With their main goalscorer unavailable, Rangers had a dismal end to the season, winning only three of the last seven games and losing to Airdrie, Dundee United and Dundee in March and April. Celtic won the league five points ahead of Rangers.

Rangers had drawn Newcastle United in the semi-final of the Fairs Cup. Centre-half Ronnie McKinnon and left-back Willie Mathieson were injured for the first leg at Ibrox and Johnston was suspended. A crowd of 75,000 filled Ibrox. In the 34th minute Newcastle keeper Ian McFaul leapt to his right to save a Penman penalty, and shortly after denied Penman again from thirty yards. A confident Rangers surged forward in the second period but could not score against the defensive Geordie side.

In Newcastle the first half was goalless but, in the second half, Jim Scott (Alex's brother) and Jackie Sinclair, both members of Newcastle's sizeable Scottish contingent, made the score 2-0. A section of the Rangers fans invaded the pitch towards the end of the game in an apparent attempt to

Norrie Martin beats Billy McNeill to a high cross in the 1969 Scottish Cup final, protected by Ronnie McKinnon and Alex Ferguson

have the match abandoned, and the ensuing violence led to 32 people being hospitalised and over fifty arrested. Chairman John Lawrence said 'They are not fans. We don't want them. I am embarrassed and sickened.' The behaviour of some of their support was to bring further embarrassment to the club over the coming decade.

Having failed in the Fairs Cup, League Cup and Scottish league championship, the last chance Rangers had for any redemption from the season was the Scottish Cup. In the semi-final they turned over Aberdeen 6-1 at Hampden, Johnston scoring a hat-trick and ex-Ger Jim Forrest netting the Dons' solitary response. In the final against Celtic, however, Rangers were outclassed. Even without the suspended Jimmy Johnstone and the injured John Hughes, Celtic won 4-0, the first goal coming from the head of Billy McNeill in the 2nd minute as a clutch of Rangers defenders looked on. Alex Ferguson was blamed by manager White for not marking the Celtic centre-half and captain, as he had been instructed to do, and the ensuing row between the two men effectively ended Ferguson's career with Rangers.

Ferguson had an unhappy time at Rangers. Initially angry at what he perceived to be the club's hostile attitude to the fact that he was married to a Catholic, he could not get on with White and he had a deep dislike for certain members of the board. After the Celtic game he was relegated to reserve and even third-team football, and he moved to Falkirk in November for £20,000. In his autobiography *Managing My Life*, he wrote: 'No other experience in nearly forty years as a professional player and manager has created a scar comparable to that left by the treatment I received at Ibrox.'

(The issue of players marrying Catholics and whether this affected their place in the team was to be revived in the 1980s. Forward Graham Fyfe, often used as a substitute, claimed that his career had been affected by his marriage across the 'religious divide', while Derek Johnstone and Bobby Russell denied any sectarianism on the part of Rangers on the subject. Indeed, Johnstone was made captain shortly after his marriage. Although there may have been some truth in the *Sunday Mail*'s Allan Herron's comment that 'the real reason why (Fyfe) left Rangers was that he wasn't quite good enough', the fact that the issue was being discussed at all is a revealing one.)

White was now under the Ibrox microscope. The board were becoming restless with their new manager and the fans were angrily demanding results. Excellent side although Celtic were, the continuing subordination of Rangers to Parkhead was unacceptable. Willie Johnston, in his autobiography *On the Wing*, described the mood of despondency at Ibrox: 'Believe me, it was heart-breaking for the players and management. We grafted for success but it

remained elusive, and it seemed the harder we tried, the more elusive it became'.

White bought time by announcing, on 28 May 1969, that he would be bringing back to Ibrox Jim Baxter who had been made available by Nottingham Forest. Baxter had an unhappy time at Forest and admitted that 'I let Nottingham down. I didn't play at all'. However, the hero was returning and the fans and the manager were hoping that the old genius was still there.

Over the summer of 1969, Alex Willoughby and Alex Smith moved to Aberdeen, and Roger Hynd to Crystal Palace, all for £25,000 fees. Gerhard 'Gerry' Neef, the first German to play for Rangers and who had joined the club the previous year, opened the season in goal. In the first League Cup sectional match against Celtic, Baxter was once more the dominant figure, and Persson and Johnston scored in Rangers' 2-1 win. In the second game a week later at Parkhead, Neef could not hold a Murdoch free kick and Gemmell was on hand to score the only goal of the game. Rangers could only draw with Raith Rovers and were out of the League Cup at the sectional stage for the third year in succession. The bad start to the season continued with Celtic winning at Ibrox – again by 1-0 – in September, the first time for twelve years that Rangers had lost a home league match to Celtic.

Davie White was now an increasingly beleaguered manager. Although his tactical gifts were generally sound, he was unable to impose his will on the senior players and seemed unwilling to bring through the younger players into the first team. He lacked firmness and authority and was accused of not standing up to some of the stronger characters at the club, which led to indiscipline and sloppiness on and off the pitch. His support on the terracing and in the boardroom was dwindling and, unless he could introduce dramatic changes, White's days were numbered.

Rangers had again entered the European Cup Winners Cup. Although they were losing finalists the previous season, the fact that Celtic had won the league and the Cup allowed Rangers into the tournament, as Celtic obviously preferred the attractions of the European Cup. In the first round Rangers beat Romania's Steaua Bucharest 2-0 on aggregate, thanks to Johnston's two goals at Ibrox, and they faced Polish champions Gornik Zabrze in the second round in November.

They lost the first leg in Poland 3-1 to a skilful Polish side, and on 26 November lined up at Ibrox for the second leg. Baxter and Henderson had slept in on the morning before the match and had missed training, but were still included by White in the line-up, evidence perhaps of Sandy Jardine's observation in his book *Score and More*: 'I think Davie White

Left: *Jim Baxter back in the Rangers strip*

Above: *Jim Baxter re-signs for Rangers, with Davie White and Willie Thornton in attendance*

Below: *Jim Baxter (no 6) is congratulated by teammates after scoring Rangers goal in the second round second leg match against Gornik Zabrze at Ibrox*

Zabrze keeper Kostra clears from Colin Stein at Ibrox

was a little in awe of some of the bigger names and found it tricky to deal with situations when they stepped out of line.' Baxter, however, gave the fans heart with an excellently-taken goal in the 18th minute from a Persson cross, and Olek replied for Gornik early in the second half. Then Gornik's star forward Lubanski created a brilliant individualistic goal, weaving the ball from the halfway line through the Rangers defence to score, and he made another for Skowrowek shortly after. Rangers were eliminated with a humiliating 6-2 on aggregate. This defeat, against a side that Rangers could have been expected to beat, combined with their position of sixth in the league, was the final straw for the board. On 27 November 1969 Davie White was dismissed as manager of Rangers.

White is the only manager of Rangers never to have won a major trophy, and the pressures of the job may have been too much for him, but he cannot entirely be blamed for the team's decline. He was plunged into the job too early in his coaching career and he never received the support, advice and, critically, time to grow into the position. Although the board had little option other than to sack him when they did, White was unfortunate that, like Scot Symon, he presided over the club during the reign of Celtic's greatest side and, to an extent, the more Jock Stein achieved at Parkhead, the more magnified became White's failings.

Rangers acted quickly to replace and the man they selected – a great hero from Rangers' past and one of

New manager Willie Waddell, accompanied by Willie Thornton, watches his first game in charge from the dugout

White's most vociferous critics – was Willie ('the Deedle') Waddell. Waddell, a legendary right-winger with the club between 1938 and 1955, had managed Kilmarnock from 1957 till 1965, when he steered Killie to the league title. Since then he had been a sportswriter with the *Scottish Daily Express*, where he had forcefully expressed his doubts about White's ability to run Rangers. In his column the day following White's sacking, Waddell opened with the headline 'Why the boy David had to go'. Waddell was seen by the fans and the board as a true Rangers man, a man with the footballing knowledge, strength of character and stature in the game to bring success back to the club. John

Rangers players on the sand dunes at Gullane

Lawrence announced the appointment on 3 December, stating 'He is in full charge on all team matters. We are naturally delighted William has come to us.'

Waddell took up his appointment on 8 December and succinctly revealed his Struthian philosophy after a private meeting with the players: 'Rangers must have pride in themselves, in their character and in their image. The greatness of a club is not always judged on what the team is doing on the field but how everyone is judged off it as well'. Baxter and Henderson knew what was in the air, as they had shaved off their moustaches before the meeting. 'They have both been thanked for their clean-shaven look', said Waddell.

Waddell retained his friend and ex-colleague Willie Thornton as assistant manager. Jock Wallace, player-manager at Berwick Rangers in 1967 and then assistant manager of Hearts, had impressed Thornton and Waddle with his tough approach to training and his man-management skills, and Wallace was appointed first team coach in April 1970 to replace David Kinnear.

One of Waddell's first acts at Rangers was to arrange meetings with the Supporters Association in order to explain his plans for the future. So many representatives turned up that Waddell had to hold two meetings on the same evening. He also held meetings with the players, emphasising that under the new wage structure all players in the first team would be paid the same. And several of the older players

were eventually eased out of Ibrox. Baxter retired – at the absurdly early age of 30 – to open a pub. Davie Provan joined Crystal Palace, Eric Sorensen rejoined Morton, Norrie Martin received a free transfer and later in the year Orjan Persson returned to Orgryte in Sweden. To fill the goalkeeping vacancy, 6 foot 4 inch Peter McCloy – the 'Girvan Lighthouse' – arrived from Motherwell in the spring of 1970.

The 1969/70 season, however, had been undistinguished. Although Rangers had produced a 12-game unbeaten run after Waddell's arrival, they only won two games out of seven in March and they ended the campaign twelve points behind winners Celtic. They had also been defeated in the League Cup qualifiers and knocked out of the Scottish Cup by Celtic.

Wallace and Waddell had both noted the lack of fitness in the team, the legacy of Davie White's lax managership. Wallace, an ex-commando and fitness fanatic, installed a new training programme. He took the players once a week to the steep Gullane sand dunes, to the east of Edinburgh, and put them through arduous and exhausting running exercises up and down the dunes. He coupled this with strenuous physical exercises back at Ibrox and, by the beginning of the new season, Rangers were back to peak fitness. Although at the time the Gullane training methods were often ridiculed in the press, it is probable that Wallace's fitness regime

16-year-old Derek Johnstone leaps between Celtic's Billy McNeill and Jim Craig to score the winning goal in the 1970 Scottish League Cup final

The bodies are laid out on the pitch after the 1971 Ibrox disaster

extended the careers of some of the older players and provided extra endurance to the team generally.

They were also a younger side. Waddell had signed 6 foot tall, powerfully built Derek Johnstone, a 16-year-old Dundonian striker who was equally at home in the centre of defence. Other new arrivals included Alfie Conn, an 18-year-old inside-right whose father had played in the famous Hearts team of the early 1950s; Graham Fyfe, a talented 19-year-old forward; and 17-year-old Derek Parlane, a promising centre-forward from Queen's Park. Waddell had also converted Sandy Jardine from midfield to right-back and had brought in the dependable defender Colin Jackson.

Rangers qualified unbeaten from their League Cup section, scoring sixteen goals and conceding only one. However, they lost their third league game 2-0 to Celtic at Parkhead, Murdoch and Hughes doing the damage. In the next game, Johnstone served notice of his potential by scoring twice in their 5-0 win over Cowdenbeath. In September they met Bayern Munich in Germany in the first

leg of the Fairs Cup. The Light Blues produced a splendid performance but the athletic goalkeeping of Sepp Maier denied them a goal. A Beckenbauer strike from the edge of the box gave the Bavarian side a 1-0 lead in the tie. At Ibrox, with 83,000 in attendance, McKinnon fouled Gerd Muller in the 80th minute and the referee quite clearly awarded an indirect free kick. Muller took the kick and scored, and the referee awarded a goal, having decided that it was direct after all. A goal from Stein a minute later was insufficient for Rangers to progress in the competition.

The side had reached the final of the League Cup, by beating Hibs and Cowdenbeath, and they faced Celtic at Hampden on October 24 in front of over 106,000 spectators. Alfie Conn was in the team in place of the unwell John Greig, and Derek Johnstone was playing up front. Rangers took the game to Celtic in the first half with Willie Johnston, in particular, having the beating of the Celtic defenders. Five minutes before the interval, Willie Johnston sent in a high cross from the right and the tall figure of Derek Johnstone soared above Billy McNeill and Jim Craig to power a header down past Celtic keeper Evan Williams into the bottom right-hand corner of the Celtic goal. Celtic

The buckled railings on Stairway 13

improved in the second period, with Murdoch and Macari going close and Jimmy Johnstone creating openings from the right, but they ran up against the impregnable defensive rock of Jardine, McKinnon and Jackson. Johnstone's goal turned out to be the winner and he had become, at the age of 16 years and 355 days, the youngest ever player to score in a national final. 'I felt great when the ball hit the net', said Johnstone. 'What about the ones you missed?', replied Wallace, keeping the youngster's feet on the ground.

The *Sunday Mail*'s headline – 'It's Silver Days Again At Ibrox' – summed up the mood of celebration and Waddell's Rangers had won their first major trophy for four and a half years. The team was: McCloy, Jardine, Miller, Conn, McKinnon, Jackson, Henderson, MacDonald, Johnstone, Stein, Johnston.

This form was not to be replicated in the league, and an inconsistent season saw the club finish fourth in the championship, fifteen points behind Celtic. The season, however, was not to be remembered for Rangers' performance on the pitch.

They had played their rivals in the Ne'er Day fixture at Ibrox on 2 January. A crowd of 85,000 attended the game, which

was not particularly eventful until the final minutes. With one minute to go, Bobby Lennox shot from twenty yards, the ball rebounded from the crossbar and Jimmy Johnstone headed it into the net. It seemed all over for Rangers and many of their disappointed fans began to stream out of the ground. With only a few seconds left, however, Colin Stein scored an equaliser but what should have been a celebration for the Rangers fans turned into an horrific disaster.

Stairway 13 – at what is now the eastern end of the Govan Stand – was a popular exit for Rangers fans, as it was the nearest exit to the Ibrox subway and the supporters' buses. Consequently, it was packed with supporters. Either someone stumbled at the top of Stairway 13 or some fans tripped on the way down. Whatever the initial reason, the densely packed crowd toppled and collapsed and, as the pressure continued, people were being heaped on top of one and other with no means of escape. Within five minutes, Stairway 13 was a mass of bodies and buckled steel barriers. People had been crushed to death, either on the ground or standing up, and the toll was 66 dead and over 140 injured. The emergency rescue services laid the bodies on the pitch and on the running track.

There had been three previous accidents on Stairway 13 – in 1961 (when two people died), 1967 and 1969 – but little had been done by Rangers to make it safer. The inquiry into the disaster criticised Rangers but decided to take no action against an individual or the club. Waddell immediately became the public face of Rangers, reading the club's statement the morning after the tragedy and organising his staff and players into attending funerals and visiting hospitals. He was also charged with the responsibility of rebuilding Ibrox, once the directors realised that all the steep terracings at the ends of the terraces would have to be demolished. The eventual remodelling of Ibrox, based on Borussia Dortmund's Westfalen Stadium, was to turn the ground into one of the finest stadiums in Europe.

The players had been traumatised by the disaster, and had devoted much of their time to help the victims and families, but there was still work to do on the pitch. They had a good Scottish Cup run and ended the season in the final of the Scottish Cup on 8 May against Celtic. Bobby Lennox scored in the 40th minute but Derek Johnstone, on for Penman in the middle of the second half, headed the equaliser with three minutes to go. In the replay the following week, 21-year-old right-back Jim Denny made his debut for the first team – something of a baptism of fire. Lou Macari and Harry Hood had Celtic 2-0 ahead by the interval but an own goal from Celtic right-back Jim Craig in the 58th minute could not help swing the game Rangers' way.

Above: Tommy McLean skips through the Celtic defence

Opposite: Colin Stein scores Rangers first goal in the European Cup Winners Cup final against Moscow Dynamo in May 1972

Below: Sandy Jardine plants a firm header, watched by Celtic's Lou Macari

Waddell had a new forward in place for the 1971/72 season. He had paid out £60,000 for Kilmarnock's Tommy McLean, a 24-year-old outside-right, renowned for his accurate passing and crossing. He was to become an ace provider for the 'two Dereks', Parlane and Johnstone. The manager had also perceptively moved Dave Smith from midfield to sweeper, from which position this season he was to pick up the award of Scotland's Player of the Year. It was again pretty much a so-so season for the Light Blues. They were beaten twice by Celtic in the League Cup sectionals and failed to reach the quarter-finals. They were also eliminated from the Scottish Cup by Hibs at the semi-final stage. And they finished third in the league, a massive sixteen points behind Celtic who had beaten them in their two league encounters. However, this season was all about Europe.

Wallace and Waddell took European football very seriously. They travelled on scouting trips to assess the opposition, made detailed notes on their opponents' capabilities and shortcomings and prepared dossiers on the teams and individual players. Rangers were nothing if not prepared for their European adventures this season. They began their European Cup Winners Cup campaign against French side Rennes and followed up an away 1-1 draw, the goal scored by Willie Johnston, with a 1-0 win at Ibrox, Alex MacDonald scoring in the first half.

In the second round against Sporting Lisbon at Ibrox, Rangers played some fine football in the first half, going in at the interval 3-0 up through Stein (2) and Henderson. Complacent Rangers' defending in the second half, however, allowed Sporting to pull back two goals. In front of a 60,000 crowd in Lisbon, Sporting went ahead half way through the first period but Stein equalised a minute later. Early in the second half Stein scored again and the score was now 2-2. With seven minutes to go Gomes headed Sporting into a 3-2 lead on the night and the game went into extra time. In the 10th minute of extra time, Henderson put Rangers ahead but Perez levelled the aggregate score within four minutes. The tie ended 6-6.

Although Rangers believed they had won on the away-goals rule, the Dutch referee Leo Horn thought otherwise, arguing that away goals did not count after extra time, and ordered a penalty shoot-out. Rangers missed four out their five penalties and Sporting celebrated. A group of Scottish journalists showed Waddell the UEFA rule book which quite clearly stated that away goals did count after extra time. In an evening of high drama, UEFA officials at the game agreed with Waddell, and Rangers had won the tie. Unfortunately for Rangers, however, long-standing centre-half Ronnie McKinnon was the victim of an over-the-top tackle during the match and his leg was broken. He was to miss the rest of the season.

Rangers were fortunate to have Dave Smith back from injury, and he deputised for McKinnon in the quarter-final against Torino. Waddell put out a strong defensive team against the Italians in Turin, with Smith acting as sweeper

and Colin Jackson and Derek Johnstone in the centre of defence. In an excellent performance from Rangers, Johnston scored from a Mathieson cross in the 12th minute and Torino could only manage to score one goal, through Toschi, in the second half. In Glasgow an Alex MacDonald strike was the difference between the sides, and Rangers were through to the semi-finals to play their old European rivals Bayern Munich.

In the first leg in Munich, with Jackson effectively policing centre-forward Muller and Johnstone closely marking Uli Hoeness, Rangers turned in a disciplined performance under fierce pressure from the Germans, but were 1-0 down by half time after a 23rd minute strike from international star Paul Breitner. Just after the interval, Stein sent in a low cross, which was headed into his own net by Zobel, and Rangers took a 1-1 draw back to Ibrox. John Greig had been injured in Rangers' 2-0 defeat by Hibs in the Scottish Cup semi-final a few days before and his place was taken in the second leg by Derek Parlane. A thunderous left-foot shot from the edge of the area from Sandy Jardine gave Rangers the lead in the 1st minute and young Parlane volleyed in the second twenty minutes later after a Willie Johnston corner had been punched away by Sepp Maier. Rangers held on to win the game 2-0 and reach the final of the Cup Winners Cup.

Nearly 30,000 Rangers supporters made the trip to the Nou Camp stadium in Barcelona for the final against Moscow Dynamo on 24 May. The security before the game was poor and the spectator area abutted the pitch, with no ditch or fence to separate the crowd from the players. An hour before kick-off, hundreds of Rangers fans wandered across the pitch to have their photos taken with the police, who escorted them back to their seats. Relations between the two groups were to deteriorate markedly after the game.

Rangers had John Greig back from injury, but neither McKinnon nor Jackson were available. Rangers moved straight into attack from the kick-off, controlling the first half and scoring twice, both goals made by Dave Smith. In the 24th minute Smith sent Stein through to smash the ball past Moscow keeper Pilugi, sparking a pitch invasion, and within fifteen minutes Johnston flicked in a header from a Smith chip for Rangers' second.

In his autobiography *Rangers: My Team*, Derek Johnstone, playing in defence on the night, recalls the crowd's reaction to Stein's goal: 'The fans were carried away by their own euphoria, totally oblivious to the fact that their actions could threaten the continuation of the match and, even more important, the safety of the players they adored so much'.

Four minutes after the interval, Johnston took advantage of a trademark long kick from Peter McCloy to sidefoot a third and Rangers were well on top. Moscow fought back, however, and substitute Eschtrekov in the 59th minute and Makovikev with three minutes to go made it 3-2, but Rangers managed to

withstand the Moscow attack. The Light Blues had won their first European trophy. Thousands of Rangers supporters ran onto the pitch to congratulate their heroes and to share in the jubilation but the Spanish police, misreading the situation, drew their batons and attacked the fans. Enraged, the fans regrouped and hurled torn-up seats, bottles and cans at the police, and charged at them again. The police charged twice more before the crowd withdrew from the stadium and the fans then went on the rampage in the city. The 'battle of Barcelona' gradually came to an end with dozens in jail and at least 150 in hospital. With all this mayhem occurring, John Greig had been unable to accept the trophy on the pitch and the ceremony was conducted in a dressing room. Two-goal hero of the game, Willie Johnston, wrote: 'The Spanish military police grossly over-reacted to a natural and spontaneous gesture of celebration by the Rangers supporters.'

UEFA eventually handed Rangers a two-year European ban, reduced to one year after an appeal by Waddell. The violence marred the club's celebrations, but Rangers had taken on some of the best club sides in Europe to win the Cup and deserved all the plaudits they received from European football. The team in the final was: McCloy, Jardine, Mathieson, Greig, Johnstone, Smith, McLean, Conn, Stein, MacDonald, Johnston.

Two weeks after the final, on June 7 1972, Willie Waddell announced that he was moving into the position of general

Opposite: Willie Johnston powers home Rangers' second goal in the final in Barcelona

Above Left: John Greig relaxes with the trophy in the bath at the Nou Camp stadium

Above Right: The Rangers team parades the European Cup Winners Cup around Ibrox

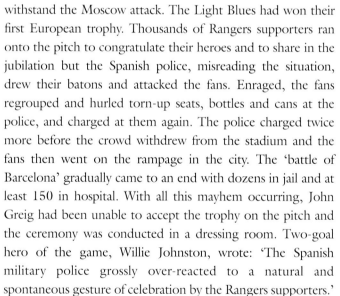

Right. Alfie Conn scores Rangers' second goal in the 1973 final

Below right: Tom Forsyth races away to celebrate his goal in the 1973 final

Below: New manager Jock Wallace

manager at Ibrox and that the new team manager was to be Jock Wallace. Many fans of the club felt disappointed by his decision and felt that he could have remained at the reins for more than two and a half years, but he was to stay a hugely influential presence at the club right up until his death in 1992.

Wallace, a single-minded, tough individual, had his own ideas about which players he wanted at the club. With McLean the now permanent right-winger, there was no place for Willie Henderson and he left to join Sheffield Wednesday on a free transfer in July 1972. Wallace also doubted the motivation of two of his stars, Colin Stein and Willie Johnston, considering them 'prima donnas'. Johnston's indiscipline on the pitch did not help his case for regular inclusion and, after he received a nine-week suspension from the SFA in September for yet another dismissal, he was sold to West Bromwich Albion in December 1972 for £135,000. Stein had gone to Coventry City in September/October for £90,000 plus winger Quinton 'Cutty' Young. 'We have lost two players but found a team', commented Wallace. From Motherwell came Tom Forsyth for £40,000. Forsyth, nicknamed 'Jaws' for the ferocity of his tackling, was originally a midfield player whom Wallace converted into a centre-half, and he was to link up with Colin Jackson in Rangers central defence for several years to come.

Season 1972/73 began badly, with Rangers winning only two of their first six games – going down to Ayr, Kilmarnock and Celtic – but they lost only one more game during the entire season when they were defeated 1-0 by Hearts at Ibrox. They finished in second place to Celtic, one point behind their rivals. Their poor start cost them any realistic chance of winning the title, but they gained revenge on their early defeat by the Parkhead side on January 6 at Ibrox when goals from Parlane and a last-minute strike from Conn gave them a 2-1 win.

To compensate for their absence from European football, Waddell had arranged for a home and away fixture against Ajax to be played in mid-January. Ajax had won the European Cup the previous year and Rangers, as Cup Winners Cup holders, were to meet the Dutch side to determine the direction of the new European Super Cup.

Ajax were, without doubt, the finest club side in the world. Captained by the brilliant Johan Cruyff, and bristling with such outstanding Dutch international players as Johan Neeskens, Ruud Krol, Johnny Rep and Gerry Muhren, they had won the European Cup the last two years in succession. The first leg was played at Ibrox and the game was ceremoniously kicked off by former Rangers legend Andy Cunningham. Cruyff's side produced a superb example of attacking 'total football' in the first half. Rep scored from a Cruyff pass in the 35th minute while Alex MacDonald equalised from a narrow angle seven minutes later. Just on half time, a glorious piece of skill on the run from Cruyff completely deceived Johnstone and the Dutch 'total footballer' struck a powerful left-foot shot past McCloy. Although Johnstone, Parlane and McLean went close in the second half, Arie Haan sealed an Ajax win with a fine strike in the 76th minute.

Eight days later at the Olympic Stadium, Amsterdam, Rangers went ahead when MacDonald crashed home a left-foot shot from twenty yards in the 3rd minute. Haan levelled the score soon after, but in the 35th minute Young headed a McLean free kick past keeper Heinz Stuy. Muhren equalised just on the interval from a penalty, however, and in the 78th minute Cruyff left Johnstone standing and swerved in the winner. Rangers were beaten but had provided genuine and sustained opposition to the world's best. In May, Ajax were to become the first team since Real Madrid in the 1950s to win the European Cup three years in succession.

Rangers reached the Scottish Cup final against Celtic on 5 May, Parlane's two goals in the semi-final seeing off Ayr United. The final was billed as the Centenary Cup Final, as it was one hundred years since the formation of the SFA, and the trophy was to be presented by Princess Alexandra. In a compelling, thrilling game at Hampden, in front of an official

attendance of 122,714, Kenny Dalglish put Celtic ahead in the 24th minute with a left-foot strike from the edge of the box and Parlane pulled one back ten minutes later, heading in a chip from Alex MacDonald. Conn put Rangers 2-1 up when he slid the ball into the Celtic net just after the interval, but Connelly equalised from the penalty spot within ten minutes after Greig had palmed the ball round the post to prevent a goal. Then, in the 60th minute, a McLean cross found Johnstone in the Celtic area and he headed the ball against the post. The ball then rolled along the line, hit the other post and came out. The unlikely figure of Tom Forsyth, having a commanding game in defence, was on hand to stab the ball over the line with his studs, and the Scottish Cup came back to Ibrox for the first time since 1966.

At the beginning of the 1973/74 season, John Lawrence had resigned as chairman and Matt Taylor had taken over from Lawrence in the board room. On the pitch, Rangers in August played Arsenal to mark the Ibrox club's centenary. Admission prices ranged from 5p to 20p, and not unsurprisingly attracted a crowd of over 70,000 to Ibrox. Before the game, some of Rangers' great players – including McPhail, Waddell and Baxter – saluted the fans. Also present was the then-oldest ex-Ranger, 97-year-old Alex Newbigging, who had signed for the club in 1906! The London side won 2-1 and, after the match, Alan Ball stated that 'Rangers would be a formidable side once they got a few English league players in the team'. Patronising, maybe, but the little redhead was to be proved correct in a few years' time.

The title chase started in dreadful fashion, with Rangers losing three of their first six league games – to Celtic, Hearts and East Fife – gaining just five points. Although Alex McDonald scored in the League Cup semi-final against Celtic, a Harry Hood hat-trick eliminated Rangers from the tournament, 3-1. Curiously, the SFA had changed the rules of the competition to allow the top two teams from each section to qualify. Rangers had been top of their group and, under the old rules, would have eliminated Celtic from the League Cup.

Although Rangers had made some new signings – particularly keeper Stewart Kennedy from Stenhousemuir, inside-forward Johnny Hamilton from junior football and striker Ally Scott from Queen's Park – the team could not win a trophy in the season. A hat-trick from Parlane had helped defeat Queen's Park in the third round of the Scottish Cup but Rangers were knocked out of the tournament 3-0 by Dundee in the next round.

They had played in the European Cup-Winners Cup earlier in the season, and had eliminated Turkish side Ankaragucu in the first round 6-0. Two Turkish players were sent off in the second leg at Ibrox where two goals from Greig helped Rangers progress to the second leg against Borussia Moenchengladbach. Two goals from West German international Juup Heynckes and one from Rupp gave Borussia a 3-0 win in Germany. McCloy prevented Heynckes' hat-trick by saving a penalty. A 10th minute goal from Conn at Ibrox gave some hope to the team and, by the 70th minute, Rangers were 3-1 ahead, with Jackson and MacDonald also getting on the scoresheet, and they were still in the tie. However, a Jensen goal brought the score back to 3-2 and Rangers were out of Europe for the season.

The Light Blues finished the season third in the league and Celtic won the title for the ninth season in succession. The booing and jeering at Ibrox escalated, and attendances suffered as the fans stayed away, frustrated by the team's inability to emulate the successes now being taken for granted at Parkhead. Wallace had probably one season left to reverse the decline, the last season before the Scottish league was to be restructured into the Premier League and three lower divisions. Before season 1974/75 began Wallace sold Alfie Conn to Tottenham Hotspur for £140,000. Dave Smith was also to leave the club in November, going to Arbroath as player-coach. Although Wallace was shrewd in the transfer market, he preferred to train up youngsters to fit alongside the settled, older players – Jardine, Jackson, Greig and McLean – in his team. He

Above: *Derek Parlane goes for goal in the 1973 Scottish Cup final*

Left: *Peter McCloy rises to catch the ball in the 1973 final while Kenny Dalglish looks on*

did, however, buy attacking midfielder Bobby McKean for £40,000 from St Mirren.

Rangers opened the 1974/75 season by taking part in the 'Juan Camper' tournament in Barcelona. They were defeated 4-1 in the final by Barcelona. In their third league game they beat Celtic 2-1 at Parkhead, the goals coming from reserve half-back Ian McDougall and Colin Jackson and in October they beat Dunfermline 6-1, with Parlane claiming five. The Celtic victory was important symbolically to the Rangers side as it was their first win at Parkhead for six years. Perhaps the balance of power in Glasgow was beginning to shift?

By their next meeting with Celtic at Ibrox on January 4, Rangers had lost only twice, to Airdrie and Hibs (who had also knocked them out of the League Cup), and were two points behind Celtic. At Ibrox, Johnstone headed in from a McLean cross in the 6th minute. Five minutes into the second half McLean made the score 2-0 with a left-foot shot, and Parlane added a third from another McLean cross. Celtic could not score and Rangers had done the double over their rivals, in their biggest victory over Celtic for twelve years. From that game till the end of the season Rangers did not lose a match until the last day. With eight games to go, Wallace brought back Colin Stein for £80,000 from Coventry, who were having difficulty in making their agreed transfer payments for the player. As if to prove to Scottish football fans that his brief sojourn in England hadn't changed his attitude, he was sent off in his second match, against Dundee. His moment, however, was to come.

Rangers needed one point from their game against Hibs at Easter Road on March 29 to clinch the championship for the first time since 1965. Nearly 40,000, of whom around three-quarters were Rangers' supporters, packed into the stadium. Hibs' Ally McLeod threatened to spoil the party by heading in past Stewart Kennedy, having a fine season in goal for Rangers, within the first twenty minutes, and Scotland's Player of the Year, Sandy Jardine, missed a penalty. However, McKean crossed in the 61st minute and Stein was waiting to head in the equaliser, his first goal since his return from Coventry. With two minutes to go, Wallace sent on an injured John Greig in place of Jardine to give his captain the opportunity to savour the moment of success, and the manager ran on to the pitch after the final whistle to perform a victory dance with his delighted players. Although they were beaten 1-0 at home by Airdrie in the last game of the season, Rangers won the title by seven points and they had prevented Celtic from collecting their tenth league title in succession.

John Greig with the league trophy and Jock Wallace in April 1975

CHAPTER SEVEN:

WALLACE AND GREIG: 1975-1986

Alarmed by the decline in attendances at football matches in the early 1970s, the Scottish football authorities decided to restructure the league, which had maintained the same format for almost 100 years. The Premier League was inaugurated in season 1975/76, with the intention of introducing more competition and excitement and thereby attracting more fans to the grounds. There were to be ten teams in the Premier and fourteen each in the First and Second Divisions. The ten top sides that season were Aberdeen, Ayr United, Celtic, Dundee, Dundee United, Hearts, Hibs, Motherwell, Rangers and St Johnstone, and they were to play each other four times in the course of the season, with the bottom two clubs relegated at the end of the season and replaced by the top two teams in the First Division.

Jock Wallace's team was looking increasingly formidable and a good bet for the new league title. Peter McCloy and Stewart Kennedy were the choices in goal. The defence was strong and dependable, with the elegant Sandy Jardine and the now-veteran John Greig linking up with Tom Forsyth and Colin Jackson as the centre-backs. The competitive Alex MacDonald was in midfield, while the wings were patrolled by Tommy McLean, Quinton Young and Bobby McKean. Wallace had moved Derek Johnstone from centre-half to centre-forward and he shared the goalscoring with Derek Parlane.

They opened their first Premier League season with a win against Celtic at Ibrox in front of just under 70,000 spectators. With intermittent fan trouble at both ends of the stadium, and Rangers' league championship flag fluttering in the breeze, Celtic commanded the first half. McCloy was outstanding although the tall keeper could do little about Dalglish's 42nd minute goal. In the second period Alex O'Hara replaced an injured Jardine and effectively nullified the contribution of Dalglish, and Rangers scored twice. Quinton Young found Johnstone twenty-five yards from the Celtic goal and the big forward fizzed the ball past keeper Peter Latchford. Then, in the 68th minute, Rangers won the game through a tremendous left-foot shot from Young.

Although Rangers lost five games in the autumn in the league, from December 6 until the end of the season they were unbeaten, a total of 21 matches. In October they

suffered a fright in the League Cup semi-final, when they were 1-0 down to Montrose at half-time. However, they came back to score three goals – through Parlane, Johnstone and Alex Miller – in the first fifteen minutes of the second period, and added two more, from Scott and Jardine.

The Light Blues had re-entered the European Cup – their first season in Europe for eleven years – and played Bohemians Dublin in the first round, winning 4-1 at Ibrox and drawing 1-1 in Eire. The second round drew them away against France's top side St Etienne, parading the exceptional talents of young winger Dominique Rocheteau and forward Patrick Revelli. McCloy unfortunately suffered an injured wrist from a Stein practice shot just before the kick-off and his place went to Kennedy at the last minute. Rangers adopted a defensive line-up, with McLean and MacDonald pushed back deep, but Revelli scored before half time. MacDonald almost equalised with a diving header in the second half, but Bathenay scored another for the French.

Three days later they met Celtic in the League Cup final. Celtic had also played in Europe the previous Wednesday, against Boavista, and the match was a poor one. Wallace commented ' They looked like two tired teams to me', while Celtic's acting manager Sean Fallon, in charge while Jock Stein was recovering from a serious car crash, described the game as 'one of the worst finals I have seen'. MacDonald won the game for Rangers with a header from a Quinton Young cross in the 67th minute.

Rangers played their second leg against St Etienne just over one week later at Ibrox. The French side were composed, confident and quick on the counter-attack, and they controlled the game throughout. Parlane nearly scored with a firm header in the 37th minute but it was well saved by keeper Yvan Curkovic. Midway through the second half, with 'What a load of rubbish' ringing out around Ibrox and aimed at Rangers, Rocheteau slid past Jardine to send a low, right-footed shot into the Rangers net. Then in the 70th minute the speedy Rocheteau again eased through the defence, slipping a Forsyth tackle, ran 50 yards unchallenged, drew Kennedy and passed to Herve Revelli, Patrick's brother, who could not miss. MacDonald replied with a consolation two minutes from the end but Rangers

John Greig in typical pose

were well beaten 4-1 on aggregate. The tactics seemed curious, with Forsyth at left-back and Johnstone and Stein both playing in a dense midfield, and the attack was minimal. The *Glasgow Herald*, noting the game was played on Guy Fawkes Night, ran the headline 'Rangers go out like damp squib'. St Etienne were to return to Glasgow in May where they contested the European Cup final at Hampden against Bayern Munich, going down 1-0.

In the league, by the spring Rangers were one point behind Celtic with seven games to go. Celtic, however, slumped and won only one of their last seven games. In this season's Old Firm tussles, Rangers had the upper hand, winning twice and drawing twice. A Johnstone goal in the first minute against Dundee United on 24 April at Tannadice gave Rangers the league title, six points ahead of Celtic. Rangers were now on course for their third 'treble'.

In the fourth round of the Scottish Cup they eliminated Aberdeen 4-1, helped by two goals from tall centre-forward Martin Henderson, having an influential season for the club. In the semi-final they found themselves 2-0 down against Motherwell at half-time. However, a disputed second-half penalty from Alex Miller and two late Johnstone strikes, one direct from a McCloy clearance and the other from a Greig free kick with two minutes remaining, steered them into the final against Hearts on 1 May.

On an afternoon of pouring rain, the referee, for some reason, blew for the kick-off two minutes early. Johnstone was immediately fouled by Jim Jeffries and headed McLean's free-kick into the Hearts net after only 42 seconds. Rangers were 1-0 up before the game was due to begin! Rangers were dominant but spurned several easy chances until an Alex MacDonald goal just before the interval. A Bobby McKean corner kick was cleared and the ball ran to MacDonald who cracked in a low, left-foot shot from 20 yards through a ruck of players. Johnstone claimed the third from a McKean cross in the 81st minute and, although Hearts scored shortly afterwards, Rangers won the Cup 3-1 and had again secured the 'treble'. Greig was singled out for special praise in the *Sunday Mail* headline – 'Greig: Captain Marvel'. The newspaper continued 'The bionic man of football inspired, nursed and even bullied Rangers to their 21st Scottish Cup win'. The team was: McCloy, Miller, Greig, Forsyth, Jackson, MacDonald, McKean, Hamilton (Jardine), Henderson, McLean, Johnstone.

Rangers began 1976/77 in the expectation of another successful season but surprisingly ended the year without a trophy. Although the side was virtually unchanged from the treble-winning team of the previous season, the players were affected by injuries and loss of form. In the league they drew four out of their first five games and never really got to grips

with Celtic, who won the championship by nine points with Rangers in second place. They also reached the semi-final of the League Cup but were outplayed by Aberdeen who routed them 5-1.

Their opponents in the first round of the European Cup were FC Zurich, which seemed an easy enough tie for the Ibrox men. Not so, however. In the first leg at Ibrox, Zurich were one up within 50 seconds when Cucinotta capitalised on sloppy passing by Rangers. Derek Parlane equalised in the 30th minute, when he headed against the crossbar and converted the rebound, but Zurich held on to the draw. In Zurich, the Swiss side scored another early goal, from Martinelli in the 8th minute. Rangers pressed forward but could not find their way past keeper Carl Grob, in inspired form for Zurich. In the second half, Grob saved brilliantly from Johnstone and Parlane, and the sending-off of Johnstone for dissent at the end of the game sealed a miserable night for the Light Blues.

On 9 October Rangers visited Villa Park to play a friendly against Aston Villa and some of the travelling support yet again disgraced the club. In the 53rd minute, with Villa 2-0 ahead, some fans invaded the pitch and ran riot. The rampage continued that evening in Birmingham, with drunken hooligans breaking shop windows, picking fights and smashing up pubs. The *Glasgow Herald* condemned the 'pack of marauding, drink-sodden louts under the guise of football fans', while Waddell confessed 'these louts are crucifying us'. Ian Archer, writing in the *Glasgow Herald* conflated the issues of sectarianism and hooliganism. 'As a Scottish football club they (Rangers) are a permanent embarrassment and an occasional disgrace. They are a permanent embarrassment because they are the only club in the world which insists that every member of the team is of one religion. They are an occasional disgrace because some of their fans, fuelled by bigotry, behave like animals.' Archer added 'I am not a Roman Catholic'. The *Evening Times* agreed with Archer and stated that Rangers have to 'change their die-hard, blue-nosed Protestant policy'.

Although Waddell did then state that Rangers would sign a Catholic, it was not until 1989, thirteen years later, that catholic Maurice Johnston joined the club under the more liberal regime of David Murray and Graeme Souness. And the hooliganism was far from over.

Rangers' last chance of getting anything out of the season was in the Scottish Cup and they met Celtic in the final on 7 May. The game was televised live and the heavy rain helped keep down the attendance to just over 54,000. The game was drab and uneventful, the only goal coming when

Opposite: Davie Cooper

Above: Bobby Russell outjumps Celtic's Danny McGrain

Below: Jock Wallace with the Scottish Cup after Rangers' 3-1 win over Hearts in the 1976 final

Celtic's Andy Lynch scored a penalty after Johnstone had handled in the box. The pressure was now beginning to build up again on Jock Wallace.

In the League Cup quarter-final Rangers had played four times against First Division Clydebank before progressing in the tournament. Wallace had been impressed by Clydebank's 21-year-old left winger Davie Cooper, who had scored in three of the four games. Wallace moved to secure his services and Cooper joined Rangers in June 1977 for £100,000. Cooper was a hugely gifted, if frustratingly inconsistent, player with a genius on the dribble and a powerful shot. His talent with his left foot drew comparisons with Jim Baxter and he was to become just as much a legend at Ibrox as 'Slim Jim'. Wallace also bought Gordon Smith from Kilmarnock for £65,000. A tall, speedy left-winger with Killie, he was converted into a deep-lying inside-forward by Wallace. Twenty-year-old Bobby Russell, from Shettleston Juniors, was another newcomer. An inside-right, the stylish Russell was to develop into a highly skilful creator and goalscorer, with vision and a delicate touch on the ball. Wallace's revamped and strengthened team was about to help the manager answer his growing band of critics.

The clouds gathered over Wallace when Rangers lost the first two games of the 1977/78 season, 3-1 to Billy McNeill's Aberdeen and 2-0 to Hibs. The following week they beat Partick Thistle 4-0, and they then met Celtic at Ibrox on 10 September. The first half belonged to Celtic, for whom Johannes Edvaldson scored twice with no reply from Rangers. There must have been some typical Wallace bollocking in the dressing room during the interval, as the Light Blues' second-half display was unrecognisable from that of the opening period. Greig came on for the injured Parlane and dropped back into defence, while Johnstone moved into the centre-forward position from centre-half. Rangers then turned on the style. In the 53rd minute, Johnstone chipped on to Smith who placed the ball past Peter Latchford. Then Latchford was forced into two spectacular saves from the effervescent Davie Cooper. In the 65th minute Cooper found Johnstone in point-blank range and the score was 2-2. With nine minutes remaining, substitute Tommy McLean sent a lovely pass to Russell whose high cross was fumbled by Latchford, and Smith was on the line to claim the winner. The *Sunday Mail* praised the Light Blues' second-half performance saying 'Rangers rose from the dead to stage one of the greatest fightbacks in their history.'

After this stirring victory Rangers were then virtually unstoppable, losing just one out of their next twenty-three games. The hooliganism persisted, however. In the game following the Celtic triumph – St Mirren at Love Street – bottles and cans were thrown onto the pitch during the 3-3

Above: *Gordon Smith*

Right: *Derek Johnstone jumps over the ball for Davie Cooper to score in the 1978 Scottish League Cup final*

draw and there was fighting on the terraces. Forty-three 'fans' were arrested in the ruckus.

By October the Light Blues led the Premier League and they were to remain there for the remainder of the season. Their nearest rivals, Aberdeen, fought back in the Spring but, in spite of beating Rangers 3-0 at Ibrox in March, the Dons could not prevent the Light Blues' unstoppable march towards the championship. Gordon Smith and Derek Johnstone scored 65 goals between them and had revelled in the chances created by wide men Cooper and McLean and the midfield probings of Russell and the industry of MacDonald.

In the League Cup, Rangers destroyed Aberdeen 6-1 in an exceptional performance, with Gordon Smith scoring a hat-trick, although they lost the return leg 3-1. They then defeated Forfar Athletic in the semi-final to play Celtic in the final. Rangers went ahead in the 38th minute when Cooper drove home a pass from Smith but, with five minutes of normal time remaining, Celtic's Edvaldsson headed in the equaliser. With three minutes to go in extra time, Alex Miller's cross was met by the head of Gordon Smith and Rangers had won the trophy. Their celebrations were muted, however, as Bobby McKean had tragically died in his fume-filled car just two days before the final.

Earlier in the season Rangers had played in the preliminary round of the European Cup Winners Cup, their first match being against Young Boys Berne at Ibrox in

August. Rangers, without the suspended Derek Johnstone, battled against a dour and defensive Swiss side without success until the 40th minute when John Greig smashed home a fifteen-yard shot off the post. The Swiss offside trap held firm and there were no further goals. Rangers continued on the attack in Berne and scored two minutes before half time when the returned Johnstone headed in a Cooper cross. Three minutes after the interval, however, Jackson turned the ball into his own net and Jost Leuzinger equalised on aggregate in the 60th minute. With McLean and Russell having been substituted with injuries, Rangers now had a fight on their hands, although Smith secured the tie in the 75th minute when he finished off a pass from Bobby McKean. In the last few minutes, Johnstone was sent off for retaliation for his second successive game in European football. Holland's Twente Enschede, with Dutch internationals Arnold Muhren and Franz Thijssen, held Rangers to a 0-0 draw at Ibrox in the next round and outplayed them in Holland, winning 3-0.

With the League Cup and the Premier League Championship under their belt Rangers now only had to beat Aberdeen in the Scottish Cup final to achieve their second 'treble' within three years and the fourth in their history. Bobby Russell was Rangers' star performer at Hampden and he made the first goal for Alex MacDonald in the 34th minute, MacDonald diving to head into the net.

Johnstone headed in the second from a Tommy McLean cross in the 60th minute and, although Aberdeen scored near the end of the game with a Steve Ritchie miskick which looped over McCloy and left the big keeper swinging from the crossbar, Rangers won 2-1 and the 'treble' was secure. The team for the final was: McCloy, Jardine, Greig, Forsyth, Jackson, MacDonald, McLean, Hamilton (Miller), Johnstone, Smith, Cooper (Parlane).

Wallace was now at the peak of his success. The only Rangers manager in the history of the club to have landed two 'trebles', he had built a strong, skilful team which seemed assured of further successes under his direction. Which made his resignation on 23 May – seventeen days after the Cup final – even more surprising. The reason why Wallace decided to leave the club has never been fully explained. A personality clash with Waddell has been suggested, as has Waddell's refusal to supply the manager with the money to bring in new players for his side. Wallace was also unhappy with his salary at Ibrox which was significantly lower than what was on offer in the English game. This last suggestion was given credence when he joined Leicester City a matter of days after his resignation for £20,000 per annum, £8,000 more than he was receiving at Rangers.

On 24 May, 35-year-old John Greig was appointed manager of the club. Recently a recipient of the MBE, Greig was Rangers personified. He had played his 857th game for the club in the Cup final against Aberdeen and had made his Rangers debut in 1962. He had been an inspirational captain and possessed five League championship, six Scottish Cup and four League Cup medals, as well as the European Cup Winners Cup medal, but he had no managerial experience. 'I haven't sat behind a desk since I was at school', said Greig. However, Greig had long been a keen student of the game and had closely observed the differing styles and tactics employed by the four managers under whom he had played. He immediately decided to stop playing and to devote himself to full-time management. He faced his first crisis the day after he took over when Derek Johnstone, top scorer with 39 goals and Scottish Player of the Year, submitted a transfer request. Johnstone declared that he wanted to play in the USA but Greig eventually persuaded the star striker to remain at Ibrox and appointed him captain for the 1978/79 season.

Greig's team was now an aging one but the board were unwilling to provide him with much money to refresh his squad. To replace himself in the left-back position he acquired Alex Forsyth, initially on loan but then on a permanent basis, from Manchester United, and he also brought in forward Billy Urquhart from Inverness Caledonian.

Rangers had a terrible start to the new season, losing their first game to St Mirren at Ibrox, and had to wait a further five games for a league win. Their progress, however, was much more encouraging in Europe. In the first round of the

Above: *Derek Johnstone heads in Rangers' second goal in the 1978 Scottish Cup final*

Right: *Alex MacDonald opens the scoring for Rangers in the 1978 Scottish Cup final*

European Cup they were drawn against Italian giants Juventus, who had provided nine of the Italian squad for the1978 World Cup finals. In that side were players of the quality of Dino Zoff, Marco Tardelli and Roberto Bettega, and Greig's side were to play them away, in the Stadio Communale, in the first leg. There were over 60,000 in the huge stadium and Rangers fielded a defensive line-up in an attempt to thwart the Italian attack. Johnstone was unavailable through suspension, McLean and Cooper were on the bench and Sandy Jardine operated as sweeper alongside full-backs Forsyth and Miller and centre-backs Jackson and Forsyth. Parlane and Smith were up front. Juventus went ahead in the 8th minute through Pietro Virdis, but thereafter the Rangers defence held solid against the surging attacks from the 'Zebras'. Towards the end McCloy made a superb save from a Bettega header and the game finished 1-0.

Rangers had never in their European history managed to come back from a first-leg deficit, and it seemed unlikely that they would do so against one of Europe's top club sides. McLean was back in the team at Ibrox, as was Johnstone, playing in the forward line, and Rangers produced one of their best ever European performances. In the 17th minute keeper Zoff parried a Gordon Smith shot and Alex MacDonald was on hand to head in the opening goal. In the second half, Smith headed in a Russell free-kick and Rangers held on for a famous 2-1 aggregate victory.

Dutch champions PSV Eindhoven, UEFA Cup holders with six Dutch internationals in the team, were the opponents in the second round. In the first leg at Ibrox, PSV, without injured star player Rene Van Der Kerkhof, settled into defence and keeper Van Egelen was instrumental in securing a 0-0 draw. In the Philips Stadium in Eindhoven, where PSV were unbeaten in European football, the Dutch team scored through Harry Lubse after only 34 seconds. Early in the second half a McLean cross found the head of MacDonald and Rangers were level. Although Gerrie Deyckers gave PSV the lead three minutes later, a Derek Johnstone header equalised the score. Rangers now had the advantage under the away goals rule and PSV besieged McCloy's goal. With only three minutes remaining, Gordon Smith on the break passed to McLean on the right, and the winger sent an accurate pass, splitting the Dutch defence, to Bobby Russell running through the centre. Russell advanced to the edge of the area and bent a glorious shot round Van Egelen. Willy Van Der Kerkhof said of Rangers after the game: 'They deserved to win. They were the better team with tremendous discipline'. Hugh Taylor in the *Evening*

John Greig talks to his players before extra time in the second replay of the 1979 Scottish Cup final

Tommy McLean takes on Hibs' Arthur Duncan in the 1979 Scottish Cup final

Times commented: 'It was Rangers' greatest victory in Europe – perhaps the best in their history. No praise is too high enough for Rangers.'

Rangers were now through to the quarter-final to meet Cologne. In the first leg in Germany, Rangers were without Johnstone and succumbed to a 1-0 defeat, the goal coming from Dieter Muller in the 58th minute. At Ibrox, Muller again scored early in the second period and a McLean strike with three minutes to go was too late. Billy Urquhart missed two chances and Rangers were out of Europe.

In the League Cup, Rangers had progressed well and met Celtic in the semi-final. John Doyle scored for Celtic early on but Tommy Burns was sent off for dissent in the 26th minute. Jardine levelled the score with a penalty. Early in the second half Alex Miller was sent off and shortly after Tom MacAdam put Celtic in front. With ten minutes to go Colin Jackson volleyed in from a Russell cross. In extra time Johnstone was culpable in not scoring, but with seven minutes remaining Johnstone shot and the ball was deflected into his own net by Celtic's Jim Casey.

In the final against Aberdeen Duncan Davidson opened the scoring for the Dons in the 57th minute but MacDonald made it 1-1 with thirteen minutes to go. A headed goal from Jackson deep in injury time gave Rangers the trophy.

Rangers had recovered from their nervous start in the league and were battling for the title with Dundee United and Celtic. On May 21 Rangers visited Parkhead. It was Celtic's last game of the season and, if they won, the title went to Parkhead. If Rangers could get a draw they had three games remaining to win the championship. Russell scored in the 9th minute and Aitken equalised in the 66th minute, after Celtic's Johnny Doyle had been sent off for retaliation. McLuskey and then MacDonald made the score 2-2. With five minutes on the clock, Jackson headed into his own net and Murdo MacLeod added a fourth with almost the last kick of the game to give Celtic the league title. In the Scottish Cup final, Rangers played three games against Hibs in the final, the first two ending in undistinguished 0-0 draws. The replay went Rangers's way, with Arthur Duncan heading past his own keeper from a Cooper cross in extra time to give Rangers a 3-2 win and their third Scottish Cup within four years.

In spite of the age of his team, the unwillingness or inability of the Rangers board to allow him to enter the transfer market in a meaningful way and the abruptness of his appointment, Greig had succeeded in bringing the club two major trophies and had significantly raised the club's profile in Europe that season. However, he faced some major problems in 1979/80. Tom Forsyth was increasingly sidelined by injury and Greig bought the volatile Gregor

Stevens from Leicester City in September for £150,000 as a replacement. Also, Alex MacDonald's influence was beginning to wane in midfield, and Smith and Cooper were suffering dips in form.

Rangers began the season by winning the Drybrough Cup, held at the start of the season in the 1970s. In the final against Celtic, they won 3-1 with two magnificent goals. The first came from Jardine who ran from one penalty area to another to crash the ball into the Celtic net, and the second came from Cooper who demonstrated his brilliant ball control by juggling the ball around four Celtic players before volleying it past the bewildered keeper Latchford.

The team's performance in the league, however, was well below what was required. Their away form was abysmal, winning only four away league games all season and finishing in fifth place, eleven points behind Aberdeen who had also knocked them out of the League Cup 5-1 on aggregate. Nor was there much comfort in Europe. They had beaten Lillestrom 3-0 on aggregate in the preliminary round of the European Cup Winners Cup and met Fortuna Dusseldorf in the first round at Ibrox where two second-half goals from MacDonald and McLean were countered by a late strike from Wentzel for the Germans. A 0-0 draw in Dusseldorf, with keeper McCloy in outstanding form and making some superb saves, saw them through to play Valencia.

The Spanish side fielded German international Rainer Bonhof and the Argentinian striker Mario Kempes, star of the 1978 World Cup finals. In Valencia Kempes opened the scoring with a free kick in the first half but Tommy McLean equalised just on half time. In the 81st minute McCloy produced a fine save from a Bonhof penalty to keep the score 1-1. At Ibrox, Jardine deflected a Bonhof free kick past McCloy but Johnstone equalised midway through the first half. In the second half, Kempes scored twice, the second a shot from fully thirty yards, to put the result beyond dispute. Gordon Smith recalls in Roddy Forsyth's *Blue and True* that, so powerful and accurate was Kempes' left foot, the players received instructions to keep him on his right. In the 78th minute Kempes on the attack was 'pushed onto his right foot so that he was more or less making a diagonal run across the defence – right foot, right foot. And then – and I will never forget this – from 30 yards he hit a right foot shot, top corner, which gave Peter McCloy no chance. My abiding memory of that moment was really the whole of our defence looking towards the dug-out as if to say, well we put him on the right foot boss, what more can we do?'. Rangers had been outfoxed by a truly world-class player.

In February Greig paid Dundee £210,000, a transfer record between two Scottish clubs, for midfielder Ian Redford, and a month later he sold Derek Parlane to Leeds

Jim Bett brushes aside Dundee United's Eamon Bannon in the 1981 Scottish Cup final

United for £160,000. Redford was in the team that played Celtic in the Scottish Cup final on 10 May 1980, as was young striker John MacDonald. An entertaining match went into extra time goalless, and Celtic scored the winner in the 107th minute when a deflected Danny McGrain shot was turned past McCloy by George McCluskey. At the final whistle some Celtic fans climbed over the perimeter fence to salute their team and this provoked some Rangers fans to invade the pitch at the other end. The two sets of fans clashed on the pitch and a riot resulted, with most of the police outside the stadium in an attempt to prevent violence as the fans left. Bottles, iron bars and stones were used in the melee and it was eventually cleared by mounted police. Over two hundred supporters were arrested and both clubs were fined £20,000. The 'Hampden Riot' was instrumental in the establishment of the Criminal Justice Act (Scotland) 1980 which, among other things, barred drinking in coaches on the way to the ground and in the ground itself.

Over the summer of 1980 Greig was busy in the transfer market trying to buy success and consistency for his team. Gordon Smith went to Brighton and Hove Albion for £400,000 and he was to achieve notoriety with the club in the 1983 FA Cup Final when he missed an open goal for the winner against Manchester United. The Sussex club's fanzine is still called 'And Smith Must Score', after Peter Jones' commentary. Alex MacDonald, who had played over 500 games for the club, also left to go to Hearts, where he was to become a successful manager. Colin MacAdam, a big, bustling centre-forward, came from Partick Thistle for £80,000 and was the first Scottish player to have the fee decided by a transfer tribunal. Ex-Aberdeen player Jim Bett joined from Belgian side SK Lokoren for £180,000. Bett was a skilful, intelligent player who would provide quality and stylish distribution in midfield. And 33-year-old Willie Johnston returned from Vancouver Whitecaps for £40,000 in August. The hot-tempered Johnston was sent off against Aberdeen one month after rejoining Rangers, the sixteenth booking of his career.

Rangers began the 1980/81 season well, unbeaten in their first 15 games, including two wins over Celtic. They also beat Kilmarnock 8-1, with John MacDonald scoring a hat-trick. Their cup form was, however, less convincing. In the Anglo-Scottish Cup, the only non-domestic tournament they entered that season, they were embarrassingly knocked out by English Third Division Chesterfield, a 1-1 draw at Ibrox followed by a 3-0 defeat at Chesterfield. They were also eliminated from the League Cup by Aberdeen. Although a 1st minute Colin MacAdam goal at Ibrox had given them a 1-0 first leg lead, two contentious penalties at Aberdeen – both scored by Gordon Strachan – saw them go down 3-1.

The New Firm – Aberdeen and Dundee United – were now rivalling Celtic as the main competition in Scotland, and United's emergence was confirmed when they beat Rangers 4-1 at Ibrox, a match which saw Gregor Stevens yet again ordered off. Making his unhappy debut in goal in the match was the £115,000 signing from Middlesbrough, keeper Jim Stewart. Rangers ended the season third in the league, twelve points behind Celtic and five behind Aberdeen. The only silverware for which they could now compete was the Scottish Cup.

Rangers had a scare in the fourth round of the competition when they squandered a 2-0 lead at Perth against St Johnstone to find themselves 3-2 down. Ian Redford's injury time goal ensured a replay which they won 3-1 at Ibrox. The

Opposite: *The scenes after the game at the 1980 Scottish Cup final*

Tommy McLean in the 1982 Scottish Cup final

quarter-final drew Hibs, now in the First Division, and Russell, MacAdam and MacDonald scored in the 3-0 win. In the semi-final they beat Morton 2-1 and met Dundee United in the final. Rangers tactics were defensive and Davie Cooper, striker John MacDonald and Derek Johnstone were all absent from the opening line-up. The game was a disappointment, but it could have been sewn up when Rangers were awarded a last-minute penalty. Redford stepped up and hit his shot against keeper Hamish McAlpine's legs, and the game went into a goalless extra time. For the replay, Greig changed his game plan and included Cooper, MacDonald and Johnstone. Cooper was in outstanding form, perhaps signalling to Greig that his omission in the first game had been an error. He scored the first goal in the 10th minute with a slow-motion chip over the keeper and made two others for Russell and MacDonald. MacDonald scored a fourth to leave the score 4-1, and the game has gone down in Rangers folklore as the 'Cooper Final'.

By the beginning of the new season the rebuilding of the stadium was now virtually complete, with the Copland Road, Broomloan and Govan Stands in place and the pitch kept in playable condition with the new undersoil heating system. Rangers had spent £10 million on constructing one of the finest stadiums in Europe, much of the funding coming from the successful Rangers Pools operation. The quality of the football, however, continued to fall short of the grandeur of its surroundings. Greig had bought the tall, Northern Ireland central defender John McLelland for £100,000 from Mansfield Town and, although the attack this season was less than fruitful, Greig also had problems in defence. Midway through the season Tom Forsyth was advised to retire on medical grounds and Gregor Stevens received a six-month ban for his fifth sending-off offence, so Jackson and McLelland formed the central defensive partnership for the latter part of the campaign.

McLelland made his European debut against Dukla Prague in the first leg of the first round European Cup Winners Cup fixture in Czechoslovakia. Rangers went one down within four minutes, with McCloy at fault, and let in two more in the second half. To compound Greig's woes, Tommy McLean was sent off. At Ibrox, Rangers' attack-minded formation left the defence exposed in the 23rd minute and Stambacher, on the break, sent in a half-hearted shot which squeezed under Stewart for a goal. Bett and MacDonald both scored in a two-minute spell just before half time but there were no more goals and Rangers were out of Europe.

The League Cup was their only trophy in that season. Rangers qualified unbeaten from their section, hammering Raith Rovers 8-1 at Ibrox with Cooper again outstanding and Redford scoring four. They met Dundee United in the final without the injured Johnstone. Ralph Milne opened the scoring for Dundee just after the interval and in the 74th minute Cooper curled in a free kick for the equaliser. With just two minutes to go Redford scored the winner, chipping keeper McAlpine.

In the Scottish Cup final against Aberdeen. John McLelland scored first in the 12th minute, Alex McLeish equalised and the game went into extra time. Without Johnstone and Redford, the aging team were not only tired but toothless, and they succumbed 4-1 to a younger, fitter and more committed Aberdeen. In the league they finished in third place, twelve points behind Celtic. As an indication of the frustration and despondency of their support, only 4,500 spectators bothered to turn up at Ibrox for the penultimate home league match against St Mirren. Waddell's vision of a state-of-the-art stadium had been realised but the fans were staying away.

The Aberdeen game had shown that emergency surgery was required on the side. Greig gave free transfers to Sandy Jardine, who went to Hearts and enjoyed a successful ending to his career at Tynecastle, and to Colin Jackson. Tommy McLean retired, but remained at Ibrox as assistant to Greig. Swedish international Robert Prytz, a midfielder who had played in the 1979 European Cup for Malmo against Nottingham Forest arrived at the club for £100,000. To replace Jackson, Greig paid a club record fee of £225,000 to Hibs for the services of centre-half Craig Paterson and £30,000 to Partick Thistle for red-haired full-back Dave McKinnon to take over Jardine's position.

The team now, on paper at least, was an impressive one. McLelland and Paterson formed the central defensive unit, with a midfield of Prytz, Russell and Bett, while Cooper, Redford and Johnstone provided the firepower up front. With this revamped line-up, Rangers began 1982/83 well enough and went twenty games without defeat. They played Borussia Dortmund in the first round of the UEFA Cup in Dortmund, securing a well-earned 0-0 draw, and beat the Germans at home 2-0 through Cooper and Johnstone. The season, however, began to unravel at the end of October. First, Celtic ended their unbeaten run with a 3-2 defeat at Parkhead, Murdo Macleod scoring the winner. Then, having already beaten Cologne 2-1 at Ibrox in the second round of the UEFA Cup, Rangers travelled to Cologne for the second leg in early November. They were comprehensively humiliated in Cologne, going down 5-0 to the German side who scored four in the first twenty minutes, and it was downhill from then on.

By January they were thirteen points off the lead in the league race and the season ended with Rangers in fourth place, a massive eighteen points behind leaders Dundee United. They also lost out in the League Cup final, where a clever Bett free-kick goal early in the second period was not enough to overhaul first-half goals apiece from Celtic's Charlie Nicholas and Murdo Macleod. And an Eric Black header four minutes from the end of extra time in the Scottish Cup final saw the Light Blues go under 1-0 to Aberdeen.

Although Greig had received the support of the board, the situation at Rangers was now becoming desperate. Celtic and the New Firm were dominant in Scottish football and to the fans this was unacceptable, particularly in the case of the Parkhead team. Greig had little money available to refresh his squad and two of his senior players – Derek Johnstone and Jim Bett – left the club, Johnstone moving to Chelsea for £30,000 and Bett going back to Belgium. Johnstone was to rejoin the club in January 1985 for a season. Although he had turned down a move to Rangers twice in his young career, striker Ally McCoist came to Ibrox for £185,000 from Sunderland in June. Although he took some time to find his form and win over the fans, McCoist was to become Rangers greatest-ever goal-scorer.

The Light Blues began the next season by winning the Glasgow Cup, defeating Celtic in the final, but the now-familiar pattern of failure soon re-asserted itself. They drew their first league game with St Mirren and were beaten in the second game 2-1 by Celtic, where McCoist made his Old

Firm debut and scored within 27 seconds. They then lost to Hearts and Aberdeen. After the latter game several hundred fans demonstrated outside the ground and called for Greig to be sacked. The board had no comment to make and Greig defiantly stated 'I can assure you that nobody will fight harder than me and the players to put Rangers where they should be'. In October Motherwell, now managed by Jock Wallace, came to Ibrox and went away with a 2-1 win, leaving Rangers with only seven points from nine games. A crowd gathered outside the stadium and jeered the players and the directors as they left the ground, and this proved to be the nadir of Greig's misfortunes. Six days later, on October 24 1983, Greig resigned, and Tommy McLean took over as temporary manager. In his five years as manager Greig had won four domestic trophies but he had failed to win the league and, critically, he had been unable to challenge Celtic's authority. In the end, although the board apparently put him under no pressure to leave, the mounting criticism from the media and Rangers fans led to his resignation. 'I am finished with football', said Greig, but he would be back at Ibrox in a few years' time.

The Rangers board turned to Aberdeen's Alex Ferguson and Dundee United's Jim McLean but both managers turned down the opportunity to manage the club. It was now evident that being the boss at Rangers was no longer considered the top job in Scottish football. There was now only one realistic

Colin Jackson watches the ball during the 1982 Scottish Cup final

candidate – Jock Wallace – and on 10 November Wallace returned to Ibrox as the new manager. He acted quickly to rejuvenate the squad, buying his old Motherwell keeper Nicky Walker in a £100,000 deal and centre-forward Bobby Williamson from Kilmarnock for the same amount. In his first game in charge, Rangers were beaten 3-0 by Aberdeen but they only lost one more game – a 3-0 defeat by Celtic at Parkhead – the rest of the season. They could not, however, catch up on their miserable start and ended in fourth place in the league, 15 points behind Aberdeen.

Although Rangers made little impact on the Scottish Cup that season, they did reach the League Cup final against Celtic. Shortly before half time, McCoist converted from the penalty spot after a McLeod foul in the area. Early in the second half McCoist claimed his second, taking advantage of a long kick from Peter McCloy, but a Brian McClair volley and a Mark Reid penalty in the last minute forced extra time. In the extra period McCoist was fouled by Aitken in the box, took the penalty, the ball was blocked by Packie Bonner, and McCoist forced home the rebound for his hat-trick. Rangers won 3-2 and McCoist had demonstrated his goalscoring potential. The team was: McCloy, Mitchell, Dawson, McLelland, Paterson, McPherson, Russell, McCoist, Clark, MacDonald, Cooper.

Greig had been in charge for the club's European Cup Winners Cup first round game against Malta's Valetta. Towering young central defender David McPherson, a product of the youth system, made his European debut in Malta and scored four in Rangers' 8-0 win. At Ibrox, John MacDonald claimed a hat-trick in a 10-0 routing of Valetta. Porto were next in the second round. With three minutes to go at Ibrox, Rangers were two ahead, through a first half strike from Sandy Clark and an 83rd minute goal from Australian centre-forward Dave Mitchell, but a McCloy error, when he punched the ball out to a Porto forward, gave Porto a vital away goal. In the second leg, with McLean now in charge, Gomez scored the only goal of the game and Porto went through on away goals.

Wallace was benefiting from the emergence from the youth team of the talented young midfielders Derek Ferguson and Ian Durrant, and he augmented his squad at the end of 1983/84 with the acquisition from Dundee of forward Iain Ferguson and competitive midfielder Cammy Fraser. In October 1984 he bought Kevin 'Ted' McMinn, a tall winger with a somewhat unorthodox, gangling style, from Queen of the South for £100,000. Wallace had given Gregor Stevens a free transfer that summer and Sandy Clark moved to Hearts early in the season. John McLelland was stripped of the captaincy in September after a financial dispute with Wallace, and he moved to Watford in November for £265,000. Craig Paterson was given the captain's armband.

In mid-September the team travelled to Dublin to play Bohemians in a first round tie in the UEFA Cup and were unexpectedly beaten 3-2 by the Irish side. Trouble, fuelled by sectarian hatred, erupted on the terraces and Wallace had to appeal to the fans to halt the violence, while Nicky Walker was bombarded by missiles throughout the game. Back at Ibrox Rangers were on the verge of a humiliating elimination with the score 0-0 and only six minutes remaining, but Paterson and Redford with a last-minute header rescued the game.

The second round found Rangers at the San Siro stadium to play Inter Milan, parading such talents as West Germany's Karl-Heinz Rummenigge, Liam Brady and Franco Baresi. With only fifteen minutes to go, Rangers were 2-0 down and McCoist missed a sitter which could have been crucially important for Rangers had it gone in. As he recalls in his autobiography, *My Story*: 'Ian Redford smacked in a tremendous shot which hit the bar and spun back in the air to me. Their keeper was still on the ground and I had an empty net to head into. But I jumped too early, met the ball when I was on the way down and the header missed'. Buoyed by McCoist's profligacy, Rummenigge scored a third goal with three minutes to go. At Ibrox, an excellent display from Rangers saw them 3-1 ahead by the 55th minute but they could not add to their total and Inter progressed to the third round. Two goals came from Iain Ferguson, replacing the dropped McCoist.

Although Rangers lost only two out of their first twenty league games, they lost their momentum in mid-season and were beaten nine times in their remaining matches. They were fourth in the table by the end of the season, 21 points behind champions Aberdeen and they were knocked out of the Scottish Cup 1-0 by Dundee (the goal scored by John Brown, soon to become a Rangers stalwart). They did, however, retain the League Cup, Iain Ferguson scoring the only goal of the game against Dundee United. This was scant consolation for Wallace and the fans. Wallace had spent heavily but had managed only one trophy in the season and he had yet to find consistency in his team.

By the end of 1985 the situation was not much better. Rangers had lost seven and drawn five of their twenty league games and were in fifth spot in the league. They were also out of the League Cup, losing 1-0 to Hibs in the semi-final. In January 1986 they went down 2-0 to Celtic at Ibrox and were eliminated from the Scottish Cup by Hearts in a thrilling 3-2 game in the third round. They were also knocked out of the UEFA Cup. Although they beat Atletico Osasuna 1-0 at Ibrox with a second-half headed goal from Craig Paterson, they lost 2-0 in Spain. With the season

Ally McCoist, who became the most prolific striker in Rangers' history

halfway through, Rangers were looking at another deeply disappointing year, and the average attendance at Ibrox dropped to only 25,000.

Important and far-reaching events were, however, occurring in the boardroom. In November Lawrence Marlborough, the grandson of ex-chairman John Lawrence, had bought out garage owner Jack Gillespie's shares and now owned a majority of the shareholding in Rangers. He moved quickly to appoint David Holmes, head of John Lawrence UK, to represent his interests on the board, and shortly after his arrival three existing board members were removed. In spite of Rangers' depressing record over the preceding few years, Holmes recognised the commercial potential of the club and he appointed Freddy Fletcher in February 1986 as director in charge of sales and marketing whose brief was to increase revenue from off the pitch

through merchandising, licensing and corporate entertainment. The Rangers commercial revolution was about to begin.

The day after a dismal 2-0 defeat by Spurs in a friendly at Ibrox on 6th April Wallace was sacked as manager. Although the result did little to improve his standing in the boardroom, the probability is that his departure had been decided several weeks previously as part of the changes about to sweep through Rangers. Wallace, a Rangers man to the core, took the news with dignity and moved to Spain to manage Seville. The appointment of his successor was to stun Scottish football but was to bring back success to Ibrox after so many barren years.

CHAPTER EIGHT:

THE SOUNESS REVOLUTION: 1986-1991

The appointment of 33-year-old Graeme Souness as player/manager of Rangers on 7 April 1986 was an imaginative decision by the new owners of the club. The combative, controversial but highly skilful Edinburgh-born midfielder had been a hugely influential player for his country and for his clubs Middlesbrough, Liverpool and Sampdoria. He had played in two World Cups, and was about to play in another as captain of Scotland, and he was the possessor of three European Cup winners' medals with Liverpool. However, he had no managerial experience. To provide the coaching experience and inside knowledge of Scottish football, Souness turned to Walter Smith, who had performed the same role at Dundee United, and appointed him as his assistant manager.

At his press conference Souness described himself as a big Rangers fan but admitted ' To say I have been thrown in at the deep end is an understatement'. He also publicly shredded Rangers' unwritten sectarian policy by pledging his intention to sign Catholic players. Souness, himself married to an Italian Catholic, said 'The best players will be signed no matter what they are. How could I possibly be in this job if I had been told I could not sign a Catholic? After all I am married to one and share my life with her. Do you think I could go home in the evening if I was under such a restriction?'

Before Souness, sectarianism was evident at Ibrox and had been an unstated pillar of the club's ethos for decades. When asked if he would buy a Protestant or Catholic player of equal ability, Jock Stein opted for the former, reasoning that he could always acquire the Catholic at a later date as his religion would preclude Rangers from signing him. Souness was effectively signalling the end to decades of religious bigotry in Scottish football, a brave but necessary step to take, but he was also acknowledging the pragmatic fact that, for Rangers to achieve the top prizes in European football, their selection policy would have to be widened.

Before he could take over at Ibrox he had to finish the Italian season as a player with Sampdoria, to whom Rangers paid £300,000 for his services. Meanwhile, Rangers finished the season with only 35 points from 36 games, their worst ever tally, although their 2-0 win over Motherwell in the final game of the season guaranteed them a place in the

Britain's then most expensive keeper, Chris Woods

following season's UEFA Cup.

Souness set about the wholesale reform of his squad. He gave free transfers to Derek Johnstone and and Dave MacKinnon. He also acquired striker Colin West for £175,000 from Watford, and in June he secured the services of keeper Chris Woods, understudy to Peter Shilton in the England team, for £600,000 from Norwich City, making Woods Britain's most expensive goalkeeper.

His most important signing came in August with the arrival of England and Ipswich Town centre-half Terry Butcher for £725,000, a Scottish record fee. A massive 6 foot 4 inch defender, Butcher was to become the club captain and leader of Souness's team. By acquiring Butcher Souness was demonstrating to British football that Rangers were intent on becoming one of Britain's top sides, a serious rival to Manchester United, Liverpool and Arsenal, and that the new board would provide the funds to bring success back to Ibrox. For Butcher's part, he was impressed by the fans, the stadium, the quality of life and the money on offer, and he

Graeme Souness and David Holmes with Terry Butcher as the big defender signs for Rangers

now had the opportunity to play in European football which he was denied in England after the UEFA five-year ban on English clubs following the Heysel Stadium disaster in 1985.

Souness bedded in his side with friendlies in Germany and a game against Spurs and, although they were beaten 2-0 at Ibrox by Bayern Munich, they impressed with their fluid, passing game. Before the start of the season, Jimmy Nicholl, who had previously played for the club on a loan basis, came to Ibrox from West Bromwich Albion in exchange for Bobby Williamson.

Rangers, with their magnificent stadium and proud tradition, had always been a team whom other Scottish clubs were desperate to beat. Now, with the expensive new signings at Ibrox, there was an increased air of resentment among other clubs towards the Light Blues, coupled with a fierce determination not to come second best and to compete to the maximum. Souness discovered this at the first league game of the season against Hibs at Easter Road on August 9. Hibs were tigerish in their tackling and scored first, while Souness was sent off in the 38th minute for kicking Hibs forward George McCluskey – causing him to have nine stitches in his leg – and nine players were booked in a brawl in which every player, except Hibs keeper Alan

Rough, was involved. Rangers lost 2-1 and were fined £5,000 by the SFA for their part in the trouble.

With Souness suspended for three games, Rangers then beat Falkirk, lost 3-2 to Dundee United at Ibrox and beat Celtic with an Ian Durrant goal at the end of August. Ally McCoist and Robert Fleck, a small, fair-haired centre-forward who had emerged through the youth team, were now the main strikers, and by the end of October Rangers were in third place in the league. They reached the Skol League Cup final on October 26 where they met Celtic. With seven minutes to go the score was 1-1, with Durrant claiming the Rangers goal. Then Roy Aitken pulled Butcher back in the area and a penalty was awarded which Davie Cooper converted. Celtic protested about the penalty and Celtic striker Mo Johnston was sent off, crossing himself as he left the pitch. Souness now had his first trophy.

Rangers had drawn Finland's Ilves Tampere in the first round of the UEFA Cup and won the game at Ibrox 4-0. Fleck contributed a hat-trick, his third goal made by Davie Cooper after the winger had waltzed his way on a dazzling run past five defenders, and McCoist, almost inevitably, scored the other. This was followed by an embarrassing 2-0 defeat away, in front of a crowd of only 2,000. The second round opposition was Portugal's Boavista, who went down 2-1 at Ibrox. A strong performance in Portugal, and a 25-yard strike from Derek Ferguson, saw them win 1-0. They met Borussia Moenchengladbach in the third round at Ibrox where an early goal from Durrant, smashing a left foot shot

Above: *Terry Butcher celebrates his goal against Aberdeen which brought the league title back to Rangers*

Left: *Graham Roberts issues instructions*

into the roof of the net, was equalised before half time and the game finished 1-1. In Germany, Borussia turned in a cynical, defensive display and ground out a 0-0 draw to progress on away goals. Davie Cooper and left-back Stuart Munro were both sent off in the game, frustrated by the Germans' negative and obdurate tactics.

In December Souness added to his squad of 'football mercenaries', as they were becoming known outside Ibrox, with the acquisition of defender Graham Roberts from Spurs for £450,000. Roberts had something of a reputation for tough tackling, and he soon settled in alongside Butcher in the centre of defence. He played in the Ne'er's Day fixture at Ibrox, which resulted in a 2-0 win with goals from McCoist and Fleck and featured Souness at his best. A 2-0 win at Hamilton later in the month saw Rangers go top of the league.

Rangers suffered a rare and humiliating reverse in their third round Scottish Cup tie against Hamilton Academicals

Souness, Durrant, Cooper, Fleck, McCoist.

Souness had succeeded in his first year in charge and the Rangers support was revitalised. Attendances at Ibrox had risen from around 15,000 to nearly 40,000, while off the pitch the new commercial ventures were bringing in significant revenues. Souness had inculcated into his players the virtues of discipline and professionalism and he did not allow anyone to step out of line. He was the boss and his word was law. He seemed particularly hard on Ally McCoist. In Souness's last season in charge McCoist went to the Cheltenham races without the manager's permission and Souness organised a press conference at which the striker was made to apologise publicly for his misdemeanour, a deep humiliation for the otherwise irrepressible striker. McCoist had also christened himself 'the judge' due to the amount of time he spent on the bench that season. However, McCoist did state that Souness had made him a better player.

Souness was concerned that physically his players were at their peak. Aided by Phil Boersma, Peter McCloy and Walter Smith, he ensured that his players were fit and well drilled in tactics, paying particular stress on training with the ball, stretching exercises and the importance of a correct diet, all of which he had picked up in Italy. He banned his players from playing golf – usually a footballer's chief recreation – in case they picked up an injury. He also installed a sauna and

Graeme Souness and Walter Smith with the league trophy

at the end of January. Although Rangers had been on top throughout, in the 70th minute Dave McPherson couldn't control a long ball and allowed Accies' Adrian Sprott to score the only goal of the game. This goal broke Chris Woods' 12-game unbeaten record. However, by the end of February Rangers were back at the top of the league and remained there until the end of the season.

On May 2 10,000 Rangers fans travelled north to Pittodrie, where they had not won a league match for five years, with the championship almost within the club's grasp. Although Souness had been sent off in the 31st minute, Butcher's second-half soaring header from a Cooper cross hurtled past Jim Leighton in the Aberdeen goal and Rangers held on to draw 1-1. With Celtic unexpectedly losing 2-1 at Falkirk, Rangers could not now be caught and were league champions for the first time in nine years. The blue-and-white support invaded the pitch in celebration and carried Butcher shoulder-high around the pitch. The captain was presented with the trophy at the following Saturday's game against St Mirren at Ibrox. The team at Pittodrie was: Woods, Roberts, Butcher, McPherson, Munro, Nicholl,

Richard Gough

an isolation bath in the dressing room, the first changes made to the room since the stadium was built in 1929.

Souness' clear-out of the older players continued in the summer of 1987 with Bobby Russell going to Motherwell on a free transfer and Ally Dawson joining Blackburn Rovers for £50,000. Ted McMinn, whose off the pitch activities had irritated Souness, joined Jock Wallace at Seville for £200,000. Souness continued to buy in players from English clubs. Strong centre-forward Mark Falco joined from Watford for £270,000, although his stay at Ibrox was to be a short one. One of Souness' first acts when joining Rangers was to make Dundee United a £600,000 offer for their tall right-back Richard Gough. He had been rebuffed by United manager Jim McLean who later sold the player to Spurs, whom Gough had captained to the 1987 FA Cup final which they lost 3-2 to Coventry City. Rangers had previously allowed Gough to slip through the net when, as an 18-year-old, he had failed a trial at Ibrox. Souness finally got his man in October 1987 for a club record £1.1 million. Gough radiated calmness and authority, was excellent in the air and was to become a pivotal

defender and captain for Rangers through the successes of the 1990s. The highly experienced, skilful midfielder Ray 'Butch' Wilkins was also recruited from Paris St Germain for £250,000. Admired for the quality of his distribution, the cool, perceptive Wilkins had amassed 84 caps for England.

Without the suspended Roberts, Butcher and Souness for the first two games of 1987/88, Rangers drew with Dundee United at Ibrox and were then beaten 1-0 by Hibs. They lost two of their next three games, with Souness sent off and picking up a five-match suspension in the 1-0 defeat by Celtic. In the next Old Firm fixture on October 17, trouble flared up again. In the 16th minute, Celtic's Frank MacAvennie, playing in his first Old Firm encounter, barged into Chris Woods and, in the ensuing melee, Roberts threw a punch at the Celtic striker and MacAvennie was sent off along with Woods. Butcher was also booked in the incident. Roberts took over in goal and let in two before half time. During the match Roberts provocatively conducted a section of the Rangers support in their rendition of sectarian songs. In the second half Butcher was dismissed for lashing out at

Above: *Ray ('Butch') Wilkins*

Left: *Souness is sent off against Celtic in August 1987*

Celtic keeper Alan McKnight, but Rangers scored twice, through McCoist and a last-gasp effort from Gough, to secure a 2-2 draw. The *Sunday Mail* had no doubt about the behaviour on the pitch, leading its match report with the single word 'Disgraceful!'. As a result of the incident, Strathclyde police charged the four protagonists with disorderly conduct likely to cause a breach of the peace. Woods and Butcher were found guilty and fined, Roberts was handed a not proven verdict and McAvennie was cleared.

In a stirring, end-to-end Skol League Cup final against Aberdeen on October 25, Aberdeen scored from a Bett penalty in the 8th minute, after Nicky Walker, in goal for the suspended Woods and playing in his first game for fourteen months, brought down Falconer in the box. By half time Rangers were 2-1 ahead through a brilliantly taken Cooper

free kick and a Durrant 40th minute strike. Hewitt, and then Falconer with nine minutes to go, put Aberdeen 3-2 ahead, and a last minute goal from Fleck levelled the score. The game went into extra time and then penalties, the first penalty shoot-out in a major final. Aberdeen missed one, Rangers converted all five and the League Cup came back to Ibrox. Dunfermline, however, put paid to Rangers' Scottish Cup aspirations by defeating them 2-0 in the fourth round.

A less than sparkling domestic season was redeemed by a good run in the European Cup. Dynamo Kiev – virtually the entire Soviet Union team, with such international players as Oleg Blokhin and Oleg Kuznetsov – were their formidable opponents in the first round. In front of 100,000 spectators in the Ukraine, Rangers survived the Kiev onslaught with a disciplined, defensive performance, and surrendered only one goal, when Alexei Mikhailichenko converted a second-half penalty. With the fast and powerful English international forward Trevor Francis, signed from Atalanta for £750,000, now in the team, Rangers surged into attack in the second leg at Ibrox. Falco scored in the 24th minute after Kiev keeper Viktor Chanov had thrown the ball against Kuznetsov's back. It bounced to McCoist who gratefully supplied Falco in front of an open goal. Five minutes after the interval, McCoist headed in the second, and Rangers went through 2-1 on aggregate. Before the game, Souness, noting Kiev's reliance on wing play, had trimmed back the width of the pitch to the legal minimum, after Kiev had

Davie Cooper (11) opens the scoring for Rangers with a free kick in the 1987 League Cup final

trained on it the day before. An incensed Kiev complained, but to no avail.

In the second round at Ibrox, Rangers were 3-0 up against Gornik Zabrze by half time, through McCoist,

McCoist and Falco turn away in triumph and Dynamo Kiev keeper Chanov holds his head after Rangers' first goal at Ibrox in the first round second leg of the 1987/88 European Cup

Mark Walters shadowed by Celtic's Paul McStay

Durrant and Falco, but a second half goal from Urban gave the Poles an away goal. In Poland, McCoist opened the scoring with a penalty and, although Gornik equalised in the second half, Rangers were through to the quarter-final.

Before the game, against Steaua Bucharest, Fleck had submitted a transfer request and had joined Norwich City for £560,000. Fleck had had a stormy personal life and his off-the-pitch behaviour had frustrated Souness, who said 'we had to let him go because of his personal problems although we didn't want him to leave'. With Falco having joined Queens Park Rangers, this left Rangers with only one recognised striker – Ally McCoist – available for European games. Worse was to come when, in a collision with Aberdeen's Alex McCleish on November 17, Butcher broke his leg and was to be out for the rest of the season. The loss of Butcher, and the fact that McCoist had to undergo an achilles operation a matter of days before the quarter-final, weakened Rangers' bid to progress in the tournament.

In torrential rain in Romania. Viktor Piturca put Steaua ahead after only two minutes and Stefen Iovan scored another in the second half. Only the excellent goalkeeping of Chris Woods prevented a bigger defeat than 2-0. The Romanians scored again within two minutes at Ibrox through Marius Lacatus and, although a McCoist penalty and a Gough header in the first half had Rangers ahead 2-1, they could not penetrate the Steaua defence again. They were eliminated 3-2 on aggregate.

Early in 1988 Souness had embarked on another spending spree. In January he bought Danish international Jan Bartram from Aarhus for £315,000. Bartram's stay at Ibrox was to be a brief one. In the summer he criticised Souness's training methods and he was soon shipped off to Brondby. The same month saw the arrival of Mark Walters from Aston Villa for £500,000. A fast, tricky winger with a powerful shot, Walters was also the first black player to play in the Premier League. The red-haired, utility defender John Brown also arrived in January from Dundee for £350,000. Brown was to enjoy a long Ibrox career and produce some courageous performances for the Light Blues. The following month, young midfielder Ian Ferguson, widely perceived as a star of the future, joined Rangers from St Mirren for £700,000

Ian Ferguson

At the end of the season a dressing room row between Roberts and Souness led to the English defender leaving the club.

Gary Stevens

After the last game of the season against Aberdeen Souness had blamed Roberts for giving a goal away and an argument developed between the two men. Souness accused Roberts of lacking in respect for the manager and Roberts retorted 'If you feel that strongly, let me go'. Souness replied 'Consider yourself sold'. Apparently the confrontation was a heated one. Roberts, a popular figure with the Ibrox support, was ostracised by the management and joined Chelsea in August. In what had been a turbulent year for Souness and Rangers, they ended the season in third place in the league and Celtic won the 'double' of Scottish Cup and league. Souness again looked south and reached for the cheque book.

The next English player to turn up at Ibrox was striker Kevin Drinkell, signed for £500,000 from Norwich, followed by Gary Stevens, an England international full-back bought from Everton for £1.25 million. Stevens was an athletic, speedy attacking defender with a particular talent for the long throw, and he was to be a regular in the team for the next six years. Souness had now brought his spending on players to over £7 million. Rangers opened the 1988/89 season with a 2-0 win over Hamilton Academicals and dropped only one point in their next seven games. They met Celtic at Ibrox on August 27 and, although Frank

Left: Ally McCoist scores the winning goal in the 1988 League Cup final against Aberdeen

Below: David Murray

Above: Souness with Mo Johnston as the forward joins Rangers

Left: Davie Cooper skips past Celtic's Roy Aitken in the 1989 Scottish Cup final

Above: Ray Wilkins in tears after his last game for Rangers

Left: Trevor Steven

MacAvennie gave Celtic the lead in the 1st minute, Rangers triumphed 5-1, the highlight being a spectacular 20-yard volley from Wilkins.

The attack was now strengthened by the arrival of ageing striker Andy Gray from West Bromwich Albion, but Ranger's 14-game unbeaten streak came to an end in a 2-1 defeat at Pittodrie on October 8. During the match a disgraceful tackle by Aberdeen's Neil Simpson resulted in Durrant suffering damaged cruciate ligaments in his right knee. Durrant was to take three years to recover from the tackle. They played Aberdeen again in the Skol League Cup final on 23 October where McCoist and Ferguson put Rangers 2-0 ahead till Davie Dodds retaliated twice for the Dons. McCoist scored the winner.

In the UEFA Cup Rangers had played the little-known GKS Katowice in the first round. In the first leg at Ibrox Katowice unexpectedly went on the attack and Rangers were relieved to score the only goal of the game through Walters. In Poland two headed goals from Butcher, plus one apiece from Durrant and Ferguson, gave them a 4-2 win. In round two they met Cologne, their fourth European encounter with the German club in twenty years. At the Mungerdorf Stadium Cologne scored two late goals and McCoist was sent off, while at Ibrox a Drinkell late goal gave the side some hope until Cologne equalised in extra time.

Back in the league Rangers beat Celtic 4-1 on Ne'er's Day and they claimed their first win at Parkhead in nine years on April 1 with a 2-1 scoreline. They won the league title on April 29 at Ibrox against Hearts, with recent arrival Mel Sterland scoring twice, the other two coming from Drinkell, fast becoming a fans' favourite. Rangers were now

chasing the 'treble' and they met Celtic on May 20 in the Scottish Cup final. In what was a poor match, Joe Miller capitalised on a poor pass-back by Gary Stevens to score past Chris Woods just before half time, and Celtic won the Cup 1-0 to deprive Rangers of the 'treble'.

In November, 36-year-old millionaire businessman David Murray had bought out Lawrence Marlborough's shareholding in Rangers. Murray commented 'I am delighted that this takeover means that a Scottish institution remains in Scottish hands. We intend to provide a strong base for the continuing development of the club and its business aspects'. Murray was a friend of Souness and the manager became a director of the holding company with a 10% shareholding. Souness now had a financial incentive in the success of the club to complement his natural drive and competitiveness.

On July 10 1989 Souness rocked Scottish football by doing what he had promised to do three years previously and sign a Catholic player. Before the Scottish Cup final, Maurice 'Mo' Johnston, a Catholic, ex-Celtic, Scottish international striker, had agreed to sign for Celtic from French club Nantes. Indeed, he had been paraded in front of the Celtic faithful prior to the Cup final. At the last moment Souness stepped in and secured the player's signature in a £1.2 million deal which made Johnston Scotland's most expensive player. Celtic were outraged, as was a bigoted section of the Rangers support who burnt scarves and programmes outside Ibrox as well as demanding season ticket refunds. Johnston became the first Catholic player knowingly to be acquired by Rangers in the modern era. The cover of the Rangers' fanzine *Follow, Follow* featured a caricature of Johnston kneeling in prayer with the caption 'Forgive me, Father, for I have signed.' In view of Souness's policy of buying English players, many felt that the real sensation was not that he bought a Catholic but a Scotsman.

However, Souness and Murray's actions were widely applauded. A *Glasgow Herald* editorial the next day summed up the view of Scottish football. 'Until yesterday', the paper commented, 'the only football club in Britain whose talent was second to religious denomination was Rangers. Now that ridiculous public posture is abandoned those who have criticised it for years should recognise that a shameful totem of Scottish religious interference is toppled...Rangers deserve congratulations because they have earned it, at long last'.

Almost forgotten in the brouhaha over Johnston was the arrival earlier that summer of classy English international midfielder Trevor Steven from Everton for £1.7 million. Steven was to enjoy two spells at Ibrox and he was to team up to great effect with Gary Stevens on the right side of the pitch.

Rangers began the 1989/90 season disastrously, winning only two out of their first eight league games and they were bottom of the table after four games. The team, however, soon began to fit together and by mid-December they were top of the league. They drew their first league game against Celtic and beat them on 4 November at Ibrox when Johnston smacked the ball from twenty yards into the Celtic net for the only goal of the game at Ibrox with two minutes remaining. Another new English signing, Nigel Spackman, joined the club in December for £500,000 from Queen's Park Rangers and promptly scored the only goal in Rangers' first win at Parkhead on Ne'er Day for twenty years. Co-incidentally, Ray Wilkins was transferred that same month to Queen's Park Rangers. Such was Wilkins' popularity with the fans that he received a standing ovation in his last game at Ibrox after Rangers' 3-0 win over Dunfermline and left the pitch in tears.

The club won the league by dint of their 1-0 win over Dundee United at Tannadice, the goal coming from a perfectly timed Trevor Steven header in the 57th minute from a Stuart Munro cross. The title was retained for the first time since 1976, seven points ahead of second-placed Aberdeen. They were less successful in the cups, however, going down 2-1 to Aberdeen in the League Cup final and being eliminated from the Scottish Cup 1-0 by Celtic in the fourth round.

They had also played in the European Cup earlier in the season. Bayern Munich, with their strong team of German internationals, were their opponents in the first round at Ibrox. Walters scored first with a penalty after Johnston was fouled but Kogl equalised three minutes later. In the second half Thon scored another for the Germans and a 35-yard shot from centre-half Klaus Augenthaler made the final score 3-1. 'It was a lesson for us,' said Souness. A desperate game then ensued in Germany when Bayern were content to pass the ball between themselves with no attempt to attack, and the crowd booed off both teams at the end of a 0-0 draw.

The single-minded, argumentative Souness had been having problems with the SFA. In February 1989 he had received a touchline ban and was fined £1,000 after an argument with a linesman at Tannadice. He was spotted on the touchline again the following month at the Scottish Cup semi-final. The SFA handed him a £2,000 fine and banned him from the touchline until the end of the 1989/1990 season. In May he was fined £5,000 and banned again from the touchline for a further season after STV cameras had caught him in the tunnel at Hearts in February. He also had a fractious and volatile relationship with the media, banning STV from Ibrox and having several dust-ups with the tabloid press. The daily frustrations of the job appeared to be affecting his health, and he was also a marked man on the

pitch. As quoted in David Mason's *Rangers: The Managers*, he said 'I used to say to Phil Boersma as I took to the field "Is the target straight on my back today?"' The intense pressures of being Rangers' manager were wearing Souness down, but he plunged back into the transfer market again in the summer of 1990.

His next acquisition was the tall, powerful striker Mark Hateley, bought from Monaco for £1 million. His arrival did not go down too well with the supporters who believed him to be a replacement for their hero Ally McCoist, with whom Souness always had an on-off relationship. Although Hateley took time to settle into the team, and received some barracking from the fans, he was soon to link up with McCoist to form a devastating goalscoring partnership. Other new arrivals were Dutchman Peter Huistra a skilful ball-playing winger who came from Twente Enschede and who quickly became known as 'Blue Peter'. Hard-tackling midfielder Terry Hurlock arrived from Milwall. They were joined in October by Oleg Kuznetsov from Dynamo Kiev for £1.4 million. Kuznetsov was a world-class central defender and sweeper who could also play in midfield and who had more than fifty caps for the USSR.

The 1990/1991 season was to be Butcher's last. The centre-half was not fully fit and still recovering from his exertions in the 1990 World Cup. After an error-strewn game against Dundee United in September, in which he scored a spectacular headed own goal, he had a row with Souness and was dropped for the Skol League Cup semi-final against Celtic. Butcher had claimed that he was injured before the game but Souness dropped him, saying 'he has refused to play'. He left the club in November to join Coventry City as player/manager. Gough was appointed captain in Butcher's place. Souness' defensive options were even more limited when, in October, Kuznetsov was badly tackled in the 6th minute of a match against St Johnstone and was out for the season. That month, however, Rangers won the League Cup with a 2-1 win over Celtic.

Rangers again disappointed in Europe. They met Valetta in the first round and Johnston scored five goals in their 10-0 aggregate defeat of the Maltese side. In the second round they faced one of the most talented, attacking teams in European football, Red Star Belgrade, featuring playmaker Robert Prosinecki, midfielder Dejan Savicevic and striker Darko Pancev. In Belgrade, John Brown helped a corner past Woods in the 8th minute, a Prosinecki free kick halfway through the second period made the score 2-0 to the free-flowing Yugoslavian side, and Pancev added a third ten minutes later. Pancev again scored at Ibrox and McCoist pulled one back with fifteen minutes to go but Rangers were well beaten 4-1 on aggregate. Red Star went on to lift the

Peter Huistra

European Cup in a tedious final against Marseille, winning on penalties.

In January Rangers beat Celtic 2-0 at Ibrox, with an improbable goal direct from a corner from Walters and a 78th minute Hateley strike, and by the end of the month they were seven points ahead in the league. In February they extended their unbeaten run in the league to fifteen games with a 1-1 draw at St Johnstone, but a 1-0 defeat by Aberdeen at Pittodrie ended their run of games without defeat, although they won their next game 2-1 against Hearts. In mid-March they faced Celtic in the quarter-final of the Scottish Cup at Parkhead. With John Brown and Nigel Spackman absent, they were 1-0 down by the 6th minute and they lost the match 2-0. Four players, three of them Rangers, were sent off. The first to go was Hurlock for an incident involving Tommy Coyne in the 63rd minute, and then Hateley and Walters were dismissed for two yellow card offences. A week later they lost again to Celtic, 3-0 in

the league. Two more wins – against Dunfermline and St Johnstone – followed, and the 0-0 draw with Hibs saw the return of Ian Durrant to first team football for the first time since 1988.

Meanwhile, Kenny Dalglish's unexpected resignation from Liverpool in February had left a vacancy at Anfield. Souness was being linked with the job but he temporarily quashed press speculation when he told the *Rangers News* on 27 February 'Right now I'm speaking to the chairman about a new contract. I have no intention of ever leaving this place.'

However, on 16 April Souness shocked Rangers and Scottish football by announcing that he was resigning to take up the Liverpool job. The frustrations and pressures associated with the Rangers stewardship were probably the dominant factors in his decision to leave Ibrox, although Liverpool were a club close to his heart and the job was one he felt he could not turn down. Also his three young children lived close to Liverpool and this was an opportunity to be with them as they grew up. The £350,000 a year, five-year contract could have been a further persuasive inducement. At a press conference he said 'I feel I've gone as far as I'm allowed to go in trying to achieve success at this football club'. The use of the verb 'allowed' was almost certainly a revealing allusion to the press and the Scottish football authorities.

Souness had wanted to stay on till the end of the season but Murray insisted he leave immediately, stating that 'it's not Graham's wish but he's free to go. We have a championship to win'. Rangers fans were angry and disappointed by Souness's sudden departure and Murray commented 'I feel personally let down. I think he is making the biggest mistake of his life.' As for the team, several leading players had joined Rangers because of Souness, and captain Gough commented 'I've spoken to a lot of the players and they are disappointed he has left'.

Although Souness wanted Walter Smith to come with him to Anfield, Smith declined and, on 19 April he was appointed the new manager of Rangers. He said 'I've supported Rangers for a great number of years and I'm delighted to take this job'. A quieter, more self-effacing figure than Souness, Smith was a popular choice among the players and the fans, many of whom had problems with Souness's confrontational manner. Smith was highly respected in club and international football for his tactical awareness and understanding of the game, and he had the experience and ability to handle the pressures at the highest level. He appointed Archie Knox, then with Manchester United, as his assistant manager.

When he took over, Rangers' league challenge was a precarious one, with the Light Blues leading the league by a single point over Aberdeen and four games to play. Smith was

Mark Hateley, Walter Smith and Chris Woods with the Scottish League trophy in May 1991

also hampered by injuries to Kuznetsov, Durrant and Trevor Steven. However, in his first game in charge, against St Mirren at Love Street, a balletic overhead goal from 20-year-old midfielder Sandy Robertson with seven minutes remaining gave Smith his first victory. Next up were Dundee United at Ibrox, where a diving header from Ian Ferguson in the 33rd minute gave the Light Blues maximum points. In the penultimate game of the season against Motherwell without a hepatitis-stricken Gough, they went down to a 3-0 defeat, with Mark Walters missing a penalty and Motherwell scoring twice on the counter-attack in the last five minutes.

Aberdeen were on the same number of points and were also level on goal difference, but had scored two more goals and the Dons went to the top of the table. By a twist of footballing fate, Rangers' last game of the season was against

Mark Hateley celebrates scoring against Aberdeen in May 1991

Aberdeen at Ibrox and Aberdeen had only to draw to win the championship, while the Gers had to win.

In a robust encounter at Ibrox, in the 40th minute Walters crossed and Hateley soared above Alex McCleish to head in the opener. Thirteen minutes into the second half Johnston burst through the Dons defence and shot at keeper Watt who could not hold the ball. Hateley was waiting, and from two yards he crashed the ball into the net. The score ended 2-0 and the celebrations began at Ibrox. Rangers had now won the league three times in a row but, with Souness gone, could this star-studded and expensively assembled team continue the momentum under Smith? The answer was to be a resoundingly affirmative one over the coming seasons.

CHAPTER NINE:

NINE IN A ROW: 1991-1998

Walter Smith faced a dilemma in 1991/92, his first full season in charge of Rangers. On one hand, it was important to maintain a strong squad to compete in Scotland, whose Premier Division that season had been expanded from ten to twelve clubs. This meant playing a total of 44 league games alone, on top of cup competitions and European involvement. However, a new UEFA directive limited the number of 'foreign' players who were permitted to play in UEFA tournaments to four and then to three. Souness and Smith had planned for this but, when Souness left Ibrox he bequeathed Smith twelve 'foreign' players in the squad. Some speedy changes had to be made in personnel.

Over the summer Englishman Trevor Steven, arguably Rangers' best player over the previous couple of seasons, joined Marseille for £5 million. Chris Woods also left, to join Sheffield Wednesday for £1.2 million, and his nationality was again an important factor in his departure. Also Mark Walters, another Englishman went to Liverpool to reunite himself with Souness.

Alexei Mikhailichenko

However, Smith moved quickly to reinforce his squad. He paid Sampdoria £2.2 million, then a Scottish transfer record, for the powerful, left-sided midfielder Alexei Mikhailichenko, an ex-Russian and now Ukranian international who had been Soviet Player of the Year in 1988. Small, stocky, English-born midfield Scottish international Stuart McCall arrived from Everton for £1.2 million. Fast, attacking left-back David Robertson joined from Aberdeen for £970,000. And, to replace Chris Woods, an English-born but Scottish international, Andy Goram, came to Ibrox for £1 million from Hibs. Goram's bravery and anticipation in goals was to be critical to Rangers' coming successes.

The Light Blues got off to a flying start in the Skol League Cup, beating Queen's Park 6-0, with Johnston scoring four, and then eliminating Partick Thistle 2-0. In the quarter-final a McCoist volley helped them to a 1-0 away win over Hearts but they stumbled in the semi, losing 1-0 to Hibs.

In Europe, UEFA had initiated the Champions League to replace the traditional structure of the European Cup. The first two rounds were to remain home and away knockouts, but the last eight clubs in the tournament were to go into two mini-leagues, the winners meeting to contest the Final. In the first round Rangers were drawn against Sparta Prague who were managed by ex-Czechoslovakian international captain Zdenek Nehoda and who had lost twelve of their players to Western clubs during the previous season. Depleted they may have been but Sparta came away from the first leg in Prague with a 1-0 win, scored by Jiri Nemec in the 18th minute when Goram misjudged a cross.

At Ibrox Goram redeemed himself with two fine saves from the adventurous Czechs in the first half. In the 48th minute Mikhailichenko found McCall in space and the midfielder scored from ten yards. The game went into extra time and, after only three minutes, a McCall volley put Rangers into an aggregate lead. Four minutes later, however, a low cross from Siegl deflected off centre-half Scott Nisbet's boot and through Goram's hands. The game ended 2-2 but Sparta progressed to the second leg on away goals.

In the Premier League Rangers began well with a 6-0 victory over St Johnstone and then beat Motherwell 2-0. In

Stuart McCall

Andy Goram

late September they lost their first game at Ibrox for ten months, succumbing 2-0 to Aberdeen but by the middle of October they were back at the top of the league with a 2-0 win over Hearts, a game in which Mikhailochenko claimed his first goal for the Light Blues.

Dale Gordon, a right-winger from Norwich City, was Smith's next purchase in November, paying the East Anglian club £1.2 million for his services. He impressed on his debut match away against Dunfermline, scoring two and making two more in the Gers 5-0 win Meanwhile, Mo Johnston, increasingly a substitute because of the free-scoring partnership of Hateley and McCoist, joined Everton in November for £1.6 million. Johnston had scored a total of 51 goals in 110 games for the Light Blues.

Having already drawn 1-1 with Celtic earlier in the season, Rangers met them again in the Ne'er Day fixture at Parkhead. McCoist opened the scoring in the 45th minute and, although Tony Mowbray equalised, a 78th minute penalty from Hateley and a last-minute 30-yard strike in off the post from John 'Bomber' Brown gave Rangers a 3-1 win. By early January they had lost only four out of their 28 league games, and their 2-0 defeat of Hibs at Ibrox – which saw the debut of striker Paul Rideout, a £500,000 buy from Notts County – meant they had already scored 68 goals in the league, 22 coming from the in-form McCoist.

The winning streak continued throughout the Spring and was brought to a halt by Celtic in mid-March when a 2-0 defeat saw Rangers lose a 16-game undefeated run. Their 4-0 win on 18 April against St Mirren, McCoist scoring another two, brought them their fourth title in succession. Manager Smith's transfer dealings had been vindicated. The club finished the league season with a total of 101 goals – the first time the century had been achieved in the Premier Division – with 51 scored in away games, and this was the fourth time in their history that they had won four successive league titles.

However, Rangers had not won the Scottish Cup since 1981. A McCoist goal at Pittodrie gave Rangers a 1-0 third round win. Phil O'Donnell put Motherwell ahead in the fourth round but two Mikhailichenko goals within two second-half minutes gave Rangers a place in the quarter-final against St Johnstone, whom they disposed of 3-0 to meet Celtic in the semi.

The Glasgow rivals had not met in a Cup semi-final for 32 years, with some cynics suggesting that this long gap had not been a coincidence. At a wet and windy Hampden, Rangers were down to ten men after only the 6th minute when Dave Robertson fouled Joe Miller and was sent off. Huistra dropped back to cover Robertson's position. Rangers defended stoutly and went ahead in the 44th minute when McCoist adroitly converted a clever sideways

Mark Hateley finds the net in the 1992 Scottish Cup final

pass from McCall with a low strike from the edge of the box. Rangers bravely resisted a Celtic wind-assisted onslaught in the second half, with the Celts hitting the woodwork three times and Andy Goram was equal to everything that Celtic could throw at him. McCoist's goal took Rangers through to the final to meet Airdrie. In an undistinguished game, Rangers went 2-0 ahead through Hateley and McCoist and, although Andy Smith pulled one back for Airdrie with nine minutes to go, Rangers had claimed the 'double' for the first time since 1978.

McCoist, in particular, had a sparkling season. The ebullient striker ended the campaign with 41 goals and, in the final league match against Aberdeen he scored Rangers' 100th goal of the season. Now that Souness had departed, the pressure was off and McCoist was in his element. He won the Sport Writers' Player of the Year award and the European 'Golden Boot' title and had formed a profitable partnership with Hateley. The coming season was to emphasise further the striking qualities of the deadly duo.

The following campaign – 1992/93 – was one of the finest seasons in Rangers' history. With Trevor Steven now back from Marseille, who were experiencing problems in meeting the terms of the transfer fee, Smith had an experienced and talented squad from which to choose. Nigel

Spackman moved to Chelsea in September for £485,000 and Paul Rideout went to Everton for £650,000, but the core of the side remained at Ibrox.

In the league Rangers were rampant. Despite losing 4-3 to Dundee at Dens Park in a shock result in August, they went on an unprecedented run of 29 unbeaten league games and 44 unbeaten matches in all competitions. This included defeating Aberdeen in the League Cup final. Stuart McCall gave Rangers the lead after some indecision by Theo Snelders in the Aberdeen goal but Duncan Shearer equalised to take the game into extra time. With only seven minutes remaining, Aberdeen defender Gary Smith deflected the ball into his own net from a David Robertson cross and Rangers claimed the trophy with a 2-1 victory.

Rangers were also to enjoy one of their best-ever seasons in Europe. They were back in the European Cup – with the league section now re-titled the Champions League – and were drawn at home in their first match against Danish champions Lyngby. A first-half header from Hateley and a second-half strike from Huistra gave the Light Blues a 2-0 lead to take to Copenhagen, where an Ian Durrant goal saw them progress to the next round 3-0 on aggregate.

Ally McCoist scores Rangers' second goal in the second round first leg European Cup match against Leeds United at Ibrox

Leeds United, who had won the English league title for the first time since 1974, were the opposition and the press dubbed the clash 'The Battle of Britain'. This was only the third time that English and Scottish champions had met in the competition (the other two being Leeds and Celtic in 1970 and Aberdeen and Liverpool in 1980), and the tie provoked huge interest both sides of the border. Leeds were rather fortunate to have reached the second round. They had been knocked out by Stuttgart in the first round on away goals but the Germans had fielded four foreign players, one more than was permitted. The game was replayed in Barcelona and Leeds won 2-1.

Both clubs had agreed that, in the interests of crowd control and safety, no tickets would be sold to away fans. In the first leg in front of over 43,000 at Ibrox, Rangers were stunned in the first minute by a superbly taken volleyed goal by Gary McAllister, and Ibrox fell eerily silent. As Andy Goram comments in *True and Blue*. 'I've only ever heard Ibrox that quiet twice. The first time was at the Leeds game and the second was when we had the minute's silence for the kids who were murdered at Dunblane'. In the 21st minute Leeds keeper John Lukic, seemingly dazzled by the floodlights, punched an Ian Durrant corner into his own net, and Rangers went on the attack, roared on by the revitalised support. Sixteen minutes later McCoist put Rangers ahead when he buried a loose ball past Lukic after the keeper had saved a Dave McPherson header. A determined Leeds resisted the Rangers forwards in the second half and the game finished 2-1.

At Elland Road Rangers repeated Leeds' start at Ibrox when in the 3rd minute Hateley connected with a Durrant header to send in a stunning twenty-five yard volley past Lukic. The Rangers defence – in particular Andy Goram, having a magnificent match – held out defiantly against the Yorkshire side, led by Eric Cantona and Lee Chapman. In the 59th minute a classic counter-attack by Rangers put them 2-0 up on the night. Hateley dummied to send Durrant free on the left, Durrant found Hateley in space and Hateley's inch-perfect cross was finished off by McCoist with a well-timed diving header. Cantona volleyed in a consolation with five minutes to go, but a superb performance by the Ibrox men saw them move into the group stage of the Champions League where they were matched with Marseille, Bruges and CSKA Moscow. The Rangers team at Elland Road was: Goram, McCall,

Robertson, Gough, McPherson, Brown, Gordon, Ferguson, McCoist, Hateley, Durrant.

In the pouring rain at Ibrox in late November Rangers were outplayed by Marseille, and with ten minutes remaining they were 2-0 down through Alen Boksic and Rudy Voller. In the 78th minute young substitute Gary McSwegan cleverly nodded the ball past keeper Fabien Barthez with his first touch of the game. Three minutes later Hateley equalised on the night with a low header from a Durrant cross and Rangers had luckily salvaged a point. The next game saw them travel to Bochum in Germany to play CSKA Moscow, technically a 'home' game for the Russians because of the wintry conditions in Moscow, and an Ian Ferguson 13th minute deflected shot gave Rangers both points.

On 14 October 1992 Willie Waddell died of a massive heart attack in a Glasgow hospital. The ex-player, manager, managing director and honorary director had been associated with the club for 56 years and was a Rangers man to the core. He had steered the club through the trauma of the 1971 Ibrox Disaster and had been the prime motivator behind the development of modern Ibrox.

At the resumption of the Champions League in March Rangers travelled to Bruges. A misshit clearance from Mikhailichenko allowed Daniel Amokachi to score before the interval but Huistra levelled the score in the 74th minute from a McCall pass. At a wet Ibrox Rangers dominated the first half against Bruges and were 1-0 ahead through a Durrant goal in the 39th minute from a precise Steven pass, and Hateley was harshly sent off for raising an arm to a Belgian defender. Lorenzo Staelens equalised early in the second half but a high cross from Scott Nisbet in the 71st minute deceived keeper Dany Verlinden. The ball swerved in the air and bounced over the keeper's head, and his frantic efforts could not stop it going over the goalline. Rangers claimed the tie 2-1.

The fifth game – against Marseille – was now a crucial one, with both sides sure of reaching the Final if they were to win. Early in the match a David Robertson error allowed Frank Sauzee in to score but a splendid Durrant strike early in the second half levelled the score. Rangers pulled into defence and the game ended 1-1.

The last two games were now critical. If both Marseille and Rangers won, then Marseille would reach the Final thanks to their superior goal tally against Rangers. Rangers had to beat CSKA Moscow at Ibrox and hope that Marseille went down to Bruges in Belgium. An early Boksic goal gave Marseille victory while Rangers, and in particular McCoist, missed several simple chances against CSKA whose keeper Plotnikov was in fine form, to end with a disappointing 0-0 draw. The absence of the suspended Hateley did not help

Ian Durrant and Mark Hateley celebrate Hateley's opening goal against Leeds United at Elland Road

the team's cause. Although they were unbeaten in all six league games and ten European games in total, Rangers had narrowly failed to reach the European Cup Final, where Marseille surprisingly beat AC Milan to collect the trophy.

Rangers duly claimed their fifth league title in succession with an away win on 1 May over Airdrie, McSwegan scoring the only goal of the game, and ended the season nine points ahead of second-placed Aberdeen. They also reached the Scottish Cup final, held at Celtic Park because of reconstruction work at Hampden, to play Aberdeen. McCoist had broken his leg in an international match against Portugal and was watching from the stand, his leg in plaster, and Trevor Steven and Gary Stevens were also injured. Young midfielder Neil Murray opened the scoring for Rangers in the 22nd minute after an error by Aberdeen defender Brian Irvine and Hateley made it two with a low shot from a tight angle near half-time. Aberdeen pulled one back through a Lee Richardson deflected shot towards the end and a tired Rangers, feeling the effects of a long season, defended grimly. However, they held off the Dons to win 2-1 and had again captured the 'treble'. Rangers' team at Celtic Park was: Goram, McCall, Robertson, Gough, McPherson, Brown, Murray, Ferguson, Durrant, Hateley, Huistra.

Over the 64 competitive games played that season Rangers had triumphantly demonstrated that they were unarguably Scotland's leading side, and Walter Smith had proven himself to be a manager fit to be compared with the great managers of Rangers' past. Hateley and McCoist scored 88 goals between them and McCoist had again picked up the Golden Boot as Europe's leading goalscorer.

The exertions of a long and draining season, however, had left Smith with injury problems as season 1993-94 began. Such influential players as Goram, McCoist, Robertson, McCall, Brown and Stevens were all carrying injuries and, although Smith had acquired the big striker Duncan Ferguson from Dundee United for £3.75 million, his squad was stretched and tired. They were back in the European Cup and played Bulgaria's Levski Sofia in the first qualifying round of the tournament, with the first leg played at Ibrox on 15 September.

Rangers were on top throughout the first half but spurned a number of chances to put the game out of Levski's reach. At the interval all they had to show for their dominance was a 1-0 lead, scored by Dave McPherson from a Durrant cross. Shortly after the restart Hateley headed in a second but Borimorov took advantage of a poor Hateley clearance to head past keeper Ally Maxwell, in for the injured Goram. Almost immediately Hateley headed in another to make the score 3-1. With eight minutes to go a mistake by Duncan Ferguson allowed Todorov to head home for a final 3-2 result. A night of wasteful finishing and error-strewn defensive play had given Rangers much to do in Sofia if they were to progress to the second round.

On a wet Bulgarian evening Rangers began well but went behind in the 36th minute, when Sirakov scored from the edge of the box. Rangers equalised on the stroke of half-time when Durrant headed in off the post and the keeper. Instead of keeping the pressure on Levski Rangers opted for defence in the second half, although a McPherson shot with fifteen minutes to go was brilliantly saved by keeper Nikolov. As the game went into injury time Rangers seemed to have done enough to gain an aggregate victory. Then, following a quick attack from Levski, Todorov smashed in a spectacular volley off the underside of the bar and Rangers were again out of the European Cup in the early stages. Their sloppy errors at Ibrox and the over-cautious nature of their tactics in Sofia had contributed to their European embarrassment.

In the League Cup the Light Blues defeated Aberdeen in the quarter-final, thanks to an Ian Ferguson extra time goal. In the semi-final against Celtic, undergoing one of the most troubled and unsettled periods in the Parkhead club's history, Huistra was sent off but a 65th minute goal from Hateley, supplied by a Durrant cross gave them victory and a place in the final against Hibernian, played at Celtic Park. With nine minutes remaining of the final and the score 1-1, McCoist, now recovering from his broken leg, volleyed in an athletic overhead bicycle kick which left Hibs' keeper Jim Leighton a spectator, and Rangers won 2-1.

In the league Rangers claimed the title for the sixth year in succession, finishing three points ahead of Aberdeen and four clear of Motherwell, assisted partly by the arrival of Gordon Durie in November from Tottenham Hotspur for £1 million. A fast, powerful striker, Durie was to score several important league goals in the season and compensate for the frequent absences of McCoist, although the Scottish Player of the Year was his striking partner Hateley who weighed in with a total of 30 competitive goals.

A second 'treble' in succession was in sight when Rangers met Dundee United in the Scottish Cup final. United had had an indifferent season, finishing in sixth place in the league, and were the underdogs. However, in the 47th minute at Hampden David McPherson underhit a backpass to keeper Ally Maxwell, who rushed out to clear. The ball hit Christian Dailly who rolled it behind Maxwell along the goalline and it rebounded off the far post where Craig Brewster was on hand to score. It was a freakish goal but one which ensured that the Cup went to Tannadice for the first time in the club's history.

The Rangers career of the talented striker Duncan Ferguson had not been the success the club had hoped for. Dogged by off-the-pitch incidents, including prosecutions for assault,

Ferguson was also injury-prone. In his 24 appearances he scored only five goals. His nadir occurred on 16 April at Ibrox when, in a match against Raith Rovers, he head-butted the Raith player John McStay. Although the referee allowed Ferguson to remain on the pitch the SFA banned him for twelve matches based on the television evidence. Worse was to come when Glasgow's Prosecutor Fiscal charged the player with assault. The fact that Ferguson was on probation when he committed the offence did not help his case and he ended up, in October of the following year, with a three-month sentence in Barlinnie Prison. In September he went to Everton on loan and subsequently was transferred to the Liverpool club for £4.1 million. David Murray said 'Every penny will be given to Walter to buy more quality players'. The following month David McPherson also left the club, signing for Hearts for £400,000, while central defender Alan McLaren made the reverse journey for £2 million. Another departure was Oleg Kuznetsov, who had played only thirty-five competitive games in four seasons for Rangers, to Maccabi Haifa.

Smith also added to the international flavour of his side with two new major signings in the summer of 1994. French international sweeper Basile Boli, scorer of Marseille's winning goal in the 1993 European Cup final against AC Milan, joined from the French club for £1.8 million. Boli was to spend only one season at Ibrox but never really gelled in the team, partly because he was played out of position in central defence or as a full back. His critical comments about Rangers to a French magazine did not endear him to Smith and helped lead to his quick departure. The other signing, however, was to become one of the finest players ever to wear the famous blue jersey.

Brian Laudrup was an explosively fast winger with delicate ball control and the ability to turn defences inside out as well as score impressive goals. His father Finn had been a Danish international and his older brother Michael was also an international, with spells at Juventus, Real Madrid and Barcelona. Brian had begun his career with Brondby before joining Bayer Uerdingen and then Bayern Munich. He then moved to Fiorentina for £2 million and joined Rangers in July 1994 for £3.5 million after Fiorentina were relegated from Serie A. Laudrup had been the recipient of abuse from many Fiorentina fans who made him the scapegoat for the club's failure, and a move away from Italy seemed sensible. Ibrox beckoned and the Dane took up the challenge.

In spite of Smith's determination to build up his squad and to challenge for major European honours, season 1994-95 began disastrously. UEFA had changed the Champions League format so that only twenty-four clubs were allowed into the tournament. Although the break-up of the former Soviet Union had led to the proliferation of new independent

states and therefore the old structure was inappropriate for the competition, this was not the overriding reason. The big European clubs were worried about early elimination from the competition and the negative commercial effects that this may have. Not wishing the big clubs to form a breakaway league, UEFA decided to ensure that they all had a decent, profitable run in the tournament, and seeded the top seven clubs and the previous year's winner in four groups of four clubs each. The winners from Italy, France, Spain, Germany and England would qualify automatically for the group stage while smaller countries, such as Scotland, would have to pre-qualify. In August 1994 Rangers were drawn against Greek champions AEK Athens.

In the first leg in Athens Rangers, fielding a new and unfamiliar 3-5-2 formation, were taken apart by AEK and were lucky to come away with only a 2-0 defeat. 'I adjusted the formation to accommodate the players we required' said Smith but his tactics were found wanting. The situation did not improve at a wet Ibrox when the Greeks took a 1-0 lead just before the interval and outplayed Rangers who failed to score. The Greek side's clever possession football won out over Rangers' long-ball tactics. The main reason for importing Boli and Laudrup had been success in Europe – and the accompanying revenue of around £5 million – and yet again Rangers had tumbled out at the first hurdle. Worse was to come. They were then knocked out of the League Cup 2-1 at Ibrox by Falkirk and, in the first Old Firm match of the season, were beaten again, two goals from McStay and Collins doing the damage at Ibrox.

Murray attempted to quell the supporters' discontent after three home defeats by saying 'this internal squabbling and bickering only provides the canon fodder for the media and other fans of other football clubs to criticise Rangers'. In the Scottish league three points were now available for a win, and Rangers began to atone for their wretched start to the season. Although they were beset by injuries – to McCoist, Gough, Durie, Boli, Brown and Ferguson – by the end of October they were two points ahead of second-equal Hibs and Motherwell, thanks to a 3-1 defeat of Celtic at Parkhead. With Laudrup in typically sparkling form and new signing McLaren solid in defence, Rangers opened the scoring with a Hateley strike from the edge of the box and Hateley claimed another just on half time. Laudrup rounded keeper Marshall to score the third half way through the second period. Rangers maintained an unbeaten run till the end of the year and by the end of January they were 14 points ahead of second-placed Hibs.

They drew with Celtic 1-1 on 4 January and two goals from Huistra, on his last game before joining San Frecce Hiroshima in the Japanese J-League, helped them to a 3-2 win over Falkirk two weeks later. They ended the month

Brian Laudrup, the 'king of the wing'

with a 1-0 win over Hearts, the goal coming from Charlie Miller in the 1st minute. The defence had been strengthened by the acquisition of Alex Cleland from Dundee United for £750,000, but they were surprisingly eliminated from the Scottish Cup by the Tynecastle side in the fourth round. Two-nil down at half time, Rangers pulled back through Laudrup and Durie early in the second half but the Tynecastle side scored two more.

On March 23rd Davie Cooper died of a brain haemorrhage at the tragically young age of 39. The outside-left, who had been such an Ibrox favourite in his time at the club, collapsed while making a coaching video with Charlie Nicholas at Clyde's stadium and died the following day in hospital. Two of his closest friend at Rangers – Derek Johnstone and Ally McCoist – were at the hospital when the decision was made to switch off the life support machine, and McCoist was a pall bearer at his funeral. Cooper's death was mourned not only by Rangers supporters, who decked the Copland gates with flowers and scarves, but also by all Scottish football fans. Cooper had spent twelve illustrious years at Ibrox before departing for Motherwell for £50,000 in 1989 and he had won three league titles, two Scottish Cups and seven Scottish league Cups in his Rangers career. The *Rangers News* printed a poem in its 5 April edition, written by William Mavers, commemorating Cooper, one verse of which reads:

'You dazzled us with brilliance, defied all logic, sense

'The man's a Scot! They don't have skill!', but you got your recompense

The world was your stage but home held your heart, and your loyalty was true

And when they speak of wingers down Govan way, all remember you'.

Although the Light Blues stuttered in March, with two draws and a defeat, they won their first two games in April and, on 16 April at Ibrox they won their seventh successive league title. Durie put the Light Blues ahead with a header in the 24th minute and Hibs drew level just before half time. With five minutes remaining Durrant played a one-two with Charlie Miller and scored the second. Two minutes later a magnificent Laudrup run culminated in the Dane finding substitute Mikhailichenko who tucked away the third. As throughout the rest of the season Laudrup – 'The King of the Wing' – was in scintillating form and the crowd rose to salute the player whose skill, surging runs, pin-point crosses and goals had done so much to retain the title at Ibrox. He was deservedly voted Player of the Year by both the players and the Scottish football writers. The Rangers team at Ibrox that day was Thomson,

Clelland, Brown (Murray), Gough, McLaren, Durrant, Steven, Miller, Durie (Mikhailichenko), Hateley, Laudrup. Rangers finished the season fifteen points ahead of Motherwell

In the close season Smith made the most audacious and risky signing of his career when he acquired Paul Gascoigne from Lazio for £4.5 million. Injuries, suspensions and controversy had coloured Gascoigne's career, but he was an enormous talent and at his best a player of genius. Doubts were expressed about his fitness – he had played only fifty games in the previous three seasons – and his tendency to indiscipline and erratic behaviour on and off the pitch, but thousands of Rangers fans crowded outside the main entrance to Ibrox to welcome the man they felt sure could link up with the irresistible skills of Laudrup and the defensive reliability of Gough and Goram to bring further success to the club. Gascoigne signed a three-year contract on £12,000 per week and became the highest paid player ever in Scottish football history. Other close season arrivals included Stephen Wright, a Scottish international right-back, from Aberdeen and Oleg Salenko a Russian international striker from Valencia. Salenko became a footballing household name at the 1994 World Cup finals, when he scored five goals in his country's 6-1 defeat of Cameroon. Gordan Petric, a Yugoslav international central defender from Dundee United, made up the list of incomers.

Rangers entered the 1995/96 season with the twin aims of edging closer to equalling Celtic's 'nine in a row' sequence of league wins established by Jock Stein's team of the 1960s and 1970s and having a decent run in the Champions League group stage. Symbolically important though overtaking Celtic's record would be, however, David Murray had spent around £10 million over the summer in strengthening his team and this would not be recouped solely by success at the domestic level. Although the club had raised money through various financial initiatives and had plans to sell 40,000 season tickets, much of this revenue was allocated to ground improvements and to cover general salaries and expenses. A good performance in Europe would help pay off the Gascoigne transfer fee and leave the club with surplus funds for further developments. Europe, then, had to be the priority. As Murray stated in *Rangers News*: 'Two years without the Champions League has meant no money for the club. We need to play in Europe from a football and financial point of view.'

They had to overcome Anorthosis Famagusta of Cyprus in the qualifying round of the European Cup. A Gordon Durie goal saw them through an awkward tie at Ibrox but they had to perform well against the tough Famagusta side in Cyprus to achieve a 0-0 draw and proceed to the group stage, which included Steaua Bucharest, Borussia Dortmund and Italian champions Juventus.

Paul Gascoigne arrives at Ibrox

Their first game was away in Romania to Steaua. Firm defending by Rangers, in particular Goram and Gough, kept the game goalless until the 84th minute when Daniel Prodan volleyed Steaua's winner. Earlier, Alan McLaren had been sent off for an off-the-ball incident. Borussia at Ibrox were next. The Germans scored first through a Heiko Herrlich header but Gough met a clever Gascoigne free kick with his head in the 62nd minute to level. Within six minutes Martin Kree headed Borussia back into the lead but Ferguson headed in a deflected Gascoigne shot four minutes later to make the final score 2-2. Rangers had played with passion and skill but an away defeat and a home draw were not the most auspicious start to the European campaign.

After several years in the doldrums, and having undergone and resolved boardroom and ownership crises, Celtic were back in real contention in Scottish football. Under the managership of Tommy Burns and guided from midfield by Paul McStay and John Collins, the old rivals were to be the main threat to Rangers this coming season. On their first meeting, in the quarter-final of the League Cup, Celtic had most of the early possession but a McCoist header from a Gascoine lob in the 75th minute – McCoist's 20th Old Firm goal – was enough to eliminate Celtic from

the competition. (McCoist had also scored his 300th competitive league goal in the opening game of the season). Rangers also won their next tussle two weeks later in the league at Parkhead, Salenko making both goals, the first headed in by Cleland, his first goal for Rangers, and the second for Gascoigne, via a McCoist cross.

In the league, October was a good month for the Light Blues. Having beaten one main rival, Celtic, they also beat another, Aberdeen, 1-0 the following week at Pittodrie. The same month saw them crush Hearts 4-1 at Ibrox and Partick Thistle 4-0 away, helped by a Durie hat-trick. In the League Cup semi-final, however, on 25 October they succumbed to two Davie Dodds goals at Ibrox and went down 2-1 to Aberdeen. By the end of October they were three points ahead of Celtic.

On 18 October they travelled to the Stadia Delle Alpi in Turin to play Juventus, coached by Marcello Lippi and containing such world-class players as Alessandro Del Piero and Gianluca Vialli. Rangers were accompanied by around 4,000 supporters but many must have wished they had stayed at home as Juventus were 3-0 ahead after only 23 minutes. A frustrated Cleland, bemused by the twisting and turning of Del Piero, kicked out at the Italian and was dismissed. Without Gascoigne and Laudrup Rangers were bereft of ideas and overrun by the speed, teamwork and

Ian Ferguson equalises for Rangers with a header against Borussia Dortmund at Ibrox

individual skill of the Italians. The game ended 4-1 – Gough scoring towards the end – although Juventus's dominance was such that the score could easily have been higher.

The second game at Ibrox on 1 November was no better. Although Rangers were missing Steven and Laudrup to injury and Durie, Cleland and McLaren to suspension, they played with more commitment than in Turin. But once again they could not match the Italians' fluency and flair and a 4-0 defeat was a fair reflection on the difference between the sides. Smith said 'it has been a bit of a nightmare for us trying to get a team on the park' but Rangers had been outclassed. With only one point from four European games, Rangers would be extremely fortunate to proceed further in the tournament.

Their fifth European game was played three weeks later at Ibrox against Steaua Bucharest and Rangers had to win. Although Gascoigne demonstrated his class by running half the length of the pitch to score in the 32nd minute, a goal by Ilie twenty minutes later produced a drawn result and, when Juventus lost at home to Borussia that same evening, Rangers were out of the Champions League. Smith admitted 'the two games against Juventus effectively killed off our hopes'.

Paul Gascoigne scores his and Rangers' second goal against Aberdeen in April 1996

They still, however, had one more game to play – against Borussia in Dortmund – in the tournament, in early December. In sub-zero temperatures, Laudrup put them ahead in the 10th minute but six minutes later Andy Moller equalised. Early in the second half Riedle scored another for Borussia and Gascoigne was sent off for a second yellow card, Durie levelled the tie with six minutes to go.

Back in the Scottish league, they drew with Celtic 3-3 in a frantic game at Ibrox on 19 November. Laudrup, McCoist and a Tosh McKinlay own goal got the points for Rangers. They were five points ahead of Celtic (who still had a game in hand) by Xmas and increased their lead to eight with a crushing 7-0 demolition of Hibs on 30 December, Durie scoring four of them. During the match, referee Doug Smith dropped his yellow card which was picked up by Gascoigne and waved at the official in a mock caution. The referee didn't see the funny side and booked the Rangers prankster.

In the New Year Old Firm match the score ended 0-0 and Rangers were now eight points ahead of Celtic, although

Rangers' undersoil heating had enabled them to play their last two matches while Parkhead had been unplayable. Celtic, therefore, had two games in hand. Four days later McCoist scored twice in Rangers 4-0 win at Brockville against Falkirk and equalled Bob McPhail's 230 league goal record. By the end of January, however, after a shock 3-0 defeat by Hearts at Ibrox, only their second league defeat of the season, Celtic had caught up and were now only one point behind Rangers.

The two clubs' next meeting was at Ibrox on 17 March and was seen as the league decider. McLaren put Rangers ahead in the 41st minute but Hughes' header equalised the game in the 87th minute. Celtic's Jackie McNamara was sent off and Gascoigne received his sixteenth caution of the season for a bad tackle on Andreas Thom. Nothing had been decided and Rangers still led by three points.

Six foot four inch Danish international striker Erik Bo

Andersen had arrived from Danish club Aarlborg at the beginning of March for £1.4 million, and he made his Rangers debut in the club's 2-0 away win against Hibs on 3 March. He then scored twice in the 3-2 win over Falkirk later in the month and also scored a hat-trick in the 5-0 win over Partick Thistle on 10 April.

Rangers met Aberdeen on 28 April at Ibrox needing a victory to retain the Scottish Premier league title for the eighth season in succession. The game was a personal triumph for Gascoigne. Although the Dons went into the lead after 20 minutes through Brian Irvine, Gascoigne shimmied his way through the Dons defence to equalise one minute later with a shot from a tight angle over keeper Michael Watt. With nine minutes remaining Gascoigne scored another when he ran on the break from ten yards inside his own half, holding off defenders' attentions, to place a firm left-foot shot past Watt. With four minutes to go Durie was fouled in the penalty area and Gascoigne took the penalty to claim his hat-trick in a frenzy of delighted celebration. The following day he was named Player of the Year for his influential and often inspirational play throughout the season and his remarkable tally of 19 goals from midfield. In his first season in Scotland, he had indelibly marked his name on football north of the border. Rangers' 3-0 win over Kilmarnock in the last league game of the season gave them the championship by four points over Celtic.

There remained the matter of the 'double'. Rangers had progressed through to the Scottish Cup semi-final (beating Highland League team Keith 10-1 in the third round) and faced Celtic at Hampden on 7 April. In the 43rd minute Celtic keeper Gordon Marshall could not hold a Robertson shot and McCoist was on hand to slot in the ball at the far post. Midway through the second half an interchange between Laudrup and Durie ended with the Dane lobbing Marshall for Rangers' second. Pierre van Hoydonk pulled back a Celtic consolation with ten minutes to go but Rangers were in the final and had ended Celtic's run of 30 undefeated domestic games.

The opponents at Hampden on 18 May were Hearts. Laudrup scored first with a volley in the 37th minute, and the game remained at 1-0 at half-time. In the 49th minute a half-hit cross from Laudrup was fumbled by Hearts keeper Gilles Rousset who allowed it to squeeze between his legs and roll across the line. Laudrup, in quite magnificent form, then made three goals for Durie within twenty minutes and the cup had come to Ibrox in a 5-1 victory. Durie's was the first hat-trick in a Scottish Cup final for 24 years and Laudrup was rightly awarded the man of the match for his brilliant display. Durie finished the season with 23 goals, the top scorer at Ibrox. The team was: Goram, Cleland,

Ally McCoist (9) scores past Celtic's Gordon Marshall in the 1996 Scottish Cup semi-final

Robertson, Gough, McLaren, Brown, Durie, Gascoigne, Ferguson (Durrant), McCall, Laudrup.

The 'nine in a row' was now the target. Smith moved again into Europe to bolster the squad in the summer of 1996. Swedish international central defender Joachim Bjorklund moved from Vicenza in Serie A for £2.2 million while Jorge Albertz arrived from Hamburg for £4 million. A tall, ginger-haired left-sided midfielder, Albertz 'The Hammer' possessed a ferocious left-foot shot, particularly from the dead ball, and was to score some thundering goals in his time at Ibrox.

Ex-manager Jock Wallace died in July from the effects of Parkinson's Disease at the early age of 60. Wallace had brought two 'trebles' to the club and Smith said 'he will always be remembered as a great Rangers man and that may be all he ever wanted.'

Rangers were again forced to qualify for a place in the Champions League. The Bosman ruling the previous year had found that the existing transfer regulations contravened the free movement of players between EEC states. Players now had the automatic right to leave clubs at the end of their contracts. As importantly, UEFA were forced to scrap the 'three foreigners' rule, which meant that nationality was no longer a barrier to selection.

The qualifying obstacle this year was Russia's Alania Vladikavaz. At Ibrox in early August, with defenders McLaren, Craig Moore and Robertson all injured and Gascoigne suspended for both legs, McInnes, McCoist and Petricall scored in the 3-1 win, having come back from 1-0 down at half time. McCoist's goal equalled Rangers' record individual tally in European football, that of Ralph Brand's twelve. A 7-2 hammering of Alania in Russia, with McCoist claiming a hat-trick within the first eighteen minutes, ensured that Rangers qualified for the Champions League, alongside Auxerre, Grasshoppers Zurich and Ajax.

Having won their first three league games in August, September was a good month domestically for the Light

Blues. In the league they beat Hearts, who had four of their team controversially dismissed by referee Gerry Evans, 3-0 and Kilmarnock 4-0. In the latter match Gascoigne scored two, with the others coming from Peter Van Vossen, an experienced Dutch forward who had arrived in the Spring from Istanbulspor in exchange for the unsettled Oleg Salenko. They also overcame Hibs in the League Cup quarter-final, Van Vossen again finding the net twice. As was becoming the norm, however, they could not replicate their domestic form in Europe.

They were outplayed and beaten 3-0 in their first test in Group A by Grasshoppers Zurich in Switzerland, and the score could have been higher had it not been for the presence of Andy Goram. They did little better in their next game. At Ibrox they were 2-0 down to Auxerre by the 68th minute and Gascoigne's 71st minute header from a Laudrup cross brought some consolation but no points. Worse was to come in mid-October in Amsterdam. Missing the injured Durie, McCoist and Andersen, and with Theo Snelders replacing Goram, Rangers were 1-0 down on the half-hour mark, when Gascoigne, suffering a rush of blood to his head, unaccountably kicked Winston Bogarde in an off-the-ball incident, much to the consternation and anger of his teammates. He was sent off and Rangers crumbled to a 4-1 defeat against superior opposition, with substitute Ian Durrant scoring towards the end. Smith commented 'our chances of qualification appear slim now'.

David Murray blamed Rangers' failures on Europe on domestic pressures, complaining that 'this nine-in-a-row achievement has become a monkey on our backs'. Had Gascoigne managed to curb his behaviour, however, at least a point may well have been achieved from the Ajax game. Gascoigne was in even deeper trouble when he arrived back in Glasgow. The press were printing stories concerning Gascoigne assaulting his wife Sheryl in an altercation at the Gleneagles Hotel. In spite of the Geordie's erratic brilliance on the pitch, many fans felt that his behaviour was unacceptable and that he had no place in a club like Rangers. The club, however, refused to take a stand on the matter and director Donald Findlay QC stated 'We are not going to interfere. It is an entirely private matter.' Gascoigne's talents were critical in this most important of years.

Rangers entered their fourth game – against Ajax at Ibrox on 30 October – without the suspended Gascoigne, Gough, Cleland, and Moore and the injured Durie, McCoist, and Andersen. Arnold Scholten scored in the 34th minute but the young, relatively inexperienced Light Blues could not find the net and the game ended 1-0 in Ajax's favour. Rangers had suffered four successive defeats in Europe, the worst record of any of the sixteen teams in the tournament and the worst

Above: Brian Laudrup opens the scoring for Rangers in the 1996 Scottish Cup final

Below: Hearts keeper Gilles Rousset after fumbling Laudrup's shot

Bottom: Gordon Durie scores for Rangers in the 1996 Scottish Cup final

European record in the club's history.

Although they were now out of the competition, two matches remained in the group. In early November on a freezing night at Ibrox, Rangers finally found European form. McCoist opened the scoring against Grasshoppers with a 65th minute penalty and converted an Albertz pass to score from 20 yards six minutes later. The penalty was McCoist's first goal in four years in the Champions League and equalled Willie Wallace's 18-goal Scottish record in Europe. Rangers took the tie 2-1. In the final game in Auxerre, a Gough header was their only consolation in a 2-1 defeat.

They could now concentrate on the domestic 'treble'. Financially, European failure did not seem to be affecting the club's performance. In September David Murray had announced record trading profits of £7 million on a turnover of £30 million, 55% up from the previous year. The chairman said: 'Securing the Double helped make season 95/96 outstanding. But while our dominance at domestic level was extremely satisfying, we continue to strive for greater success at the highest level in Europe.'

The Light Blues beat Celtic 2-0 in the season's first Old Firm encounter in mid-October, the goals coming from Gough and Gascoigne. A second-half hat-trick from Gascoigne in their 5-0 defeat of Motherwell helped them to pole position in the league, two points ahead of a resurgent Celtic. A poor draw against Raith Rovers in early November allowed Celtic to go top by virtue of one goal difference, the first time the Parkhead side had topped the league for fourteen months. Their second meeting on 14 November at a packed Parkhead saw Celtic pour into attack. However, in the 7th minute Laudrup collected a poor pass from Brian O'Neil, advanced on goal and scored from 20 yards. An exciting game continued with Celtic pressing forward and Rangers breaking on the counter. Laudrup, having another superb game, clashed with Celtic keeper Stewart Kerr in the 69th minute and was awarded a penalty which Gascoigne failed to convert. Then Van Vossen missed an open goal when it was easier to score. In the 85th minute Gough brought down Simon Donnelly but Goram saved van Hoydonk's penalty effort, turning the Dutchman's effort round his right post. Rangers were now 3 points clear.

In the League Cup, Rangers had trounced Dunfermline 6-1 in the semi-final and faced Hearts on 24 November in the final. In a splendid, attacking match, McCoist claimed two in the first half and Hearts' Fulton pulled one back just on half time from a cross from the industrious Neil McCann. John Robertson equalised ten minutes after half time but a splendid shot from Gascoigne made the score 3-2 in the 64th minute. Two minutes later, Gascoigne again, playing a

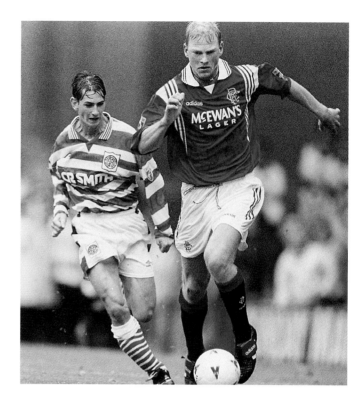

Above: Jorge Albertz moves away from Celtic's Jackie McNamara

Below: Paul Gascoigne scores against Auxerre at Ibrox

Bottom: Gascoigne sent off against Ajax in Amsterdam after fouling Winston Bogarde (on ground)

Gascoigne claims his second and Rangers' fourth goal in the 4-3 League Cup final win over Hearts in November 1996

one-two with Charlie Miller, shot over the diving keeper for his second and, although Davie Weir headed in Hearts' third in the final minute, Rangers had their first trophy of the season. Smith commented 'It was a terrific match... Gascoigne scored two great goals which effectively won the match for us'.

By December Rangers were beginning to put some distance between themselves and Celtic in the league and by Xmas they were a massive 14 points ahead, although Celtic had three games in hand. In their 4-3 victory over Hibs at Ibrox McCoist set a new post-War league goalscoring record of 265. Their wins that month also included 3-0 against Aberdeen at Pittodrie, 3-1 against Dunfermline, 4-2 against Kilmarnock (Andersen scoring a hat-trick) 4-1 away against Hearts and a 4-0 result on Boxing Day against Raith Rovers.

In early January the Ibrox dressing room was hit by a flu virus. Gough, Laudrup and Gascoigne were all absent on 2 January for the New Year game against Celtic at Ibrox, but Rangers ended with a 3-1 win, their ninth successive victory over Celtic. Albertz opened the scoring in the 9th minute with a typical free kick through the Celtic wall from 25 yards, measured by Sky TV at an unstoppable 80 mph. Di Canio replied for Celtic midway through the second half but, in the last seven minutes, Andersen, on for McCoist, scored twice.

The flu virus quickly spread and, the following day Walter Smith applied to the SFA for postponement of the forthcoming game against Hibs, producing medical certificates for no less than 28 of his squad. The application was disallowed but Rangers won anyway, Andersen and an Albertz penalty answering Kevin Harper's opener at Easter Road. In the middle of the month, in the 3-1 away win over Motherwell, Sebastian Rozental made his first appearance in the blue jersey as substitute. The first South American to play for Rangers, Rozental was a Chilean international

striker whose signing had been delayed by work permit problems. His career at Ibrox was to be badly affected by cruciate ligament problems.

On 22 January David Murray announced a far-reaching development in the financial structuring of the club. Murray had reduced his share in the club from 83% to 61% and Bahamas-based millionaire Joe Lewis had invested £40 million in Rangers through his English National Investment Company (ENIC). The investment gave ENIC a 25.1% ownership of the club and was the biggest-ever single financial investment in a British football club. The club was now valued at £160 million. Murray said 'I am excited about the opportunities which partnership with ENIC will bring and believe that Rangers is now in a much stronger position to realise our ambitions for footballing and commercial success.' The money was to be used for clearing bank borrowings, building an hotel, financing a new training centre and acquiring new players. As an indication of how Murray had changed the financial and corporate nature of Rangers, he had bought the club for £6.5 million only nine years earlier.

Australian defender Tony Vidmar signed from NAC Breda in mid-February on a Bosman transfer but would not join until July. During February and March Rangers' injury problems – including Gascoine, Goram, McCall and Wright – were affecting their performances and by the time they faced Celtic at Parkhead on 16 March, their lead had been whittled down to five points. Celtic had also put Rangers out of the Scottish Cup 2-0 at the quarter-final stage nine days beforehand with Rangers putting up a dismal performance. This was a crucial game for both clubs. In an attempt to mitigate his injury crisis and with no fully-fit striker available, Smith brought back 35-year-old Mark Hateley from Queen's Park Rangers. He also played Andy Dibble, on loan from Manchester City, in goal for Goram.

Durrant scored the only goal of the game when he lobbed the ball over Stewart Kerr. Hateley, who had an influential game, was sent off in the 67th minute after an altercation with Kerr and Celtic's Malky MacKay was also sent off thirteen minutes later. At full time some of the Rangers players went into a huddle – a practice Celtic had adopted some years earlier – and were accused of bad sportsmanship by a furious Tommy Burns. Smith defended his players' actions, saying, with some logic, 'if Celtic can do it and no-one complains, why not Rangers?'. The Light Blues were now five points ahead of Celtic.

By the end of April Rangers' lead had stretched to twelve points. When they met Motherwell at Ibrox on 5 May, they needed only one point for the title and for the 'nine in a row'. Motherwell, unfortunately for the 50,000 over-

Brian Laudrup (11) watches as Ian Durrant's lob eludes Celtic keeper Stewart Kerr in March 1997 at Parkhead

Year for the second time, an honour previously received only by John Greig and Sandy Jardine.

Early departures from the club at the end of the season were Richard Gough, off to team up with Mo Johnston in the Kansas City Wizards, and David Robertson who joined Leeds United for £500,000. In an effort to maintain the momentum and improve Rangers' status in Europe, Murray had promised that Smith would have £20 million to buy in new players. Smith moved quickly to replace Gough with the purchase of defenders Lorenzo Amoruso for £3.9 million from Fiorentina and Norwegian Staale Stensaas from Rosenborg for £1.75 million. They were followed shortly after by Sergio Porrini, a £3.5 million right-back who could also play in central defence, from Juventus, Italian striker Marco Negri, a £3.5 million striker from Perugia and Antti Niemi, a Finnish international goalkeeper. Jonas Thern, a 30-year-old midfielder from Roma and Swedish international captain, and 19-year-old Gennaro ('Rino') Gattuso, a midfield player from Perugia, also arrived on Bosman transfers.

confident fans ready to celebrate at Ibrox, won the game 2-0, and attention shifted to the next game, away to Dundee United two days later. In the 11th minute at Tannadice, Charlie Miller (on in place of the injured Albertz) sent in a precise cross from the left and Laudrup met it with a diving header from ten yards which he placed to the right of keeper Sieb Dykstra. That was the only goal of the game and, at the final whistle, Rangers had finally overcome the Celtic bogey. Injured captain Gough, in tears at the emotion of the moment and the fact that his departure was imminent, collected the trophy. Thousands of fans waited outside Ibrox that evening to celebrate the return of the players and the trophy. The team that historic day was: Dibble, Cleland, Robertson, Petric, McLaren, Bjorklund, Moore, Gascoigne (McInnes), Durie, Miller, Laudrup (McCoist).

Although Hearts beat Rangers 3-1 a few days later, the Light Blues won the league by five points over Celtic and the peerless Laudrup was voted Scottish Footballer of the

After his remarkable season, Laudrup was the focus of enquiries from Manchester United, Barcelona and Ajax – the Dutch club making a £4.5 million bid – but the Dane decided to remain at Ibrox for a further season, saying 'after positive talks I have decided to complete my existing contract with Rangers'. His contract had only one year to run so Murray was effectively waving goodbye to a substantial cash injection. However, the chairman obviously believed that Laudrup's talismanic importance to the club was of greater value. In early July Gascoigne also committed his immediate future to Rangers by signing a new three-year contract. Smith stated 'I am delighted that Paul has confirmed his commitment to the talent which has joined the club'.

The new season began on 23 July when Rangers travelled north to the Faroe Islands to play GI Gotu in the European Cup first qualifying round. On a hillside in front of 2500 spectators Rangers easily won 5-0 with new boy Negri opening the scoring and Durie and McCoist claiming a brace apiece. A week later at Ibrox Negri scored two more in the 6-0 defeat of the part-timers.

In the second qualifying round they faced IFK Gothenburg. On 14 August, without the injured defenders Amoruso and Moore and missing Laudrup, Rangers were on top in the first half in an unpleasantly hot Gothenburg. However they surrendered two goals in two minutes early in the second half and a third with two minutes to go, without reply. Once again, they seemed to have failed in the European Cup. 'All the goals were the result of basic errors' fumed Smith. Rangers' departure from the tournament was confirmed a fortnight later at Ibrox in front of almost 46,000 fans when, although Charlie Miller scored in the 24th minute, Robert Andersson equalised early in the second half and Rangers could not add another.

There was still some hope of progressing in Europe, however, as UEFA had decided that teams knocked out in the second qualifying round would drop into the UEFA Cup. Drawn away against unfancied Strasbourg in the middle of September, Rangers equalised a French first-half penalty with a 49th minute penalty from Albertz but Strasbourg scored again from the spot kick. Back at Ibrox at the end of the month, another disappointing performance by Rangers saw them open the scoring, from an 11th minute Gattuso strike but a Stensaas error allowed Strasbourg to equalise in the 37th minute, and the French sealed the tie ten minutes later.

As Rangers had been eliminated from the League Cup earlier in the month 1-0 by Dundee United in the quarter-final, this result meant that, although the season had only just begun, the Light Blues had had already been knocked out of three cup tournaments. They were, however, progressing well in the league.

By the middle of October, following a 7-0 thrashing of Dunfermline, they were two points clear of the main contenders Celtic and Hearts. Much of the reason for this was the abundant goalscoring of Negri. He scored twice in two minutes in the early August 3-1 defeat of Hearts, a game which saw the return of Goram in goal, and claimed all five in the 5-1 defeat of Dundee United later in the month, becoming the first Rangers player to score that number in one game since Derek Parlane in 1974. Negri's

Top: The goal that clinched the 'nine in a row'. Brian Laudrup rises to meet a Charlie Miller cross against Dundee United in May 1997

Left: *Laudrup celebrates his goal*

Paul Gascoigne, Alan McLaren and Ally McCoist with the Scottish league trophy in May 1997

third goal – when he combined a delicate piece of juggling with a deft lob over Dykstra – was particularly memorable. In September he scored in the 3-3 draw with Aberdeen and claimed two more apiece in the defeats of St Johnstone and Kilmarnock, with another two in the 4-3 win over Hibs at Easter Road. In the Dunfermline match he added four to his tally, giving him 22 goals in the season so far.

On 14 October the 37-year-old Gough re-signed for Rangers as a replacement for Amoruso, now out with a long-term ankle injury. He signed a two-year contract, saying ' I'd love to help Rangers to ten in a row this season'. With Gough back in the side they slipped to a 2-1 away defeat against Dundee United at the end of the month, although Negri again got his name on the scoresheet. Their 4-1 win over Kilmarnock in early November, with Negri notching another hat-trick, saw the unsmiling Italian striker set a Premier Division record by scoring in ten consecutive games.

At the AGM on 28 October Smith received a standing ovation from the shareholders and then he announced his intention to retire at the end of the season. David Murray

commented ' This is the end of an exhilarating era and all the success of the last decade would certainly not have happened without Walter. He will go down as one of the greatest managers in the history of Rangers.' Immediately speculation began as to his likely successor, with such names as Kenny Dalglish, Graeme Souness and Richard Moller-Nielsen (whose son Tommy had been appointed first team coach in June) seemingly the favourites.

The first Old Firm derby of the season took place at Ibrox on 8 November with Gough scoring the only goal of the game from a Laudrup cross in the 29th minute. Eleven days later the clubs met again at Parkhead, with Laudrup and Porrini unavailable through injury. Early in the second half Gascoigne appeared to hit Morten Wieghorst on the back and the Celtic player fell over. Although it seemed accidental and not malicious, Gascoigne was sent off and later picked up a five-match ban. In the 71st minute Durie found Negri whose left-foot shot put Rangers one up. In the very last

High scoring Italian forward Marco Negri scores against Celtic at Parkhead on 19 November 1997

minute Jackie McNamara sent a high cross into the box and Stubbs headed in the equaliser. Durie was also 'sent off' in the tunnel after the match as a result of a disagreement with referee John Rowbotham.

By the end of the month Hearts were the league leaders, one point ahead of Rangers, but a 5-2 win for Rangers, featuring a Durie hat-trick, on 20 December at Tynecastle and a 4-1 defeat of Dundee United at Ibrox one week later, with two late Negri strikes, put Rangers into top position at the year's end, two points ahead of the Edinburgh team.

Gascoigne began the year in the face of more media criticism which alleged that he had been on a drinking binge with his friend Jimmy 'five bellies' Gardner over Hogmanay, in contravention of an Ibrox 48-hour drinking ban. More trouble followed for the Geordie when he was warming up as a substitute before the New Year game on 2 January when he inflamed the Celtic support by pretending to play the flute, an instrument with Orange and Loyalist connotations. He had previously done this on his first appearance at Ibrox in 1995 and had been warned about his behaviour. After the game he was disciplined by Rangers and fined two weeks wages by the club. A few days later he apologised, saying 'I fully accept that I should think twice before such actions'. A dull game was won 2-0 by Celtic, the goals coming from Burley and Lambert, and was Rangers' first defeat in 10

league games by Celtic and the first New Year fixture which Celtic had won since 1988. Rangers, however, remained league leaders by one point.

One week later a 2-0 win over Aberdeen at Ibrox maintained their lead, with Gascoigne's replacement, 19-year-old Barry Ferguson, running midfield with assured ease. By the end of February, however, Rangers had suffered an embarrassing defeat by St Johnstone – their first win over Rangers in the league for 27 years – and had drawn with Motherwell, Dunfermline, Kilmarnock and Hearts. In the Hearts game on 28 February two bad defensive errors by Bjorklund gifted the goals and Albertz saved the point with a last-minute 25 yard rocket for his second goal of the match. Rangers' title defence was stuttering and they were involved in a three-way battle with Celtic and Hearts.

In February Rangers announced that the manager to take over from Smith would be 50-year-old Dick Advocaat, previously manager of the Dutch national team and currently overseeing PSV Eindhoven. Advocaat was widely regarded as one of the finest coaches in world football. A strict disciplinarian, Advocaat dropped Ruud Gullit before the 1994 World Cup finals, prompting a walk-out from the tournament by the player. He was to take over on 1 July on a three-year contract and become the first non-Scottish manager in the history of Rangers. Murray said 'we are delighted to be able to say that the man we saw as our number one candidate will join us'. A few days later, Brian Laudrup who had been suffering from recurring injury, declared that he would be joining Chelsea at the end of the season, although 'I will do all in my power to help Rangers win a tenth successive title before I leave'.

Speculation had been rife for several months that Gascoigne was on his way south. It was no real surprise, then, that the following month saw Gazza leave for Middlesbrough for £3.5 million. In his last game, Rangers's 2-1 win over St Johnstone at Ibrox on 21 March, he came on as a substitute with twenty minutes to go and received a loud and affectionate ovation from the Rangers support. Gascoigne, who had spent much of the season nursing injuries and was frequently absent through suspension, nonetheless was still regarded by the Ibrox fans as one of the greats in the club's modern history. Smith was criticised by many who felt it was a mistake to offload their playmaker at such a critical stage in the season, although the deal was good business for Rangers.

By the end of March, Rangers and Celtic were neck and neck in the league, level top with 63 points. They were both dropping points, Rangers most recently going down 2-1 to Motherwell in the middle of the month, and the battle seemed as if it would go to the wire. Their final league meeting was at Ibrox on 12 April. In the 24th minute, Thern volleyed in from 25 yards from a misplaced Rieper header to put Rangers ahead, and halfway through the second half Albertz ran from deep, outpacing Burley and Stubbs, to smash home the second. Although McCoist missed several chances, Rangers won 2-0 and went back to the top of the league.

The clubs had met each other the previous week in the Scottish Cup semi-final at Celtic Park. Rangers had needed a replay to get past Motherwell in the fourth round and they also had to play Dundee twice in the quarter-final, with the

Dick Advocaat

ageless McCoist scoring both goals in the 2-1 replay win. In the semi-final Goram was on magnificent form to keep out the Celtic attack, producing particularly outstanding saves from Larsson, Burley and Donnelly. His defensive endeavours were ably assisted by Gough and Amoruso, on as a substitute for Petric in the 20th minute and finally back from injury nine months after his arrival at Ibrox. In the 72nd minute a McCoist header from an Albertz cross gave Rangers the advantage, and with two minutes to go Albertz on a run shot over keeper Jonathan Gould. Burley added one for Celtic in the dying seconds

Rangers' title aspirations were hit by a 1-0 away defeat at Aberdeen on 19 April. A below-par display display by the Light Blues was compounded by the dismissal of Amoruso for an innocuous push on Eoin Jess.

At the beginning of May Celtic were one point ahead of Rangers with two games to play. Rangers met Kilmarnock at Ibrox on the 2nd and were beaten 1-0 by an injury time goal from Ally Mitchell. Celtic played Dunfermline the next day, fully expecting to be crowned league leaders, but they also faltered and allowed Dunfermline to equalise with only seven minutes left. The championship race was to go to the final games. On 9 May Laudrup scored a magnificent goal in the 31st minute against Dundee United at Tannadice. In the 52nd minute McCall weaved his way through the defence and was brought down in the box. Albertz sent the keeper the wrong way from the ensuing penalty. United scored a consolation, and Albertz was dismissed for kicking out at Steven Thompson with six minutes remaining and would miss the Cup final.

A 2-1 win was academic, however, as Celtic beat St Johnstone at Parkhead and won the title by two points. The 'ten in a row' dream was over.

On 16 May Rangers and Hearts met in the Scottish Cup final. In the first minute Ian Ferguson was judged to have fouled Steve Fulton in the box and Colin Cameron converted from the spot, although many spectators felt that the penalty was a harsh one. Early in the second half a long clearance from Rousset found Stephane Adam who evaded Amoruso to score Hearts' second. With Rangers on the attack and Hearts in defence, McCoist came on as a substitute and pulled one back for Rangers in the 80th minute. With four minutes to go, McCoist was brought down by Davie Weir apparently in the penalty box but the referee awarded a free-kick on the edge of the area. Laudrup could not take advantage of the kick and Hearts had won their first Scottish Cup for 42 years. This was the first season in eleven years that no major trophy had come to Ibrox, and new man Advocaat was determined that this depressing state of affairs would not last long.

Chapter Ten:

THE LITTLE GENERAL: 1998-2002

As soon as Advocaat ('the little general') took over the reins at Ibrox he began to build a new team. Out went old stagers McCoist, scorer of 355 goals in his fifteen years at Ibrox, and Durrant to Kilmarnock, Van Vossen to Feyenoord, Bjorklund to Valencia and McCall back to his old club Bradford City. 'The Goalie' Goram, a nickname which testified to his near-constant presence in the Rangers goal over seven years, also left to join Motherwell. Goram seemed to have a hex on Celtic, and he was in goal when Rangers put together a nine-game unbeaten sequence over their rivals. An indication of Celtic's frustration with The Goalie was Celtic manager Tommy Burns' comment that he wanted inscribed on his tombstone the words 'destroyed by Andy Goram'.

Incomers included Dutch international left back Arthur Numan from PSV Eindhoven, bought in May for a Scottish then-record fee of £5 million. Murray laid down his buying policy when he said 'The deal for Numan was more than Rangers have ever spent on a player but obviously we are going to have to pay more for other players in the future.' Other new arrivals were Daniel Prodan, a Romanian defender from Atletico Madrid; Gabriel Omar Amato, an Argentinian forward from Real Mallorca for £4.2 million; left-sided midfielder Giovanni van Bronckhorst from Feyenoord for £5 million; Lionel Charbonnier, a French international goalkeeper from Auxerre for £1.2 million; and striker Rod Wallace on a Bosman transfer from Leeds United. Rangers broke the transfer record again in July when they bought the ex-Manchester United, Everton and Fiorentina flying Russian winger Andreii Kanchelskis for £5.5 million. Advocaat added to his spending in August with the acquisition of Colin Hendry, centre-half and captain of Scotland, from Blackburn Rovers for £4 million. At the start of the season Amoruso was appointed club captain by Advocaat.

Advocaat, however, had no place for Marco Negri. The moody centre-forward, scorer of 36 goals the previous season, had been dropped after a dressing room altercation with Amoruso and disagreements with Smith. After his amazing goal run came to an end halfway through the previous season, the Italian had made no secret of his antipathy to the club and to Glasgow. The sullen Italian was to remain in limbo for nearly two years at Ibrox, claiming injury and refusing to train.

Irish club Shelbourne were the opponents in the qualifying round of the UEFA Cup. The first leg on 22 July was technically an away fixture but the Irish Garda and the FAI were concerned about playing the game in Dublin, due to the heightened political tensions at the time. The tie was played at Tranmere's ground in Birkenhead. On a wet night on the Wirral, a section of Rangers fans shamed the club by throwing missiles at the Shelbourne bus, fighting with mounted police and chanting sectarian slogans. Rangers also experienced problems on the pitch and were 3-0 down after 58th minute, the collapse starting with an early backheaded own goal by Porrini. Superior fitness and technique eventually told, however, and Rangers ended the evening 5-3 winners, Van Bronckhorst and Albertz both scoring twice, the other coming from Amato. The Scottish *Daily Express* saw the match as 'a nerve-wracking debut for new coach Dick Advocaat who slammed his players for treating the first half as a friendly'. At Ibrox, two from Finnish forward Jonatan Johansson, his first goals for the club, took them comfortably to the first round proper to play PAOK Salonika.

At Ibrox on 12 August, the Greek side went down to two Rangers goals within ten minutes early in the second half. First Wallace crossed for Kanchelskis to head in to the net and then Wallace rammed home a 30-yard shot. Durie, however, fell victim to PAOK's rough tactics as early as the 6th minute when he was carried off with a suspected broken ankle. It was later found to be only badly bruised but the injury was to sideline Durie for two months. Two weeks later in Greece, in an intimidating and provocative atmosphere, an effective defensive performance by Rangers and some excellent goalkeeping by Charbonnier resulted in a 0-0 draw.

This was the first season of the new, 10-club Scottish Premier League which had broken away from the Scottish League in order to maximise control of TV and sponsorship

Top left: Arthur Numan.

Top right: Andrei Kanchelskis.

Bottom: Giovanni van Bronckhorst and Sergio Porrini

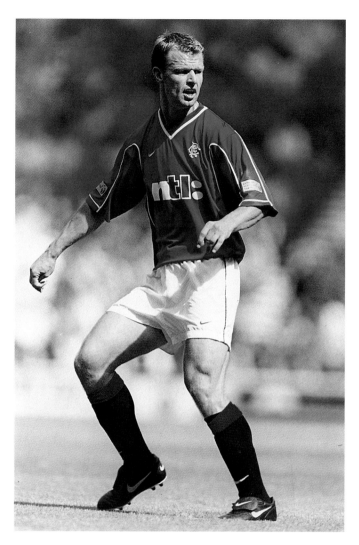

Barry Ferguson

money. Although Rangers lost their first fixture 2-1 to Hearts at Tynecastle on 2 August, by the end of the month they were top of the league, having disposed of Motherwell, Kilmarnock away and St Johnstone. Young ex-Rangers Boys Club midfielder Barry Ferguson was flourishing under Advocaat, and his impressive performances in the 3-1 win against Kilmarnock and in the 4-0 St Johnstone victory, where he created three goals, resulted in his elevation to the Scottish international squad. *Scotland on Sunday* described Ferguson as 'an astute and blossoming player to gladden the indigenous heart'.

On a hot evening in mid-September Rangers were away to Beitar Jerusalem in the UEFA Cup first round. Although they went down to a 15th minute penalty, a trademark long-range effort from 78th minute substitute Albertz with six minutes to go brought them the draw. Four days later they played Celtic at Ibrox in the first Old Firm derby of the season. The game ended in a goalless draw and Rangers had Charbonnier to thank for his two fine saves from Larsson and McKinlay, although Amato missed several simple chances and was replaced by Charlie Miller midway through the second half.

Rangers eased their way into the third round of the UEFA Cup on 1 October, beating Beitar 4-2 at Ibrox with an opening goal from Gattuso in the 1st minute and met Bayer Leverkeusen in Germany on 22 October. Although without the injured Numan and the suspended Amoruso, Rangers turned in an exceptional performance, and created two well-

taken goals, to beat the German side 2-1. In the 45th minute Ferguson brilliantly slipped four Bayer players and found Johansson whose pass to van Bronckhorst was smacked by the Dutchman into the far corner of the net. Just under twenty minutes later, Wallace drew the defence and Johansson side-footed in the second. Bayer scored a goal in injury time, but Rangers had beaten one of Europe's top sides away from home and restored their reputation in European football. The *Sunday Mirror* commented 'rampant Rangers proved the nights of European misery are well and truly over', in what was to prove a somewhat optimistic prediction.

In early November Bayer came to Ibrox for the second leg. The Germans were a much-improved side and controlled the first half. Rangers went ahead, however, when an Amoruso clearance reached Johansson whose searing shot from twenty yards early in the second half defeated the keeper. Ulf Kirsten equalised in the 79th minute but Rangers held on for the remaining nervy ten minutes to go through on aggregate 3-2. Charbonnier banged into the post and damaged his ligaments in the second half. This was to be his last game of the season.

Rangers were cruising in Scotland and their 3-0 win over Hearts in mid-October gave them a run of fifteen unbeaten games. Their unbeaten run, however, was ended later in the month when ex-Ger John Spencer's goal was the difference between them and Motherwell. By the middle of November a 2-1 home win over Aberdeen meant they were ten points ahead in the league. French international striker Stephan Guivarc'h had arrived for £3.5 million from Newcastle, a victim of Ruud Gullit's appointment as manager on Tyneside, while Rozental had returned to Chile on loan. Guivarc'h scored twice on his debut when he

Opposite: *Lorenzo Amoruso holds off Celtic's Mark Viduka*

Below: *Jonatan Johansson scores against Bayer Leverkeusen at Ibrox in the UEFA Cup*

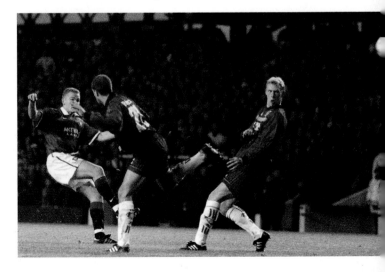

came on as a substitute in Rangers' resounding 7-0 away win over St Johnstone.

On 21 November, with 60,000 at Celtic Park and 30,000 watching on the screens at Ibrox, Rangers were beaten 5-1 by Celtic, their biggest win over Rangers for 35 years. The sending-off of Scott Wilson, on for the suspended Amoruso, in the 22nd minute did not help the Ibrox cause, but the Light Blues' defence was punished for its lack of concentration and discipline.

Rod Wallace equalises for Rangers in the third round first leg UEFA Cup game against Parma at Ibrox in November 1998

Colin Hendry prevents Hernan Crespo from scoring in the game against Parma at Ibrox

In the League Cup, Rangers had eliminated Alloa, Ayr and Airdrie, the latter by an easy 5-0 in the semi-final. No doubt seeking revenge for their 7-0 league defeat three weeks previously, St Johnstone put up an impressive display in the final on 28 November. Rangers, however, went ahead in the 6th minute when Kanchelskis played the ball across the box to Guivarc'h who drove into the net. Nick Dasovic equalised two minutes later but Albertz's superb left foot shot in the 36th minute made the final result 2-1 and Rangers had their first trophy of the season.

Four days previously Rangers had faced Parma at Ibrox in the UEFA Cup. With players of the quality of Juan Veron, Hernan Crespo, Dino Baggio and Lilian Thuram, Parma were favourites to win the tournament. Abel Balbo scored for Parma early in the second half. Advocaat replaced defender Porrini with striker Durie and Rangers equalised in the 69th minute when Hendry headed down a Barry Ferguson cross to Rod Wallace, who found the net from three yards. Rangers produced a spirited, committed display to emerge with a 1-1 draw.

In Italy on 8 December Parma, who had in between the games beaten AC Milan 4-0 and Sampdoria 2-0, now had Enrico Chiesa in the team to partner Crespo in attack while Wallace and Durie foraged upfront for Rangers. Parma began on the offensive but in the 28th minute Albertz picked up a poor pass from Sensini and scored with a long-range thunderbolt. Porrini, however, was sent off late in the first half for fouling Veron, who fell over rather too easily. After the match Advocaat commented 'I did not think the second yellow card was justified'. Ten-men Rangers were going to find it difficult to protect their lead in the second half, and so it proved. Three minutes after the interval Balbo made it 1-1, then Fiore gave Parma the lead. In the 68th minute the unpredictable Amoruso inexplicably and needlessly handled in the area and Chiesa converted the penalty. Rangers were beaten 3-1 and out of the tournament, although they displayed fighting spirit and more than a little skill. The team was cheered off the pitch by the 3,000 or so travelling fans and the stadium rang to chants of 'Advocaat's Blue and White Army'. The Light Blues' performance had shown that they could look forward with optimism to their next European campaign.

On 12 December, Advocaat bought the pacy left winger Neil McCann from Hearts for £2 million. Only the second Scottish-born Catholic, after Mo Johnston, to play for Rangers in modern times, he made his debut in mid-December in Rangers' 3-2 away win over his old club, two of the goals coming from Guivarc'h. By the end of the month,

Top left: Neil McCann

Left: Claudio Reyna

Ranger's five undefeated league games in December saw them lead the league by four points over Kilmarnock, with Celtic a distant ten points away. On Xmas Eve Advocaat revealed another new signing, the Borussia Dortmund keeper Stefan Klos who made his debut in the 1-0 win over St Johnstone.

In the New Year derby, Rangers drew 2-2 with Celtic at Ibrox. In an exciting, entertaining contest, Rangers dominated the first half, with Amoruso and Wallace going close. Celtic, however, took the lead in the 38th minute through Alan Stubbs but an Amato header equalised matters on the stroke of half time. Amato created the next goal in the 58th minute when he nutmegged Stubbs, dribbled past Jackie McNamara on the byeline and crossed for Wallace to score. Larsson tied the game seven minutes later.

The new league had decided on a three-week winter shutdown, so Rangers spent a week at a Florida training camp and played a couple of friendlies. When the league re-commenced on 27 January, a 4-0 away win over Dundee began a series of six undefeated league games, including an Albertz hat-trick in the 6-1 defeat of Dundee and a Wallace hat-trick in the 5-0 win at Kilmarnock. By the middle of February they were thirteen points ahead of Celtic.

In March Advocaat bought striker Michael Mols from Utrecht, bringing his spending to date to £40 million, and in early April US international midfielder and captain Claudio Reyna arrived from Wolfsburg for £2 million. Defender Craig Moore, who had joined Crystal Palace five months previously, also returned to the club.

In March and April Rangers had suffered two defeats – by Dundee United and St Johnstone – and their draw with

Left: Jorge Albertz scores from the spot to put Rangers 2-0 ahead at Parkhead in May 1999

Below: Referee Hugh Dallas receives attention after being struck on the head by a coin at Parkhead in May 1999

Dundee on 18 April cut their lead to four points over Celtic. However, a 3-1 win over Aberdeen at Ibrox, where Wallace scored his 26th goal of the season, meant that they were seven points clear with four games to play. If they could beat Celtic at Celtic Park in four days time, the league title would be theirs.

Sky TV had won the contract to televise the new league and had decided to screen the last few games of the season early on Sunday evenings. In spite of objections from the police, players and fans, the game at Celtic Park went ahead at 6.00pm on Sunday 2 May. Many fans had been drinking all day before what was a crucial match for both teams and sets of supporters, and an ugly atmosphere was developing at the stadium.

Rangers went ahead in the 12th minute when McCann capitalised on a cut back from Wallace to place the ball past keeper Kerr. The hostile atmosphere transmitted itself to the players and Stephane Mahe was dismissed for dissent by referee Hugh Dallas in the 31st minute. As Rangers prepared to take a free kick a few minutes later some fans ran onto the pitch towards the referee and were restrained by security guards. Suddenly Dallas fell to his knees clutching his head. He had been hit by a coin thrown from the crowd and required treatment and, eventually, five stitches. When the game restarted, van Bronckhorst sent the ball into the Celtic penalty area and Vidmar fell over in a tussle with Riseth. The referee blew for a penalty from which Albertz cooly scored to put Rangers 2-0 up. With fourteen minutes to go, McCann collected a through pass from Johansson and rounded Kerr to slot the ball into the net. As the game degenerated into indiscipline and disorder Wallace and Riseth were sent off near the end. Ten minutes after the game ended some Rangers players again mocked the Celtic huddle at the almost deserted Celtic end of the ground (although Advocaat stated that some of the foreign players were used to this ritual in their respective countries), and van Bronckhorst aggravated the situation by blowing kisses at the Celtic fans. *The Daily Mail* said 'Rangers' Championship celebrations at Parkhead were tainted and bloodied by the most shameful set of events involving the Old Firm since the 1980 Scottish Cup Final riot'.

Trouble flared after the game with street battles and 113 people arrested. A 'fan' threw two bottles through the window of Dallas's house and the referee commented: 'I have been all over the world. I have had some very difficult matches but I have never had a threat like this at all.' Scottish Home Affairs Minister Henry McLeish described the events as a 'bad, bad night for Scottish football'. Nonetheless, Rangers had won their 100th Old Firm victory and the league championship. As a result of their fans' behaviour, Celtic were later fined £45,000 by the SFA while Rangers were cleared of inciting trouble by performing the huddle.

Rangers were still on for the 'treble', having disposed of Stenhousemuir, Hamilton, Falkirk and St Johnstone to reach the Scottish Cup final. They were to face Celtic in the first official match at the newly-refurbished Hampden Park, and the first Old Firm final since 1989. Hugh Dallas was once again the referee and there was general trepidation in Glasgow about the likely outcome. In the event, it was a well-behaved occasion, and a cautious, disappointing

Rod Wallace scores the winner in the 1999 Scottish Cup final

encounter was won by a single goal from Wallace. In the 49th minute, Vidmar from the left passed to McCann who knocked it in front of Wallace. Wallace lifted the ball over keeper Gould to score the winner and his 27th goal of the season. The team was: Klos, Porrini (Kanchelskis), Hendry, Amoruso, Vidmar, McCann (Ferguson), McInnes, van Bronckhorst, Wallace, Amato (Wilson), Albertz.

In his first season in charge, the 'Little General' had won the sixth 'treble' in Rangers' history. Some of his new signings – in particular Wallace, van Bronkhorst and McCann – had vindicated Advocaat's expertise in the transfer market, although others, notably Amato and Guivarc'h, had disappointed. Nevertheless it seemed that the Dutchman was

Rangers celebrate their 1999 Scottish Cup final victory over Celtic

blending a team with the ability to dominate again in Scottish football for the foreseeable future.

Shortly after the game, the *Daily Record* obtained a video of Donald Findlay, vice-president of the club, singing sectarian songs at a private party in the Rangers Social Club to celebrate the 'treble' and Findlay was forced to resign from the board. He was also fined £3,500 by the Dean of Faculties.

In early June the underwhelming Stephan Guivarc'h was unloaded to Auxerre for £3.4 million while Colin Hendry, who had lost his place to the central partnership of Moore and Amoruso, was told he could leave for the right price. Meanwhile, Polish midfielder Darius Adamczuk arrived under freedom of contract from Dundee.

Because of the low status of Scottish football in Europe, Rangers were again forced to play two qualifying rounds in the European Cup in season 1999-2000. Mols, in his first

game for the club, scored twice in their second round 4-1 defeat away of Finland's FC Haka and made another. A further three at Ibrox drew the Light Blues against their conquerors of last season, Parma, in the final qualifying round. Parma remained a formidable side, although Veron had left for Lazio and Chiesa had gone to Fiorentina, but they had been reinforced by the arrival of Argentinian international midfielder Ariel Ortega. At Ibrox on 11 August Rangers atoned for their previous defeat with a stirring 2-0 victory. Defender Fabio Cannavaro was sent off in the 30th minute for a second yellow card, and three minutes later a wicked Vidmar shot deflected off Thuram over keeper Gianluca Buffon to give Rangers the lead. A low shot from Reyna from a McCann pass in the 76th minute secured an excellent victory and a real chance of reaching the Champions League.

Two weeks later at the Ennio Tardini stadium in Italy, with Rangers spreading five players across midfield and McCann on the bench, Charbonnier kept out efforts from Ortega and Fuser to leave the game goalless at the interval. Vidmar hit the post in the second half and a Wallace shot was brilliantly saved by Buffon, but Johan Walem gave Parma the lead in the 68th minute when his free kick was fumbled by Charbonnier. Rangers, however, held on to go through to the Champions League to meet Valencia, Bayern Munich and PSV Eindhoven in one of the strongest groups in the competition.

Michael Mols keeps possession in the away game against Parma in August 1999

Michael Mols heads in Rangers' second goal against PSV Eindhoven at Ibrox

Although Rangers had scrambled a 2-1 win over Kilmarnock in the first game of the Scottish Premier League, their form improved throughout August and, by the time their first European game kicked off on 15 September, they had gone six league games without defeat and topped the league. Michael Mols was particularly impressive, scoring all four in the 4-1 defeat of Motherwell and two in the 3-0 win over Aberdeen.

UEFA had expanded the Champions League to eight groups to counter the threat posed by Italian-based Media Partners to establish a breakaway 'super league'. As a further incentive, places would be reserved in the UEFA Cup for clubs disqualified in the third qualifying round and finishing third in the first group stage. As the fixture list was crowded to capacity, the Cup Winners Cup had been abolished. The European Cup was now unrecognisable from the simple knockout competition which Rangers had first entered in 1957.

Rangers' first game was away against Valencia, with their high-scoring forwards Claudio Lopez and Kily Gonzales and midfield playmaker and captain Gaizka Mendieta. Valencia got off to a storming start but after the first thirty minutes Rangers began to enjoy more of the possession. In the 57th minute, however, Charbonnier could not hold a cross from the right and Moore, desperately trying to clear, put the ball in his own net. Gonzalez doubled the score with fifteen minutes remaining.

A week later at Ibrox, the Light Blues faced Bayern Munich, one of the favourites to win the trophy. Rangers played with panache and determination and deserved their opening goal scored by Albertz from twenty yards in the 22nd minute. However, in injury time Michael Tarnat equalised with a fortunate deflected free kick off teammate Roque Santa Cruz.

Advocaat's previous club PSV lined up against Rangers the following week in Holland and substitute Albertz's 84th minute volley was sufficient for Rangers to collect three points. Their next two games were at home and they were in a comfortable position halfway through the group matches.

On 20 October PSV came to Glasgow for game four. Rangers poured into attack from the outset against a poor, uncoordinated PSV and McCann and Wallace spurned some early opportunities. Amoruso opened Rangers' account with an 18th minute header from a Van Bronckhorst corner and twenty minutes later Mols headed in a McCann cross. PSV striker Ruud Van Nistelrooy converted a penalty on the interval but two from McCann and Mols in the second half gave Rangers a 4-1 win. A splendid performance by the Light Blues saw them assume leadership of the group, one point ahead of Valencia and Bayern.

Although they stumbled against a fast, skilful Valencia in the fifth game at Ibrox, going down 2-1, the goal coming from a sidefoot flick from Craig Moore, they travelled to Germany on 3 November needing only one point to qualify. Rangers were dominant and bombarded the Bayern goal, hitting the wodwork three times and an inspired Oliver Kahn in goal for Bayern saved everything on target. However, in the 32nd minute Mehmet Scholl fell over Klos in the area and the referee awarded a disputed penalty. Strunz scored from the spot although Klos got a hand to the ball. Rangers could not score and were out of the competition. Their bad luck was compounded by a serious cruciate ligament injury

Lorenzo Amoruso powers in a header to open the scoring against PSV Eindhoven in October 1999 at Ibrox

to Mols when he clashed with Kahn in the 25th minute, and the tricky Dutchman, now a favourite with the fans, was to be out for the rest of the season. However, Rangers fans and neutral observers agreed with Advocaat when he commented after the game: 'I am very proud of my team. They showed that they are very strong and can compete very well with other European top teams.' And there remained the attraction of the UEFA Cup.

Rangers were still unbeaten in the league in Scotland, although Kilmarnock had ended their eight-game winning

Billy Dodds

streak with a 1-1 draw on 16 October. At the end of the month a Johansson hat-trick helped them to a 5-1 win over Aberdeen and they met Celtic at Ibrox in early November, Celtic manager John Barnes' first Old Firm match. In an enthralling match, Johansson scored in the 19th minute, taking advantage of Gould dropping the ball, but two from Berkovic had Celtic 2-1 shortly before the interval. In the third minute of first half injury time, Albertz was illegally challenged by Paul Lambert in the box and Lambert was stretchered off. Albertz scored from the spot. An Amoruso free kick deflected off Ian Wright for Rangers' third in the 49th minute and seventeen minutes later Amato squeezed the ball in from a tight angle to make the final score 4-2. Celtic had now not won at Ibrox since August 1994. By the end of November Rangers were four points clear of Celtic in the league, although Dundee's surprise 1-0 win at Ibrox ended their 12-game unbeaten league record.

Before Rangers' third round UEFA Cup tie with Borussia Dortmund at Ibrox on 25 November, Advocaat had faced a goalkeeping crisis, with Klos and Charbonnier injured and Antti Niemi on loan to Charlton. Thomas Myhre came for a month's loan from Everton and was in goal for the match. Rangers 2-0 win came courtesy of an 18th minute Jurgen Kohler own goal and a Wallace strike on half time. In the

second leg in early December, Rangers came to defend their lead. However, an unmarked Victor Ipkeba headed in Borussia's first early in the game and Bobic equalised on aggregate in injury time. The game went to penalties and Amoruso was the only Rangers player to convert. Borussia won the shoot-out 3-1.

In early December Rangers were running desperately short of strikers, with Mols, Amato, Johansson and Wallace all injured. Advocaat moved to fill the gap by buying little striker Billy Dodds from Dundee United for £1.4 million. Dodds scored twice in the 5-1 defeat of Motherwell on 18 December, and Rangers celebrated the centenary of Ibrox on 22 December by beating Hearts through a solitary late goal from Albertz.

The Light Blues had been knocked out of the League Cup 1-0 by Aberdeen but remained league leaders by four points at the end of the year, although they could only draw with Celtic 1-1 at Celtic Park, the goals scored by Viduka and Dodds.

After the January winter break Rangers took revenge for their League Cup elimination by thumping a poor Aberdeen

Above: Gio van Bronkhorst scores past Jonathan Gould at Ibrox in March 2000

Right: Fernando Ricksen

side 5-0, three of the goals coming in the ten minutes before half time. This game saw the debut of recent signing Tugay Kerimoglu, a £1.4 million buy from Galatasaray. In early February Rozental made his first start for two years and scored in the 4-0 win over Dundee United. Later in the month young striker Kenny Miller scored twice for Hibs in their 2-2 draw with Rangers at Easter Road, while at the end of the month Rangers destroyed Dundee 7-1 at Dens Park, scoring six in the first half and Wallace claiming a hat-trick.

In March they met Celtic twice and came top on both occasions. On the 8th at Celtic Park a Wallace goal four minutes from time was the only score. Thirteen days later at Ibrox a listless Celtic struggled to get into the game and went down 4-0. In the 3rd minute an unmarked Kanchelskis headed a Van Bronckhorst corner at the far post to Albertz who converted, and five minutes from the interval Kanchelskis shot low past keeper Gould for the second. Albertz added a third with six minutes remaining with an overhead kick from a McCann cross and van Bronckhorst wrapped it up. The win saw Rangers' lead over Celtic increase to fifteen points and was effectively the title decider.

At the end of March David Murray revealed plans to float the club, currently on the Ofex market, on the Stock Exchange. He also announced a £53 million share issue with £20 million coming from South African-based businessman Dave King. The money was earmarked to pay off the club's £40 million debt, buy new players and help develop the Rangers academy.

Advocaat had also been busy behind the scenes. Amato had gone to Brazilian club Cremio for £3.75 million; Hendry had finally departed for Coventry for £750,000; a new arrival was young Dutch defender Fernando Ricksen, joining from AZ Alkmar for £3.75 million; and Terro Pentilla, a tall, young defender who had impressed Advocaat when he played for FC Haka, made his debut in April.

Although the Light Blues could only draw 1-1 with bottom-placed Aberdeen on 1 April, three straight league wins brought them an 18-point lead over Celtic and to the brink of the championship. On 22 April Celtic could only draw with Hibs and Rangers were champions for the twelfth time in 14 years. The trophy was displayed amid celebrations on the pitch lasting over an hour after their next home game of the season, a 3-0 win over Dundee on 1 May. A lacklustre Rangers lost their final game 2-0 to Motherwell – only their

second league defeat of the season – but they had won the Scottish Premier League by 21 points.

Rangers had beaten First Division Ayr United 7-0 in the Scottish Cup semi-final, Dodds scoring a hat-trick and a re-energised Rozental claiming two, and met Aberdeen in the final at Hampden on 27 May. With many of the Rangers fans decked out in orange as a tribute to Advocaat, the game was an easy 4-0 victory for the Light Blues, particularly as veteran Dons keeper Jim Leighton, playing in his last senior match, collided with Wallace in the 2nd minute and was carried off with a double fracture of the jaw. Aberdeen manager Ebbe Skovdahl had not included a keeper among his substitutes and striker

Top left: Van Bronckhorst scores the first goal for Rangers in the 2000 Scottish Cup final

Left: Tony Vidmar claims Rangers' second goal in the 2000 Scottish Cup final

Right: Dick Advocaat with the Scottish Cup

Peter Lovenkrands

Robbie Winters put on the jersey. Van Bronckhorst opened the scoring in the 35th minute from a chipped Albertz free kick. The other three came in the five minutes following the interval. First Vidmar's left foot shot found Winters stranded, then Dodds headed in at the back post and finally a 40-yarder from Albertz was touched onto the crossbar by Winters but he could not prevent the ball bouncing over the line. Rangers had won the 'double' again and Advocaat had claimed five domestic trophies out of six. The team was: Klos, Reyna, Moore (Porrini), Vidmar, Numan, Kanchelskis, Ferguson, Albertz, van Bronckhorst, Wallace, (McCann), Dodds.

Although Rangers appeared to be uncatchable in Scottish football, changes were occurring at Celtic Park which would turn Celtic into a serious challenger to Rangers' dominance over the next season. John Barnes had been fired as manager for his failure to match the Ibrox club's success, the last straw being his team's humiliating 3-1 defeat by Inverness

Caledonian in the Scottish Cup ('Super Caley go ballistic, Celtic are atrocious' ran the memorable *Sun* headline). Barnes was replaced by Leicester City manager Martin O'Neill who was to inspire and cajole Celtic to one of their most successful seasons in years.

In early June further developments took place at the corporate level. NTL, who owned the Glasgow cable franchise and sponsored Rangers' strip, announced a £31 million agreement to act as Rangers' media agent. A joint venture was to be set up to run a TV channel and internet venture.

Advocaat, meanwhile, was again busy in the transfer market in June. Although Rangers had agreed a £4 million deal with Sunderland for Amoruso, the commanding, if erratic, defender decided to remain at Ibrox as he could not agree personal terms with the Roker Park club. Striker Jonatan Johansson moved to Charlton Athletic. Two new defenders arrived at the club. Scottish international Paul Ritchie joined from Bolton for £500,000 but he was to stay only 77 days at Ibrox before moving to Manchester City. Tall defender-cum-

midfielder Bert Konterman added to the Dutch contingent at Ibrox in a £4.5 million move from Feyenoord. Advocaat bolstered his attack with the acquisition of 20-year-old Peter Lovenkrands from AB Copenhagen for £1.5 million and winger Allan Johnston from Sunderland. At the end of the month he persuaded goalscoring prodigy Kenny Miller to move from Hibs for £2 million.

He capped all this in August when he announced the arrival from Barcelona of one of Europe's top players, Ronald de Boer, for £5 million. An attacking midfielder, de Boer was an experienced Dutch international who had played under Advocaat in the 1994 World Cup finals and who had won a European Cup winner's medal with Ajax when they had beaten AC Milan in 1995. His arrival was a coup for the club and demonstrated that Rangers could not only attract some of the world's finest players but were also serious about competing at the highest level in European football.

Rangers' recent performances in Europe had been of benefit to Scottish football. At the end of June UEFA allocated a second

Above Left: Ronald de Boer

Above Right: Bert Konterman

place to Scotland in the European Cup, largely because of Rangers' successes, and the league runner-up next season would enter the second qualifying round. On 26 July at Ibrox Rangers met FK Zalgiris Kaumas, the part-time Lithuanian champions, in the first leg of the European Cup second qualifying round. Van Bronckhorst was rested after Euro 2000 and Numan was injured, and Rangers made heavy weather of the game, only 2-1 ahead against nine men at the end of ninety minutes. In injury time, however, Dodds scored twice, both from Albertz passes, to save Rangers' face. A week later in Lithuania, Rangers again failed to turn their superiority into a convincing scoreline but a 0-0 draw was enough to get them through.

Herfolge, the Danish champions, were managed by ex-Arsenal player John Jensen. Rangers travelled to Denmark in the next round to play the 'little farmers', as they were nicknamed by the Danish press. Albertz opened the scoring with a 30-yard shot and Rangers won the tie 3-0. They achieved the same result at Ibrox at the end of the month, the highlight being a clever lob over the keeper by Kanchelskis for the third, and again qualified for the Champions League, in the same apparently easy group as Galatasaray, Monaco and Sturm Graz.

Rangers had a hesitant start to the new league season in 2000/01. They came from behind in their first two games – against St Johnstone and Kilmarnock – to win, Dodds scoring twice in both matches. At the end of the month they faced

Celtic at Parkhead and suffered their worst league defeat against Celtic since 1938. By the 11th minute a shell-shocked Rangers were 3-0 down but they scored through Reyna on half time. Larsson found the net twice in the second half and, although Dodds converted a penalty, Sutton scored in the last minute of the game for a 6-2 win by Celtic. To compound Rangers' woes, Ferguson was sent off in the 82nd minute. In their next league game against Dundee, which saw the return of Mols after an absence of ten months, a mistake by Amoruso, when he was caught in possession, allowed Dundee to equalise and Rangers had gained one point from their last two games. Celtic were now five points ahead of the Light Blues.

They were faring better in Europe, however. On 12 September at Ibrox they routed Sturm Graz, champions of Austria, 5-0. Mols opened the scoring in the 9th minute and ten minutes later de Boer claimed his first goal for his new club, a close range volley from a Johnston cross. Albertz added a third within ten minutes and van Bronckhorst, with a screamer from the edge of the box, and Dodds made it five towards the

end with a sweet lob over the keeper. On top of this, Rangers hit the woodwork twice and Albertz had his penalty saved. De Boer and Mols were in outstanding form and Rangers had reason to look forward to their next European encounter, against Monaco in France one week later.

In Monaco a spectacular, swerving van Bronckhorst effort from 30 yards in the 8th minute gave Rangers the only goal of the game and Rangers now had six points from their two games and had not conceded a goal. They were, however, fortunate to come away with the three points and only a strong defensive performance, particularly from Tugay in the role of sweeper, kept out the busy Monaco forwards.

Their third European game in as many weeks was in a wet Istanbul against Galatasaray who were without their star player Gheorge Hagi. The game was goalless by half time but, by the 70th minute, the Turkish side were three ahead, the last a superb volley from their Brazilian striker Mario Jardel. Kanchelskis with a deflected header and van Bronckhorst, the latter from a thunderous free kick, both scored in the last twenty minutes, but

Barry Ferguson scores the first goal in Rangers 5-1 defeat of Celtic in November 2000

Galatasaray won the game 3-2. Rangers and Galatasaray now shared the group leadership with six points apiece.

Back in the league, the out-of-favour Negri made an appearance in Rangers' 3-0 win over Dundee United at Ibrox on 1 October but they lost their next three league matches. With Mols, Wallace and McCann all injured they went down 1-0 to Hibs, with Kanchelskis sent off. They then succumbed 2-1 to St Johnstone, another Amoruso error handing the winner to the Perth club, prompting an angry Advocaat to remark 'some of my players must realise that big heads do not win games... it was a hopeless performance'. And they collapsed 3-0 at Ibrox to Kilmarnock in an abject display of gutless defending and aimless attacking, to leave the club thirteen points behind Celtic at the end of the month and in fourth place in the league. Rangers' poor form, combined with an extensive injury list, was jeopardising their chances of

retaining the league title. On top of this, rumours persisted of disharmony and discord in the dressing room and there were even calls for Advocaat to be fired.

The prospect of competing in the Champions League was also receding. Held 0-0 at home by Galatasaray in mid-October, they played Sturm Graz in Austria a week later. On new keeper Jesper Christiansen's debut Rangers again stumbled to defeat, going down 2-0 and Numan was sent off. They rounded off their league programme against Monaco in early November at Ibrox, needing to win to go through to the second stage. Kenny Miller shot Rangers ahead in the 3rd minute from a Ferguson cross but Francisco Da Costa levelled in the 37th minute. Mols scored with a low shot under the keeper just after the interval but, with thirteen minutes remaining, Amoruso was robbed as he brought the ball out of defence and Simone fired in the equaliser. The UEFA Cup was now Rangers' consolation.

They got back to winning ways, however, with a League Cup quarter-final 2-0 win over Dundee United at the end of October, Tugay the supplier to Kenny Miller and Barry Ferguson. In early November, with Barry Ferguson having taken over the captaincy from an unhappy and increasingly criticised Amoruso, new signing Kenny Miller proved his worth. In only his third start for Rangers, the young striker scored five goals in the 7-1 hammering of St Mirren, the first after only 50 seconds with three more in the first thirty minutes. However, a 0-0 away draw with Dunfermline in the middle of the month left them in fourth place in the league, fifteen points behind Celtic.

The tall Norwegian international striker Tore Andre Flo joined the club from Chelsea on 24 November, two days before their next meeting with Celtic, for a Scottish record transfer fee of £12 million, increasing Advocaat's options in attack. The Dutchman had brought his spending on players to £74 million in thirty months. Flo made his club debut in the Celtic game. In a bad-tempered match at Ibrox, Rangers achieved some revenge for their 6-2 mauling two months later. Ferguson, in his first Old Firm match as captain, scored first in the 34th minute when he collected the ball on the run from Reyna and lobbed it over Celtic keeper Rab Douglas. Larsson equalised early in the second half but Flo cleverly flicked in a back heel from two yards to put Rangers ahead. Celtic's Alan Thompson was sent off in the 64th minute. Then de Boer and Amoruso headed in two more from Albertz corners and Mols from the six-yard line added Rangers' fifth five minutes from time for a 5-1 win. Celtic were still twelve points clear but Rangers had demonstrated that they were going to fight the Parkhead club all the way. Advocaat commented after the match 'The team showed what they can do. I was pleased for both our players and fans.'

Van Bronckhorst was ruled out for three months in late November. He had picked up a groin injury in a World Cup match against Cyprus and had played only one game in the previous ten weeks. His influential presence was again missed in a frenetic third round UEFA Cup tie against Kaiserslautern at Ibrox on 30 November when a right foot shot by Albertz in the 88th minute was the only difference between the sides. The following week in Germany Rangers could not take their chances while Kaiserslautern converted what came their way. A 3-0 defeat saw the Ibrox club yet again out of Europe before Xmas.

By the middle of December three straight wins – over Hearts, Motherwell and Aberdeen – saw Celtic's lead cut to ten points. Although yet another Amoruso defensive error gave away the only goal of the game to Dundee United, another three wins in succession, the last a 3-1 away victory over St Mirren when Flo scored twice in the first half, allowed Rangers to begin their winter break in good heart.

Rangers and Celtic had long complained about the lack of revenue in Scottish football. With a regular attendance of 50,000 at Ibrox and 60,000 at Parkhead, and a huge domestic and international fan base, the clubs nonetheless received only around £3 million per year from TV rights,

compared to the far higher sums which much smaller Premier League clubs, such as Leicester, received. Earlier in the year the clubs had proposed to UEFA plans for a new Atlantic League. This would involve 16 teams from seven countries – Holland, Portugal, Scotland, Belgium, Sweden, Norway and Denmark – in a league which would be in place by 2003. Both Celtic and Rangers would contest the Scottish Cup but they would withdraw from the Scottish Premier league. The top six clubs would enter the Champions league every season. The intention was to secure a much bigger television market than Rangers or Celtic could reach in Scotland with significantly higher TV revenues. Although UEFA had been making encouraging noises about the new league, on 16 December chief executive Gerhard Aigner rejected the proposal. The following year Celtic and Rangers, still determined that they receive the TV revenue which their stature in the European game merits, proposed that they join the English Premiership. a suggestion welcomed by several English chairmen, but later vetoed.

Before the winter break began, a service was held at Ibrox to commemorate the victims of the 1971 Ibrox Disaster thirty years on, and football grounds across Scotland held a minute's silence. David Murray unveiled a bronze statue of

Far left: Kenny Miller shoots for goal

Left: Tore Andre Flo

Below: The memorial to the dead of the 1971 Ibrox disaster unveiled in January 2001 by David Murray

John Greig, who was captain on the day of the tragedy, with the names of the dead and the names of those who perished in the 1902 disaster and the two fans killed in 1962 inscribed on it. He said 'The club has publicly stated its commitment to the families of the bereaved and the shareholders that when the overall modernisation of the stadium was complete a fitting memorial to all those who tragically lost their lives would be erected'. The memorial stands at the eastern end of the Main Stand.

On 27 January the lowest crowd for ten years at Ibrox saw an unconvincing Rangers beat a defensively-minded Third Division Brechin City 2-0 in the third round of the Scottish Cup. Tugay scored the only goal in their 1-0 win over Aberdeen four days later, although McCann was sent off, and Tugay again, with a cracking 25-yard drive, scored in the 2-0 home win over Dunfermline, the first Sky TV pay-per-view game televised in Scotland.

Rangers faced Celtic twice within four days in early February. The first match, in the League Cup semi-final at Parkhead, saw Celtic two ahead within the first 18 minutes. Albertz pulled one back with a penalty before half time, but Larsson fell over in the box after a seemingly innocuous challenge from Scott Wilson and the Swede converted the

Tributes to Jim Baxter at the Copland Road gates at Ibrox

Before the Dundee game a minute's silence was held for Jim Baxter. The brilliant left-half of the 1960s had died of liver cancer a few days earlier at the age of 60, and his funeral had been held the previous Friday. Football fans across Scotland mourned his passing and fondly remembered his glorious contributions to Scot Symon's legendary side of the early 1960s and his destruction of the 'Auld Enemy' at Wembley in 1963 and 1967.

penalty for a 3-1 win for Celtic. Towards the end of the game Reyna and Mols were both sent off. In the league at Ibrox Alan Thompson scored the only goal of the game, leaving Rangers a virtually unreachable twelve points behind Celtic. In this match it was Ricksen's turn for an early bath. Rangers' debilitating injury list was being compounded by the growing number of suspensions which the players were gathering.

A 62nd minute winning goal from Ferguson and two earlier goals from Flo in front of 6,000 at Dingwall helped Rangers to a 3-2 victory over a determined and unlucky Ross County in the Scottish Cup fourth round in mid-February. On 11 March they were knocked out of the competition in the quarter-final by Dundee United 1-0 in a match in which the Light Blues managed to avoid a single shot on target and in which Konterman contrived to get himself dismissed. Rangers also suffered mixed fortunes in the league in March, beating Hearts and Motherwell but losing to Dundee and Dundee United. In the Motherwell game Fabrice Fernandes, on loan from French club Rennes, scored a dramatic equaliser with his first touch of the ball for the club only fifteen seconds after coming on as a substitute.

With the squad now reinforced by the arrival of Wimbledon striker Marcus Gayle for £1 million, April began with a goalless draw with Hibs at Easter Road. A 2-1 away win followed at Kilmarnock, Flo scoring both, and they laid their Tayside jinx with a 3-0 victory at Dens Park, the goals coming from Wallace, Flo and Albertz in the first half hour.

Runaway league leaders Celtic visited Ibrox on 29 April for the last Old Firm match of the season and achieved their first win at Ibrox in seven years, Larsson scoring his 50th goal of the season in the 3-0 victory. A 4-1 win at Hearts one week later confirmed Rangers as runners-up to Celtic in the league and assured them of a place in the qualifying round of next season's European Cup. Wallace, Albertz and Flo all scored in the second half, although Ferguson was dismissed in the 30th minute, his fifteenth booking of the season and the twelfth Rangers player to be sent off during the term. With little left to play for, Rangers upped a gear in their last two matches, beating Kilmarnock 5-1 and Hibs 4-0, but Celtic completed the 'treble' and asserted their temporary superiority in Scottish football.

One of the first things Advocaat had noticed when he arrived at Ibrox was the lack of a modern training facility. David Murray had agreed on the need to invest in appropriate facilities for the players and to bring on youngsters and so, twelve months after work began, the new complex at Auchenhowie to the north of Glasgow was complete. Named Murray Park, the complex cost around £12 million and was opened on 4 July 2001. Within its 38 acres are to be found a high-tech gym, indoor pitches and a total of ten pitches, six of which are full size. The pitches are heated undersoil and are exact replicas of the surface at Ibrox. Murray Park is one of the most advanced training grounds in Europe and tangible evidence of Rangers' ambitions to compete at the highest level in continental football.

Murray Park, Rangers' new 38 acre training ground contains state-of-the-art facilities, including ten pitches and a high-tech gym

Although constrained by spending limits, Advocaat added three new names to his squad in the early summer of 2001. From Dundee came Claudio Caniggia, an Argentinian forward whose previous clubs included Roma, Benfica and Boca Juniors. Now 34 years old, the long-haired striker was still capable of displaying the skills which had made him such a star for his country at the 1990 World Cup finals. Christian Nerlinger, an experienced German international midfielder, arrived from Borussia Dortmund for £1.8 million, while Russell Latapy, a 33-year-old Trinidad and Tobago international midfielder who was given a free transfer from Hibs after a disagreement with the Edinburgh club, also joined the Light Blues.

Although the influential and popular Gio van Bronckhorst opted for the English Premier League in a £8.5 million move to Arsenal, in August Advocaat secured the services of Shota Arveladze and Michael Ball. Arveladze was a fast and tricky Georgian international striker for whom Rangers paid Ajax £2 million while Ball was a highly rated young English defender who arrived from Everton for £6.5 million.

In the first league game of the season against Aberdeen at Pittodrie, newcomers Caniggia, Nerlinger and Latapy all scored in the Gers 3-0 victory. Nerlinger had also scored two days previously in the 3-0 away win over Slovenia's Maribor in the qualifying round of the European Cup. A week later at Ibrox Maribor went ahead in the first half but a Flo equaliser and two from Caniggia secured a third qualifying round tie against Fenerbahce. Young midfielder Stephen Hughes, compared to Barry Ferguson at the same age, made a strong case for a regular first team place with his confident performances early in the season.

The following week at Ibrox Rangers could only draw 0-0 with the Turkish side and Mols, on as a second half substitute for Caniggia, was sent off after a clash with Samuel Johnston. On 22 August in Turkey Rangers were two down by the 71st minute and, although Ricksen scored with a deflected goal two minutes later and Rangers piled on the pressure in the last fifteen minutes, Fenerbahce won the game 2-1. Rangers were out of the European Cup. As consolation they dropped into the UEFA Cup.

In late August Rangers were drawn away against Anzhi Makhachkala in the first round of the UEFA Cup. Makhachkala, in Dagestan in the south west of Russia, is situated around 100 miles from Grozny in Chechnya, the scene of fierce fighting between Russians and Chechens, and the Foreign Office advised fans not to travel to the game. A stand-off developed between Rangers and UEFA, who insisted that Rangers meet their commitments and travel to Dagestan while Rangers, with a team valued at fifty million pounds, would find it almost impossible to find insurance

Argentinian forward Claudio Caniggia

even if they were convinced the journey was safe. The players were at best apprehensive, with Barry Ferguson saying 'I'm certainly not going. I want to see my children growing up'. In the face of Rangers' insistence that the club would rather pull out of the UEFA Cup than play the game, Uefa conceded on 16 September that the match was potentially too dangerous and agreed to a one-off tie at a neutral venue. Rangers travelled to Warsaw on 27 September and beat Anzhi 1-0 in a somewhat scrappy game through an 85th minute drive from Konterman.

Rangers were feeling the effects of an alarming injury list in August and September, and by the time they met Celtic at Ibrox in the first Old Firm game of the season at the end of September they were four points behind the league champions. Their results included a 0-0 draw at Ibrox with newly-promoted Livingston and away draws with Hibs and Hearts, although the week before the Celtic game they destroyed Dundee United 6-1 in an excellent performance. Flo scored the first hat-trick of his Ibrox career in the match. After the Celtic game Rangers were seven points adrift, going down 2-0 to the old enemy and Amoruso sent off.

Stephen Hughes controls the ball in the game against Feyenoord at Ibrox

Arveladze and Ball made their debuts on 9 October with the Georgian scoring, twice, the first a stunning 5th minute opener in the 3-0 defeat of Airdrie in the third round of the League Cup. In the next match – a home league game against Kilmarnock – Arveladze emphasised his talent by scoring the first goal and making the other two in a 3-1 victory.

Rangers met Moscow Dynamo in the second round of the UEFA Cup at Ibrox on 16 October, watched by the 'Barcelona Bears', the team which had beaten Dynamo in the 1972 European Cup Winners Cup final. Comfortably ahead 3-0 – through Amoruso, a Ball free-kick and De Boer – with a minute to go, Rangers gave away an away goal to Rolan Gusev in the 90th minute. Advocaat commented 'we still make the same mistakes that have cost us in the last two years of the Champions league'. In the second leg on 1 November Rangers were two ahead by the 15th minute through a De Boer left foot shot and a Ferguson cross which

the Dynamo keeper fumbled into the net. Dynamo equalised but Flo made the score 3-1 at half time, with substitute Lovenkrands dancing past the keeper to score the fourth, his first Rangers goal, in the 78th minute, to leave the aggregate score a satisfying 7-2.

The third round opponents in the UEFA Cup were Paris St Germain, with the first leg played at Ibrox on 22 November. With Arveladze cup-tied, De Boer and Caniggia missed first half chances and the game ended 0-0 with Ricksen sent off. In Paris two weeks later, with 10,000 Rangers fans in attendance at the Parc des Princes, the game was again goalless, although De Boer missed a penalty with four minutes remaining of extra time, and went to penalties. Ferguson scored the first sudden death penalty and Mauricio Pochinetto's effort hit the bar. Rangers were through to the fourth round. This game marked Claudio Reyna's last match for Rangers as he joined Sunderland later in the week for £4.75 million. As with Van Bronckhorst, Rangers were finding it difficult to keep their best players when the English Premier League came calling.

Celtic had beaten Rangers for the fifth time in a row in late November at Parkhead and were now ten points ahead of the Ibrox club. Lovenkrands scored in the 76th minute but Celtic ran out 2-1 winners. Ball sparked a touchline altercation with Advocaat when he was subbed, and was later fined £10,000. 'I don't like that kind of reaction from players', said the Dutchman. Advocaat's future at Ibrox was increasingly coming under question in the press, although the manager stated 'I will definitely stay till the end of the season'. After Ranger's 3-1 win over Hearts on 9 December, however, he admitted 'There will be a new manager'. Two days later Alex McLeish was appointed the new Ibrox boss.

McLeish had been a doughty defender for Aberdeen and had gained 77 caps for Scotland. His managerial career began with Motherwell and then Hibs, and Rangers are by far the biggest club with which he has been involved. Many fans considered that he lacked the experience and the status within football to take over at an institution like Rangers, and his welcome from the stands was initially lukewarm. Nor was he particularly popular with some of the Hibs support who felt betrayed by his departure. His first game as a Rangers man was, ironically, against Hibs whose opening goal was greeted by the Hibs fans with chants of 'Judas, what's the score?'. McLeish, however, was to settle in quickly and prove himself a shrewd motivator and tactician.

With Advocaat now director of football, and soon also to become part-time manager of Holland, Rangers won three and drew one of their last four games in December but by the end of the year were an almost uncatchable 15 points behind Celtic. Although McLeish's side were unbeaten in the league until a shock away 2-1 defeat by Livingston in the middle of April, Celtic claimed the title by 18 points. Rangers were in second place 27 points clear of third placed Livingston, a statistic which emphasises the increasing gulf between the Old Firm and the rest of Scottish football.

With the Championship virtually ceded to the Parkhead side by the beginning of 2002, Rangers now had to concentrate on the UEFA Cup and the two Scottish Cups. In

Shota Arveladze scores against Kilmarnock

the League Cup they had progressed to the final against Celtic with a 2-1 victory over Ross County in Dingwall. In McLeish's first Old Firm encounter, Lovenkrands scored on half time while Balde equalised midway through the second half. Arveladze missed a penalty, hitting the crossbar, three minutes later. In extra time Bert Konterman cracked a magnificent shot from 25 yards for the winning goal. A 4-0 win in the final over Ayr United – with two coming from Caniggia – secured Rangers' first trophy since the 2000 Scottish Cup.

On 21 February the Light Blues met Feyenoord at Ibrox in the UEFA Cup 4th round. In a passionate atmosphere, and with fighting erupting between some Rangers and Feyenoord fans, Feyenoord went ahead late in the game through Shinji Ono and Ferguson equalised with an 81st minute penalty after Lovenkrands had been brought down in the box. In Rotterdam a week later, McCann opened the scoring but Van Hoydonk had the Dutch team 2-1 up by the interval. Kalou made the score 3-1 early in the second half and a Ferguson penalty was not enough to prevent Rangers' elimination from the tournament.

In what was almost a replay of the 1967 debacle, Rangers met Berwick Rangers in the Scottish Cup third round. The 'wee Rangers' were bottom of the Second Division but they held a poor Rangers side 0-0 at home. Amoruso smashed a 25-yard goal in the second half at Ibrox and Konterman and Arveladze made the final score 3-0. A storming performance against Hibs at Ibrox in the next round saw Rangers beat Hibs 4-1, with late substitute Dodds netting his first goal for 13 months. A hat-trick from Dodds in the quarter-final against outclassed Forfar Athletic helped Rangers to a 6-0 win, while two goals from a now fit and back to form Nerlinger, who had missed most of the season through injury, and one from Ferguson brought a 3-0 victory over Partick Thistle in the semi-final.

They met Celtic in the Scottish Cup final on 4 May. In a tense and exciting game Celtic went ahead in the 19th minute with a Hartson header at the far post, and two minutes later Lovenkrands spun the Celtic defence to drill home a low left foot shot from the edge of the box. Rangers were playing with skill and determination, with Ferguson and McCann particularly inspirational. Celtic went ahead through Balde early in the second half but in the 68th minute

New manager Alex McLeish takes up his appointment

Barry Ferguson celebrates winning the 2002 Scottish Cup

Ferguson scored with a delightful free kick over the wall and into the top corner of the net. In the 92nd minute, and with the referee about to blow for extra time, McCann floated in a perfect cross which was well met by Lovenkrands for a deserved winner. McLeish had gained his second trophy of the season and the celebrations began around Hampden.

Whether the new manager can match the achievements of his predecessors remains to be seen. But there is little doubt that there is now a renewed air of confidence and self-belief around Ibrox which promises well for the future. In May 2002 stories emerged in the media that Rangers and Celtic were hoping to play in the English Nationwide League in season 2002-2003 with the expectation of promotion to the Premier League the following season, but the Football Association subsequently voted against such a move. It seems clear that the Old Firm have outgrown Scottish football so perhaps the idea of the Atlantic League, or some variant, will be revived. However, whether the Light Blues remain in Scottish football, take up the challenge of the English leagues or become part of a new competition it seems likely that, under McLeish, they are set to maintain the high standards which have been expected of Rangers throughout the old club's illustrious history.

SCOTTISH LEAGUE 1890-2002

		P	W	D	L	F	A	Pts
1890/91	Dumbarton (1)	18	13	3	2	61	21	29
	Rangers (1=)	18	13	3	2	58	25	29
1891/92	Dumbarton (1)	22	18	1	3	78	27	37
	Rangers (5th)	22	11	2	9	59	46	24
1892/93	Celtic (1st)	18	14	1	3	54	25	29
	Rangers (2nd)	18	12	4	2	41	27	28
1893/94	Celtic (1st)	18	14	1	3	53	32	29
	Rangers (4th)	18	8	4	6	44	30	20
1894/95	Hearts (1st)	18	15	1	2	50	18	31
	Rangers (3rd)	18	10	2	6	41	26	22
1895/96	Celtic	18	15	3	0	64	25	30
	Rangers (2nd)	18	11	3	4	57	39	26
1896/97	Hearts	18	13	3	2	47	22	28
	Rangers (3rd)	18	11	4	3	64	30	25
1897/98	Celtic	18	15	0	3	53	13	33
	Rangers (2nd)	18	13	2	3	71	15	29
1898/99	Rangers (1st)	18	18	0	0	79	18	36
	Hearts	18	12	4	2	56	30	26
1899/1900	Rangers (1st)	18	15	1	2	69	27	32
	Celtic (2nd)	18	9	2	7	49	27	25
1900/01	Rangers (1st)	20	17	1	2	60	25	35
	Celtic (2nd)	20	13	3	4	49	28	29
1901/2	Rangers (1st)	18	13	2	3	43	29	28
	Celtic (2nd)	18	11	4	3	38	28	26
1902/3	Hibernian (1st)	22	16	5	1	48	18	37
	Rangers (3rd)	22	12	5	5	56	30	29
1903/4	T Lanark (1st)	26	20	3	3	61	26	43
	Rangers (3rd)	26	16	6	4	80	33	38

		P	W	D	L	F	A	Pts
1904/5	Celtic (1st)	26	18	5	3	68	31	41
	Rangers (2nd)	26	19	3	4	83	28	41
1905/6	Celtic (1st)	30	24	1	5	76	19	49
	Rangers (4th)	30	15	7	8	58	48	37
1906/7	Celtic (1st)	34	23	9	2	80	30	55
	Rangers (3rd)	34	19	7	8	69	33	45
1907/8	Celtic (1st)	34	24	7	3	86	27	55
	Rangers (3rd)	34	21	8	5	74	40	50
1908/9	Celtic (1st)	34	23	5	6	71	24	51
	Rangers (4th)	34	19	7	8	90	37	45
1909/10	Celtic (1st)	34	24	6	4	63	22	54
	Rangers (3rd)	34	20	6	8	70	35	46
1910/11	Rangers (1st)	34	23	6	5	90	34	52
	Aberdeen (2nd)	34	19	10	5	53	28	48
1911/12	Rangers (1st)	34	24	3	7	86	34	51
	Celtic (2nd)	34	17	11	6	58	33	45
1912/13	Rangers (1st)	34	24	5	5	76	41	53
	Celtic (2nd)	34	22	5	7	53	28	49
1913/14	Celtic (1st)	38	30	5	3	81	14	65
	Rangers (2nd)	38	27	5	6	79	31	59
1914/15	Celtic (1st)	38	30	5	3	91	25	65
	Rangers (3rd)	38	23	4	11	74	47	50
1915/16	Celtic (1st)	38	32	3	3	116	23	67
	Rangers (2nd)	38	25	6	7	87	39	56
1916/17	Celtic (1st)	38	27	10	1	79	17	64
	Rangers (3rd)	38	24	5	9	68	32	53
1917/18	Rangers (1st)	34	25	6	3	66	24	56
	Celtic (2nd)	34	24	7	3	66	26	55
1918/19	Celtic (1st)	34	26	6	2	71	22	58
	Rangers(2nd)	34	26	5	3	86	16	57

		P	W	D	L	F	A	Pts
1919/20	Rangers (1st)	42	31	9	2	106	25	71
	Celtic (2nd)	42	29	10	3	89	31	68
1920/21	Rangers (1st)	42	35	6	1	91	24	76
	Celtic (2nd)	42	30	6	6	86	35	66
1921/22	Celtic (1st)	42	27	13	2	83	20	67
	Rangers (2nd)	42	28	10	4	83	26	66
1922/23	Rangers (1st)	38	23	9	6	67	29	55
	Airdrie (2nd)	38	20	10	8	58	38	50
1923/24	Rangers (1st)	38	25	9	4	72	22	59
	Airdrie (2nd)	38	20	10	8	72	46	50
1924/25	Rangers (1st)	38	25	10	3	77	27	60
	Airdrie (2nd)	38	25	7	6	85	31	57
1925/26	Celtic (1st)	38	25	8	5	97	40	58
	Rangers (6th)	38	19	6	13	79	55	44
1926/27	Rangers (1st)	38	23	10	5	85	41	56
	M'well (2nd)	38	23	5	10	81	52	51
1927/28	Rangers (1st)	38	26	8	4	109	36	60
	Celtic (2nd)	38	23	9	6	93	39	55
1928/29	Rangers (1st)	38	30	7	1	107	32	67
	Celtic (2nd)	38	22	7	9	67	44	51
1929/30	Rangers (1st)	38	28	4	6	94	32	60
	M'well (2nd)	38	25	5	8	104	48	55
1930/31	Rangers (1st)	38	27	6	5	96	29	60
	Celtic (2nd)	38	24	10	4	101	34	58
1931/32	M'well (1st)	38	30	6	2	119	31	66
	Rangers (2nd)	38	28	5	5	118	42	61
1932/33	Rangers (1st)	38	26	10	2	113	43	62
	M'well (2nd)	38	27	5	6	114	53	59
1933/34	Rangers (1st)	38	30	6	2	116	41	66
	M'well (2nd)	38	29	4	5	97	45	62

		P	W	D	L	F	A	Pts
1934/35	Rangers (1st)	38	25	5	8	96	46	55
	Celtic (2nd)	38	24	4	10	92	45	52
1935/36	Celtic (1st)	38	32	2	4	115	33	66
	Rangers (2nd)	38	27	7	4	110	43	61
1936/37	Rangers (1st)	38	26	9	3	88	32	61
	Aberdeen (2nd)	38	23	8	7	89	44	54
1937/38	Celtic (1st)	38	27	7	4	114	42	61
	Rangers (3rd)	38	18	13	7	75	49	49
1938/39	Rangers (1st)	38	25	9	4	112	55	59
	Celtic (2nd)	38	20	8	10	99	53	48

(No league games were contested between seasons 1939/40 and 1945/46)

		P	W	D	L	F	A	Pts
1946/47	Rangers (1st)	30	21	4	5	76	26	46
	Hibs (2nd)	30	19	6	5	69	33	44
1947/48	Hibs (1st)	30	22	4	4	86	27	48
	Rangers (2nd)	30	21	4	5	64	28	46
1948/49	Rangers (1st)	30	20	6	4	63	32	46
	Dundee (2nd)	30	20	5	5	71	48	45
1949/50	Rangers (1st)	30	22	6	2	58	26	50
	Hibs (2nd)	30	22	5	3	86	34	49
1950/51	Hibs (1st)	30	22	4	4	78	26	48
	Rangers (2nd)	30	17	4	9	64	37	38
1951/52	Hibs (1st)	30	20	5	5	92	36	45
	Rangers (2nd)	30	16	9	5	61	31	41
1952/53	Rangers (1st)	30	18	7	5	80	39	43
	Hibs (2nd)	30	19	5	6	93	51	43
1953/54	Celtic (1st)	30	20	3	7	72	29	43
	Rangers (4th)	30	13	8	9	56	35	34
1954/55	Aberdeen (1st)	30	24	1	5	73	26	49
	Rangers (3rd)	30	19	3	8	67	33	41
1955/56	Rangers (1st)	34	22	8	4	85	27	52
	Aberdeen (2nd)	34	18	10	6	87	50	46

		P	W	D	L	F	A	Pts
1956/57	Rangers (1st)	34	26	3	5	96	48	55
	Hearts (2nd)	34	24	5	5	81	48	53
1957/58	Hearts (1st)	34	29	4	1	132	29	62
	Rangers (2nd)	34	22	5	7	89	49	49
1958/59	Rangers (1st)	34	21	8	5	92	51	50
	Hearts (2nd)	34	21	6	7	92	51	48
1959/60	Hearts (1st)	34	23	8	3	102	51	54
	Rangers (3rd)	34	17	8	9	72	38	42
1960/61	Rangers (1st)	34	23	5	6	88	46	51
	K'nock (2nd)	34	21	8	5	77	45	50
1961/62	Dundee (1st)	34	25	4	5	80	46	54
	Rangers (2nd)	34	22	7	5	84	31	51
1962/63	Rangers (1st)	34	25	7	2	94	28	57
	K'nock (2nd)	34	20	8	6	92	40	48
1963/64	Rangers (1st)	34	25	5	4	85	31	55
	K'nock (2nd)	34	22	5	7	77	40	49
1964/65	K'nock (1st)	34	22	6	6	62	33	50
	Rangers (5th)	34	18	8	8	78	35	44
1965/66	Celtic (1st)	34	27	3	4	106	30	57
	Rangers (2nd)	34	25	5	4	91	29	55
1966/67	Celtic (1st)	34	26	6	2	111	33	58
	Rangers (2nd)	34	24	7	3	92	31	55
1967/68	Celtic (1st)	34	30	3	1	106	24	63
	Rangers (2nd)	34	28	5	1	93	34	61
1968/69	Celtic (1st)	34	23	8	3	89	32	54
	Rangers (2nd)	34	21	7	6	81	32	49
1969/70	Celtic (1st)	34	27	3	4	96	33	57
	Rangers (2nd)	34	19	7	8	67	40	45
1970/71	Celtic (1st)	34	25	6	3	89	23	56
	Rangers (4th)	34	16	9	9	58	34	41

		P	W	D	L	F	A	Pts
1971/72	Celtic (1st)	34	28	4	2	96	28	60
	Rangers (3rd)	34	21	2	11	71	38	44
1972/73	Celtic (1st)	34	26	5	3	93	28	57
	Rangers (2nd)	34	26	4	4	74	30	56
1973/74	Celtic (1st)	34	23	7	4	82	27	53
	Rangers (3rd)	34	21	6	7	67	34	48
1974/75	Rangers (1st)	34	25	6	3	86	33	56
	Hibs (2nd)	34	20	9	5	69	37	49

(the Scottish Premier League was established at the beginning of 1975/76)

		P	W	D	L	F	A	Pts
1975/76	Rangers (1st)	36	23	8	5	60	24	54
	Celtic (2nd)	36	21	6	9	71	42	48
1976/77	Celtic (1st)	36	23	9	4	79	39	55
	Rangers (2nd)	36	18	10	8	62	37	46
1977/78	Rangers (1st)	36	24	7	5	76	39	55
	Aberdeen (2nd)	36	22	9	5	68	29	53
1978/79	Celtic (1st)	36	21	6	9	61	37	48
	Rangers (2nd)	36	18	9	9	52	35	45
1979/80	Aberdeen (1st)	36	19	10	7	68	36	48
	Rangers (5th)	36	15	7	14	50	46	37
1980/81	Celtic (1st)	36	26	4	6	84	37	56
	Rangers (3rd)	36	16	12	8	60	32	44
1981/82	Celtic (1st)	36	24	7	5	79	33	55
	Rangers (3rd)	36	16	11	9	57	45	43
1982/83	Dundee U (1st)	36	24	8	4	90	35	56
	Rangers (4th)	36	13	12	11	52	41	38
1983/84	Aberdeen (1st)	36	25	7	4	78	21	57
	Rangers (4th)	36	15	12	9	53	41	42
1984/85	Aberdeen	36	27	5	4	89	26	59
	Rangers (4th)	36	13	12	11	47	38	38
1985/86	Celtic (1st)	36	20	10	6	67	38	50
	Rangers (5th)	36	13	9	14	53	45	35

		P	W	D	L	F	A	Pts
1986/87	Rangers (1st)	44	31	7	6	85	23	69
	Celtic (2nd)	44	27	9	8	90	41	63
1987/88	Celtic (1st)	44	30	10	4	78	24	70
	Rangers (3rd)	44	26	8	10	85	34	60
1988/89	Rangers (1st)	36	26	4	6	62	26	56
	Aberdeen (2nd)	36	18	14	4	51	25	50
1989/90	Rangers (1st)	36	20	11	5	48	19	51
	Aberdeen (2nd)	36	17	10	9	56	33	44
1990/91	Rangers (1st)	36	24	7	5	62	23	55
	Aberdeen (2nd)	36	22	9	5	62	27	53
1991/92	Rangers (1st)	44	33	6	5	101	31	72
	Hearts (2nd)	44	27	9	8	60	37	63
1992/93	Rangers (1st)	44	33	7	4	97	35	73
	Aberdeen (2nd)	44	27	10	7	87	36	64
1993/94	Rangers (1st)	44	22	14	8	74	41	58
	Aberdeen (2nd)	44	17	21	6	58	36	55
1994/95	Rangers (1st)	36	20	9	7	60	35	69
	M'well (2nd)	36	14	12	10	50	50	54
1995/96	Rangers (1st)	36	27	6	3	85	25	87
	Celtic (2nd)	36	24	11	1	74	25	83
1996/97	Rangers (1st)	36	25	5	6	85	33	80
	Celtic (2nd)	36	23	6	7	78	32	75
1997/98	Celtic (1st)	36	22	8	6	64	24	74
	Rangers (2nd)	36	21	9	6	76	38	72
1998/99	Rangers (1st)	36	23	8	5	78	31	77
	Celtic (2nd)	36	21	8	7	84	35	71
1999/2000	Rangers (1st)	36	20	6	2	96	26	90
	Celtic (2nd)	36	21	6	9	90	38	69
2000/01	Celtic (1st)	38	31	4	3	90	29	97
	Rangers (2nd)	38	26	4	8	76	36	82
2001/02	Celtic (1st)	38	33	4	1	94	18	103
	Rangers (2nd)	38	25	10	3	82	27	85

SCOTTISH CUP 1874-2002

1874/75	0-1 v Dumbarton (2nd rd replay)	1919/20	0-2 v Albion Rovers (semi-final 2nd replay)
1875/76	0-2 v Third Lanark (2nd rd replay)	1920/21	0-1 v Partick Thistle (Final)
1876/77	2-3 v Vale of Leven (Final, second replay)	1921/22	0-1 v Morton (Final)
1877/78	0-5 v Vale of Leven (4th rd replay)	1922/23	0-2 v Ayr United (2nd rd)
1878/79	1-1 v Vale of Leven (Final, Rangers did not appear for replay)	1923/24	1-2 v Hibs (3rd rd)
		1924/25	0-5 v Celtic (semi-final)
1879/80	1-5 v Queen's Park (1st rd replay)	1925/26	0-1 v St Mirren (semi-final)
1880/81	1-3 v Dumbarton (quarter-final replay)	1926/27	0-1 v Falkirk (quarter-final replay)
1881/82	1-5 v Dumbarton (quarter-final replay)	**1927/28**	**Won 4-0 v Celtic**
1882/83	2-3 v Queen's Park (2nd rd)	1928/29	0-2 v Kilmarnock (Final)
1883/84	0-3 v Vale of Leven (semi-final)	**1929/30**	**Won 2-1 v Partick Thistle (replay)**
1884/85	3-5 Renton (quarter-final)	1930/31	1-2 v Dundee (2nd rd)
1885/86	0-1 v Clyde (1st rd)	**1931/32**	**Won 3-0 v Kilmarnock (replay)**
1886/87	0-2 v Cambuslang (3rd rd)	1932/33	0-1 v Kilmarnock ((3rd rd)
1887/88	1-2 v Partick Thistle (2nd rd)	**1933/34**	**Won 5-0 v St Mirren**
1888/89	0-3 v Clyde (2nd rd replay)	**1934/35**	**Won 2-1 v Hamilton Academicals**
1889/90	2-3 v Vale of Leven (3rd rd replay)	**1935/36**	**Won 1-0 v Third Lanark**
1890/91	0-1 v Celtic (1st rd)	1936/37	1-0 v Queen of the South (1st rd)
1891/92	3-5 v Celtic (4th rd)	1937/38	3-4 v Kilmarnock (semi-final)
1892/93	2-3 v St Bernards (3rd rd)	1938/39	1-4 v Clyde (4th rd)
1893/94	**Win 3-1 v Celtic**		
1894/95	1-2 v Hearts (1st rd)		
1895/96	2-3 v Hibs (3rd rd)	**the tournament was suspended between**	
1896/97	**Win 5-1 v Dumbarton**	**1939/40 and 1945/46**	
1897/98	**Win 2-0 v Kilmarnock**		
1898/99	0-2 v Celtic (Final)	1946/47	0-2 v Hibs (2nd rd replay)
1899/1900	0-4 v Celtic (semi-final replay)	**1947/48**	**Won 1-0 v Morton (replay)**
1900/01	0-1 v Celtic (1st rd)	**1948/49**	**Won 4-1 v Clyde**
1901/02	0-2 v Hibs (semi-final)	**1949/50**	**Won 3-0 v East Fife**
1902/03	**Win 2-0 v Hearts (2nd replay)**	1950/51	2-3 v Hibs (2nd rd)
1903/04	2-3 v Celtic (Final)	1951/52	1-2 v Motherwell (quarter-final replay)
1904/05	1-3 v Third Lanark (Final replay)	**1952/53**	**Won 1-0 v Aberdeen (replay)**
1905/06	0-1 v Port Glasgow Athletic (3rd rd)	1953/54	0-6 v Aberdeen (semi-final)
1906/07	0-3 v Celtic (3rd rd)	1954/55	1-2 v Aberdeen (6th round)
1907/08	1-2 v Celtic (2nd rd)	1955/56	0-4 v Hearts (quarter-final)
1908/09	1-1 v Celtic (Final replay, cup withheld)	1956/57	0-2 v Celtic (6th round replay)
1909/10	0-2 v Clyde (2nd rd)	1957/58	1-2 v Hibs (semi-final replay)
1910/11	1-2 v Dundee (3rd rd)	1958/59	1-2 v Celtic (3rd rd)
1911/12	1-3 v Clyde (2nd rd)	**1959/60**	**Won 2-0 v Kilmarnock**
1912/13	1-3 v Falkirk (3rd rd)	1960/61	2-5 v Motherwell (3rd rd replay)
1913/14	1-2 v Hibs (3rd rd)	**1961/62**	**Won 2-0 v St Mirren**
		1962/63	**Won 3-0 v Celtic (replay)**
		1963/64	**Won 3-1 v Dundee**
The tournament was suspended between		1964/65	1-2 v Hibs (3rd rd)
1914/15 and 1918/19		**1965/66**	**Won 1-0 v Celtic (replay)**

1966/67	0-1 v Berwick Rangers (1st rd)
1967/68	0-1 v Hearts (quarter-final replay)
1968/69	0-4 v Celtic (Final)
1969/70	1-3 v Celtic (quarter-final)
1970/71	1-2 v Celtic (Final replay)
1971/72	0-2 v Hibs (semi-final replay)
1972/73	**Won 3-2 v Celtic**
1973/74	0-3 v Dundee (4th rd)
1974/75	1-2 v Aberdeen (3rd rd replay)
1975/76	**Won 3-1 v Hearts**
1976/77	0-1 v Celtic (Final)
1977/78	**Won 2-1 v Aberdeen**
1978/79	**Won 3-2 v Hibs (2nd replay)**
1979/80	0-1 v Celtic (Final)
1980/81	**Won 4-1 v Dundee United (replay)**
1981/82	1-4 v Aberdeen (Final)
1982/83	0-1 v Aberdeen (Final)
1983/84	2-3 v Dundee (quarter-final replay)
1984/85	0-1 v Dundee (4th rd)
1985/86	2-3 v Hearts (3rd rd)
1986/87	0-1 v Hamilton Academicals (3rd rd)
1987/88	0-2 v Dunfermline (4th rd)
1988/89	0-1 v Celtic (Final)
1989/90	0-1 v Celtic (4th rd)
1990/91	0-2 v Celtic (quarter-final)
1991/92	**Won 2-1 v Airdrie**
1992/93	**Won 2-1 v Aberdeen**
1993/94	0-1 v Dundee United (Final)
1994/95	2-4 v Hearts (4th rd)
1995/96	**Won 5-1 v Hearts (Final)**
1996/97	0-2 v Celtic (quarter-final)
1997/98	1-2 v Hearts (Final)
1998/99	**Won 1-0 v Celtic**
1999/2000	**Won 4-0 v Aberdeen**
2000/01	0-1 v Dundee United
2001/02	**Won 3-2 v Celtic**

LEAGUE CUP

1946/47	**Won 4-0 v Aberdeen**
1947/48	0-1 v Falkirk (semi-final)
1948/49	**Won 2-0 v Raith Rovers**
1949/50	1-2 v East Fife (semi-final)
1950/51	did not qualify
1951/52	2-3 v Dundee (Final)
1952/53	0-1 v Kilmarnock (semi-final)
1953/54	0-2 v Partick Thistle (semi-final)

1954/55	2-3 v Motherwell (quarter-final)
1955/56	1-2 v Aberdeen (semi-final)
1956/57	did not qualify
1957/58	1-7 v Celtic (Final)
1958/59	did not qualify
1959/60	did not qualify
1960/61	**Won 2-0 v Kilmarnock**
1961/62	**Won 4-2 v Hearts**
1962/63	2-3 v Kilmarnock (semi-final)
1963/64	**Won 5-0 v Morton**
1964/65	**Won 2-1 v Celtic**
1965/66	1-2 v Celtic (Final)
1966/67	0-1 v Celtic (Final)
1967/68	did not qualify
1968/69	did not qualify
1969/70	did not qualify
1970/71	**Won 1-0 v Celtic**
1971/72	did not qualify
1972/73	0-1 v Hibs (semi-final)
1973/74	1-3 v Celtic (semi-final)
1974/75	did not qualify
1975/76	**Won 1-0 v Celtic**
1976/77	1-5 v Aberdeen (semi-final)
1977/78	**Won 2-1 v Celtic**
1978/79	**Won 2-1 v Aberdeen**
1979/80	1-5 v Aberdeen (3rd rd)
1980/81	2-3 v Aberdeen (3rd rd)
1981/82	**Won 2-1 v Dundee United**
1982/83	1-2 v Celtic (Final)
1983/84	**Won 3-2 v Celtic**
1984/85	**Won 1-0 v Dundee United**
1985/86	0-1 v Hibs (semi-final)
1986/87	**Won 2-1 v Celtic**
1987/88	**Won 3-3 (5-3 penalties) v Aberdeen**
1988/89	**Won 3-2 v Aberdeen**
1989/90	1-2 v Aberdeen (Final)
1990/91	**Won 2-1 v Celtic**
1991/92	0-1 v Hibs (semi-final)
1992/93	**Won 2-1 v Aberdeen**
1993/94	**Won 2-1 v Hibs**
1994/95	1-2 v Falkirk (3rd rd)
1995/96	1-2 v Aberdeen (semi-final)
1996/97	**Won 4-3 v Hearts**
1997/98	0-1 v Dundee United (quarter-final)
1998/99	**Won 2-1 v St Johnstone**
1999/2000	0-1 v Aberdeen (quarter-final)
2000/01	1-3 v Celtic (semi-final)
2001/02	**Won 2-1 v Celtic**

EUROPEAN CUP

1956/57 2-1 v Nice (1st rd, Ibrox), 1-2 v Nice, 1-3 v Nice (play-off, Paris)

1957/58 3-1 v St Etienne (preliminary rd, Ibrox), 1-2 v St Etienne; 1-4 v AC Milan (1st rd, Ibrox), 0-2 v AC Milan

1959/60 5-2 v Anderlecht (preliminary rd, Ibrox), 2-0 v Anderlecht; 4-3 v Red Star Bratislava (1st rd, Ibrox), 1-1 v Red Star Bratislava; 3-2 v Sparta Rotterdam (quarter-final, Rotterdam), 0-1 v Sparta Rotterdam, 3-2 v Sparta Rotterdam (play-off, London); 1-6 v Eintracht Frankfurt (semi-final, Frankfurt), 3-6 v Eintracht Frankfurt

1961/62 3-2 v AS Monaco (preliminary rd, Monaco), 3-2 v AS Monaco; 2-1 v ASK Vorwaerts (1st rd, Berlin), 4-1 v ASK Vorwaerts (played as a 'home' tie in Malmo); 1-4 Standard Liege (quarter-final in Liege), 2-0 v Standard Liege

1963/64 0-1 v Real Madrid (preliminary rd, Ibrox), 0-6 v Real Madrid

1964/65 3-1 v Red Star Belgrade (preliminary rd, Ibrox), 2-4 v Red Star Belgrade, 3-1 v Red Star Belgrade (play-off, London); 1-0 v Rapid Vienna (1st rd, Ibrox), 2-0 v Rapid Vienna; 1-3 v Inter Milan (quarter-final, Milan), 1-0 v Inter Milan

1975/76 4-1 v Bohemians (1st rd, Ibrox), 1-1 v Bohemians; 0-2 v St Etienne (2nd rd, St Etienne), 1-2 v St Etienne

1976/77 1-1 v FC Zurich (1st rd, Ibrox), 0-1 v FC Zurich

1978/79 0-1 v Juventus (1st rd, Turin), 2-0 v Juventus; 0-0 v PSV Eindhoven (2nd rd, Ibrox), 3-2 v PSV Eindhoven; 0-1 v Cologne (quarter-final, Cologne), 1-1 v Cologne

1987/88 0-1 v Dynamo Kiev (1st rd, Kiev), 2-0 v Dynamo Kiev; 3-1 v Gornik Zabrze (2nd rd, Ibrox), 1-1 v Gornik Zabrze; 0-2 v Steaua Bucharest (quarter-final, Bucharest), 2-1 v Steaua Bucharest

1989/90 1-3 v Bayern Munich (1st rd, Ibrox), 0-0 v Bayern Munich

1990/91 4-0 v Valetta (1st rd, Malta), 6-0 v Valetta; 0-3 v Red Star Belgrade (2nd rd, Belgrade), 1-1 v Red Star Belgrade

1991/92 0-1 v Sparta Prague (preliminary rd, Prague), 2-1 v Sparta Prague (Rangers eliminated on away goals)

1992/93 2-0 v Lyngby (1st preliminary rd, Ibrox), 1-0 v Lyngby; 2-1 v Leeds United (2nd preliminary rd, Ibrox), 2-1 v Leeds United

Champions League: 2-2 v Marseille (Ibrox), 1-0 v CSKA Moscow (Germany), 1-1 v Bruges (Bruges), 2-1 v Bruges (Ibrox), 1-1 v Marseille (Marseille), 0-0 v CSKA Moscow (Ibrox)

	P	W	D	L	F	A	Pts
Marseille	6	3	3	0	14	4	9
Rangers	6	2	4	0	7	5	8
Bruges	6	2	1	3	5	8	5
CSKA Moscow	6	0	2	4	2	11	2

(Marseille qualified for the Final)

1993/94 3-2 v Levski Sofia (preliminary rd, Ibrox), 1-2 v Levski Sofia (Levski qualified on away goals)

1994/95 0-2 v AEK Athens (preliminary rd, Athens), 0-1 v AEK Athens

1995/96 1-0 v Anorthosis Famagusta (preliminary rd, Ibrox), 0-0 v Anorthosis Famagusta

Champions League: 0-1 v Steaua Bucharest (Bucharest), 2-2 v Borussia Dortmund (Ibrox), 1-4 v Juventus (Turin), 0-4 v Juventus (Ibrox), 1-1 v Steaua Bucharest (Ibrox), 2-2 v Borussia Dortmund (Dortmund)

	P	W	D	L	F	A	Pts
Juventus	6	4	1	1	15	4	13
Borussia Dortmund	6	2	3	1	8	8	9
Steaua Bucharest	6	1	3	2	2	5	6
Rangers	6	0	3	3	6	14	3

(Juventus and Borussia Dortmund qualified for the quarter-finals)

1996/97 3-1 v Alania Vladikavkaz (preliminary round, Ibrox), 7-2 v Alania Vladivkavkaz

Champions League: 0-3 v Grasshoppers Zurich (Zurich), 1-2 v Auxerre (Ibrox), 4-1 v Ajax (Amsterdam), 0-1 v Ajax (Ibrox), 2-1 v Grasshoppers Zurich (Ibrox), 1-2 v Auxerre (Auxerre)

	P	W	D	L	F	A	Pts
Auxerre	6	4	0	2	8	7	12
Ajax	6	4	0	2	8	4	12
Grasshoppers	6	3	0	3	8	5	9
Rangers	6	1	0	5	5	13	3

(Auxerre and Ajax qualified for the quarter-finals)

1997/98 5-0 v GI Gotu (Faroe Islands), 6-0 v GI Gotu; 0-3 v IFK Gothenburg (Gothenburg), 1-1 v IFK Gothenburg

1999/2000 4-1 v FC Haka (1st preliminary round, Finland), 3-0 v FC Haka); 2-0 v Parma (2nd preliminary rd, Ibrox), 0-1 v Parma (Parma)

Champions League: 0-2 v Valencia (Valencia), 1-1 v Bayern Munich (Ibrox), 1-0 v PSV Eindhoven (Eindhoven), 4-1 v PSV Eindhoven (Ibrox), 1-2 v Valencia (Ibrox), 0-1 v Bayern Munich (Munich)

	P	W	D	L	F	A	Pts
Valencia	6	3	3	0	8	4	12
Bayern Munich	6	2	3	1	7	6	9
Rangers	6	2	1	3	7	7	7
PSV	6	1	1	4	5	10	4

(Valencia and Bayern Munich qualified for the second group round)

2000/2001 4-1 v FK Zalgiris Kaumas (1st preliminary rd, Ibrox), 0-0 v FK Zalgiris Kaumas); 3-0 v Herfolge (2nd preliminary rd, Denmark), 3-0 v Herfolge

Champions League 5-0 v Sturm Graz (Ibrox), 1-0 v Monaco (Monaco), 2-3 v Galatasaray (Istanbul), 0-0 v Galatasaray (Ibrox), 0-2 v Sturm Graz (Graz), 2-2 v Monaco

	P	W	D	L	F	A	Pts
Sturm Graz	6	3	1	2	9	12	10
Galatasaray	6	2	2	2	10	11	8
Rangers	6	2	2	2	10	7	8
Monaco	6	2	1	3	13	10	7

(Sturm Graz and Galatasaray qualified for the second group stage)

2001/02 3-0 v Maribor (2nd preliminary rd, Maribor), 3-1 v Maribor; 0-0 v Fenerbahce (3rd preliminary rd, Ibrox), 1-2 v Fenerbahce

EUROPEAN CUP WINNERS CUP

1960/61 4-2 v Ferencvaros (1st rd, Ibrox), 1-2 v Ferencvaros; 3-0 v Borussia Moenchengladbach (2nd rd, Germany), 5-0 v Borussia Moenchengladbach; 2-0 v Wolves (semi-final, Ibrox), 1-1 v Wolves; 0-2 v Fiorentina (Final, Ibrox), 1-2 v Fiorentina

1962/63 4-0 v Seville (1st rd, Ibrox), 0-2 v Seville; 2-5 v Tottenham Hotspur (2nd rd, White Hart Lane), 2-3 v Tottenham Hotspur

1966/67 1-1 v Glentoran (1st rd, Belfast), 4-0 v Glentoran; 2-1 v Borussia Dortmund (2nd rd, Ibrox), 0-0 v Borussia Dortmund; 2-0 v Real Zaragoza (quarter-final, Ibrox), 0-2 v Real Zaragoza (Rangers win on toss of coin); 1-0 v Slavia Sofia (semi-final, Sofia), 1-0 v Slavia Sofia; 0-1 v Bayern Munich (Final, Nuremberg)

1969/70 2-0 v Steaua Bucharest (1st rd, Ibrox), 0-0 v Steaua Bucharest; 1-3 v Gornik Zabrze (2nd rd, Poland), 1-3 v Gornik Zabrze

1971/72 1-1 v Rennes (1st rd, Rennes), 1-0 v Rennes; 3-2 v Sporting Lisbon (2nd rd, Ibrox), 3-4 v Sporting Lisbon (Rangers progress on away goals); 1-1 v Torino (quarter-final, Turin), 1-0 v Torino; 1-1 v Bayern Munich (semi-final, Ibrox), 2-0 v Bayern Munich; 3-2 v Moscow Dynamo (Final, Barcelona)

1973/74 2-0 v Ankaragucu (1st rd, Turkey), 4-0 v Ankaragucu; 0-3 v Borussia Moenchengladbach (2nd rd, Germany), 3-2 v Borussia Moenchengladbach

1977/78 1-0 v Young Boys Berne (1st round, Ibrox), 2-2 v Young Boys Berne; 0-0 v Twente Enschede (2nd rd, Ibrox), 0-3 v Twente Enschede

1979/80 1-0 v Lillestrom (preliminary rd, Ibrox), 2-0 v Lillestrom; 2-1 v Fortuna Dusseldorf (1st rd, Ibrox), 0-0 v Fortuna Dusseldorf; 1-1 v Valencia (2nd rd, Valencia), 1-3 v Valencia

1981/82 0-3 v Dukla Prague (1st rd, Prague), 2-1 v Dukla Prague

1983/84 8-0 v Valetta (1st rd, Malta), 10-0 v Valetta; 2-1 v Porto (2nd rd, Ibrox), 0-1 v Porto (Porto progress on away goals)

FAIRS CUP (UEFA Cup from 1972)

1967/68 1-1 v Dynamo Dresden (1st rd, Dresden),
2-1 v Dynamo Dresden; 3-0 v Cologne (2nd rd, Ibrox),
1-3 v Cologne; 0-0 v Leeds United (quarter-final, Ibrox),
0-2 v Leeds United

1968/69 2-0 v Vojvodina Novi Sad (1st rd, Ibrox),
0-1 Vojvodina Novi Sad ; 6-1 v Dundalk (2nd rd, Ibrox),
3-0 v Dundalk; 2-0 v DWS Amsterdam (3rd rd, Ibrox),
2-1 v DWS Amsterdam; 4-1 v Athletic Bilbao (quarter-
final, Ibrox), 0-2 v Athletic Bilbao; 0-0 v Newcastle
United (semi-final, Ibrox), 0-2 v Newcastle United

1970/71 0-1 v Bayern Munich (1st rd, Munich),
1-1 v Bayern Munich

1982/83 0-0 v Borussia Dortmund (1st round,
Dortmund), 2-0 v Borussia Dortmund; 2-1 v Cologne
(2nd rd, Ibrox), 0-5 v Cologne

1984/85 2-3 v Bohemians (1st rd, Dublin),
2-0 v Bohemians; 0-3 v Inter Milan (2nd rd, Milan),
3-1 v Inter Milan

1985/86 1-0 v Atletico Osasuna (1st rd, Ibrox),
0-2 v Atletico Osasuna

1997/98 1-2 v Strasbourg (1st rd, Strasbourg),
1-2 v Strasbourg

1998/99 5-3 v Shelbourne (qualifying rd, Birkenhead),
2-0 v Shelbourne; 2-0 v PAOK Salonika (1st rd, Ibrox),
0-0 v PAOK Salonika;1-1 v Beitar Jerusalem (2nd rd,
Jerusalem), 4-2 v Beitar Jerusalem; 2-1 v Bayer Leverkusen
(3rd rd, Leverkusen), 1-1 v Bayer Leverkusen; 1-1 v Parma
(4th rd, Ibrox), 1-3 v Parma

1999/2000 2-0 v Borussia Dortmund (3rd rd, Ibrox),
0-2 v Borussia Dortmund (Borussia won 3-1 on penalties)

2000/2001 1-0 v Kaiserslautern (3rd rd, Ibrox),
0-3 v Kaiserslautern

2001/02 1-0 v Anzhi (1st rd, played in neutral ground);
3-1 v Dynamo Moscow (2nd rd, Ibrox), 4-1 v Dynamo
Moscow; 0-0 v Paris St Germain (3rd rd, Ibrox), 0-0 v
Paris St Germain (Rangers progress 4-3 on penalties;
1-1 v Feyenoord (4th rd, Ibrox), 2-3 v Feyenoord

FURTHER READING

So far as books are concerned, such general publications as Kevin McCarra's *Scottish Football* (1984), John Cairney's *Scottish Football Hall of Fame* (1993), back issues of *The Scottish Football Book* and the *Sunday Times Illustrated History of Football* (1998) provide the context, while Brian Glanville's *Champions of Europe* (1991), John Motson and John Rowlinson's *European Cup* (1980) and my own *Illustrated History of the European Cup* (2000) chronicle the European dimension.

Rangers' early years are well covered, in a rather idiosyncratic and subjective manner, by John Allen's *History of the Rangers* 1873-1923, and the same author produced subsequent volumes entitled *Eleven Great Years, Rangers 1923-1934* and *Rangers' Eventful Years, 1934-1951*. *Rangers: The New Era*, by Willie Allison, takes the story up to 1966. Other older histories of Rangers include Hugh Taylor's *We Will Follow Rangers* (1961) and Ian Peebles' *Growing with Glory* (1973), while Stephen Halliday's *Rangers: An Illustrated History* (1989) and Ian Morrison's *Rangers* (1989) are more up-to-date. Alan Fairley's *Rangers in Europe* (1991) covers the Gers' European adventures between 1956/57 and 1990/91, while the most detailed study, complete with compendious statistics, is *Rangers: The Complete Record* (1996), by Robert McElroy and Bob Ferrier. McElroy also produced *Rangers Season by Season* in 1992.

Bill Murray's *The Old Firm* (1984) is an excellent academic analysis of the historical relationship between Rangers and Celtic but is also accessible to the interested non-academic reader. The same author has brought his analytic skills to bear on the period 1986-2000 in *The Old Firm in the New Age* (2000). Other recent titles on Rangers (most of which are published by the Edinburgh publishing house, Mainstream) include *Blue and True – The Rangers Dream Team* (1996) by Roddy Forsyth, *Rangers: The Managers* (2000), by David Mason, *Rangers: A Match to Remember* (2001), also by David Mason and *The Best of the Blues* (2001), by Bob MacCallum, a fan's memory of the team of the early 1960s. Quirkier titles – such as David Mason's *Ultimate Rangers Quiz Book* (2001) and Willie Thornton's introduction to the Ibrox Trophy Room, *Blue Heaven* (1991) – also provide interesting insights.

So far as the players are concerned, Ferrier and McElroy's *Rangers Player by Player* (updated 1996) is a comprehensive account of every Rangers player since World War II, while Dixon Blackstock's *Rangers Greats* (1988) and *More Rangers Greats* (1991) focus on the star players from the club's history. Autobiographies also abound, with the early years represented by Jerry Dawson's *Memoirs* (1949), Bob McPhail's *Legend* (1988) and George Young's *Captain of Scotland* (1951). Other titles include Willie Henderson's *Forward with Rangers* (1966), John Greig's *A Captain's Part* (1968), Derek Johnstone's *Rangers: My Team* (1979), Willie Johnston's *On the Wing* (1983), Jim Baxter's *The Party's Over* (1984), Davie Cooper's *True Blue* (1987), Sandy Jardine's *Score and More* (1987), Ally McCoist's *My Story* (1992), Richard Gough's *Field of Dreams* (1993), Andy Goram's *My Life* (1997), Stuart McCall's *The Real McCall* (1998) and Alex Ferguson's *Managing My Life* (1999) describes his time as a Rangers player. Nor are the managers forgotten, with Graeme Souness's *A Manager's Diary* (1989) and Ken Gallacher's *Walter Smith* (1994) reflecting on their Ibrox experiences. A new series – *Legends* – has individual titles on Bob McPhail, Ally McCoist, Mark Hateley and Davie Cooper.

I consulted back issues of *The Rangers Historian* magazine – an excellent source of information for the more archivally minded – and scoured issues of *Rangers News* during my researches, as well as back copies of the *Scottish Sport* and the *Scottish Referee* for information on the early days of Scottish football. For more recent happenings I referred to the *Glasgow Herald*, *Scottish Sunday Mail* and *Daily Record* for match reports and background material.

Currently available videos include *Goals, Goals, Goals (300 Great Rangers Goals)*, the last two seasons' round-ups (*One Vision and One Eck of a Double*), *Greatest Rangers*, *Wing Wizards*, *Blue Steel*, *Derek Johnstone and Jim Baxter – a Tribute* (Jim's earlier video *Jim Baxter's Rangers Memories* is still available in second hand shops). For the more ambitious (and wealthier) try *The History of Rangers* box set and the *9 in a Row* box set.

The internet can also provide much material from the seriously informative to the scurrilously wacky. Click on www.rangers.co.uk for the club's official website, www.rangers-web.com, or www.ibroxfc.co.uk and follow the links. For a view from the fanzines visit the entertaining www.followfollow.com, the website of 'Follow, Follow'.

INDEX